BOWL ECCLESIOLOGY

Smyth & Helwys Publishing, Inc.
6316 Peake Road
Macon, Georgia 31210-3960
1-800-747-3016
©2023 by Larry Gregg
All rights reserved.

Note: All Bible quotations are from the King James Version unless otherwise indicated.
Cover image created with the assistance of Midjourney

Library of Congress Cataloging-in-Publication Data

Names: Gregg, Larry (Christian Historian), author.
Title: Bowl ecclesiology : essays in Christian critical thinking / by Larry Gregg.
Description: Macon, GA : Smyth & Helwys Publishing, 2023. | Includes bibliographical references.
Identifiers: LCCN 2023018590 | ISBN 9781641734493 (paperback)
Subjects: LCSH: Catholic Church--Doctrines.
Classification: LCC BX1751.3 .G745 2023 | DDC 262--dc23/eng/20230615
LC record available at https://lccn.loc.gov/2023018590

Disclaimer of Liability: With respect to statements of opinion or fact available in this work of nonfiction, Smyth & Helwys Publishing Inc. nor any of its employees, makes any warranty, express or implied, or assumes any legal liability or responsibility for the accuracy or completeness of any information disclosed, or represents that its use would not infringe privately-owned rights.

Advance Praise for *Bowl Ecclesiology*

Larry Gregg has performed a profound service to all of us that care about the church. In *Bowl Ecclesiology*, Larry presents a theology of the church that enables us to face the future with faith and strength. In a time when people talk about the church as if it is dying, or already did, Larry lifts up a vision that can help us to face the future with fortitude and faith.

—*Charles Bugg*
Former Dean and Professor
Gardner Webb School of Divinity

Larry Gregg never ceases to amaze me with his words of inspiration. I've never been around him when I didn't learn something new. In *Bowl Ecclesiology*, you too get to stand in Larry's workshop and share his wisdom. Larry has a wonderful way of sharing deep theological thoughts so that any of us can learn and remember.

—*Dr. Nelson Granade*
Pastor, First Baptist Church
Statesville, North Carolina

Another pastor-theologian from the Carolina mountains, Carlyle Marney, once famously quipped that "being in the church is like being in Noah's ark—sometimes the stench is unbearable, but the alternative is unthinkable." Holding in view both human frailties and failings, along with an unshakable sense that the church still has relevance, Larry Gregg writes with the homespun wisdom of the proverbs. Here in abundance is the insight of a disciple who loves the church, its people, and who loves God with all his "mind." For anyone with the same commitments this work will come as welcome companionship along The Way.

—*Rev. Dr. Bart Hildreth*
Senior Pastor, First St. Charles United Methodist Church
St. Charles, Missouri

Larry Gregg is a captivating storyteller who uses the analogies of the ordinary to describe the meanings of our theologies as humans. His chapter on the varieties of Southern BBQ becomes a profound assessment of the reality of diversity in human life and experience. Every church member would profit from a reading of the chapter "Give Your Minister a Break, and You Won't Break Your Minister." Buy the book. Read it!

—*Larry L. McSwain, S.T.D.*
Retired Baptist educator
Author of Open and Closed Doors:
Memoir of a Survivor of the SBC Unholy War

This wonderful collection of essays by Dr. Larry Gregg takes the author's delightful personal stories and uses them as a springboard to critical thinking about biblical and ecclesiological issues. Dr. Gregg does an excellent job of wrestling with important theological questions in a manner that draws from his practical experience in the church and his years in academia.

—*Rev. Dr. Donald G. Scofield Jr.*
Rutherfordton Presbyterian Church

Bowl Ecclesiology is a clear-yet-nuanced confession about the challenges and benefits of commitments to the church. Gregg brings his varied experiences as a woodworker, a pastor, and a counselor to a collection of essays. With his experience as a lathe master, he exposes and highlights the grain of the life of a minister and his parishioners.

—*Richard Wilson*
Emeritus Professor of Religion, Mercer University
Macon, Georgia

BOWL
ECCLESIOLOGY

*Essays in Christian
Critical Thinking*

D. LARRY GREGG

Also by *D. Larry Gregg*

For God and Freedom: A Novel of the First Jewish Revolt

Through a Glass Darkly, but I Still See:
Reflections of a Believing Thinker and a Thinking Believer

If You Ain't Somewhere Doin' Somethin':
More Reflections of a Thinking Believer

Ten Biblical Characteristics of a Great Church

Random Musings of a Contented Old Man

Timotheus: Dearly Beloved Son

To teachers, mentors, professional colleagues, church members,
family, and friends who challenged me to heed and
seek to emulate the words of Augustine of Hippo:
*everybody who believes thinks,—both thinks in believing,
and believes in thinking.*

Contents

Bowl Ecclesiology
1

If You Want to Walk in the Sunshine,
You've Got to Expect Some Rain
7

It's Not So Much My Faith in God as It Is God's Faith in Me
13

They Give You Cash, Which Is Just as Good as Money
19

Just Musing Along with My Mind Out of Gear
25

Light the Candles and Push Back the Darkness
31

The Night I Killed the Christmas Tree
39

Any Good First Read Deserves a Second
45

The Consumer and the Consumed—A BBQ Road Trip
51

Does It Hurt When You Jump Up and Down?
57

Give Your Minister a Break, and
You Won't Break Your Minister
63

God Trims My Trees,
But God Expects Me to Clean Up the Mess
69

You Can't Catch No Fish if You Don't Go Near the Water
75

God Sees Stuff the Rest of Us Don't See
81

Sanity Ain't Necessarily All It's Cracked Up to Be
87

The Challenges to Renewal
Leave Questions to Be Answered
95

There Are Some Things I Just Plain Hate
101

Things I Want to Accomplish before I Die
107

Peggy Said, "Watch My Purse!"
I Said, "Why? What's It Gonna Do?"
113

What're Ya Huntin' For?
Nothin', I'm Just Huntin'
119

The Game Is Called *Shut-the-Box*
125

The Travelocity Gnome
131

You Can't Experience the "Power of God" and
Worship the "god of Power"
137

Only an *I* Separates *Run* from *Ruin*
143

How Deep Does the Water Have to Be?
149

Making Idols of What We Believe
155

If That Don't Just Beat a Hog a Peckin'
161

Never Push on the Hinges
167

Because I Am a Rich Man:
An Exercise in Reflective Thanksgiving
173

Just 'Cause Somebody Says "Boo!"
Don't Mean We Have to Jump
179

Between *Rosh Hashanah* and *Yom Kippur*
185

Just 'Cause You're Thinkin' about You All the Time
Don't Mean Everybody Else Is
191

To Be Announced
197

The Beach Is a Wonderful Place
if You Don't Mind Getting Sand in Your Diaper
203

Larry, You're Gonna Miss the Mandevilla this Year,
and It's Nobody's Fault but Your Own
209

If There Weren't Writers Who Aren't as Good as
Shelby Foote, There Wouldn't Be Any Shelby Footes
215

God's Family Is Larger than Just the Part of It I Know
221

Not Every Foot Leaves the Same Print in the Sand
229

Things I Gave Up when I Gave My Heart to Jesus
235

Son, They Sell Produce Down at the Grocery Store
241

You Take My Picture, and I'll Take Yours
247

It'll Be Just as Beautiful as It Ever Was;
It'll Just Be Beautiful Differently
253

Bowl Ecclesiology

In the mid-1990s a treasured senior adult friend offered to teach me the basic skills of woodworking. Over the next few years, during summers and other breaks in my teaching and pastoral schedules, we made tables, bookcases, china cabinets, toy boxes, blanket chests, and more to our heart's content. Shortly after I began developing my woodworking skills, another equally treasured senior adult friend offered to introduce me to the art of turning wooden bowls from scrap pieces of wood left over from my furniture-building projects. A number of years ago, both of these fine Christian gentlemen went home to be with the Lord, but, as long as I live, I will be indebted to them for befriending me, sharing the insights and wisdom of their diverse experiences, and teaching me basic woodworking skills that have contributed to my overall mental health for decades.

"Ecclesiology" is the fancy theological word for the study of the nature and significance of the Christian community called the "church." During the years of my formal theological training, my days and nights were filled with reading and reflection on theology (the study of God), Christology (the study of Jesus as the Christ), pneumatology (the study of the Holy Spirit), eschatology (the study of last things), ecclesiology (the study of the Church), and various other "ologies." Now I have lived for almost as many years as the beloved friends who shared with me their woodworking skills. It intrigues me to reflect on the reality that my systematic study of the various "ologies" of Christian theology and my hobby of turning bowls from wood scraps have much in common, particularly in the case of the nature and function of the Christian community—both some church somewhere and all Christians everywhere. Please indulge me as I reflect a bit about these commonalities.

First, I took up bowl turning as a way to put the scraps from my furniture building to a useful purpose beyond using them for kindling in the Greggs' wood-burning heater. In many ways the diversity of those wood scraps is similar to the diversity of the people who make up the Christian community. Species of wood are even more diverse than the racial, ethnic, cultural, and ideological diversities of human beings, yet they are all botanical products of the creativity of God as surely as we are all human beings created by that same God. This means that the scraps resulting from the creative endeavors of a woodworker are not automatically useless and worthless simply because they are flawed or oddly sized or hard to work with or damaged in some way.

In a similar way, human beings who, by our own collective and individual choices, have fallen from our original relationship to our Creator are not automatically useless and worthless simply because theologically, psychologically, sociologically, and ecologically we are flawed, oddly sized, hard to work with, and damaged by our collective and individual choices to go our own way rather than God's way. If we as human beings did not have value, despite the fact that sometimes that value is difficult to discern, there would be no need for a community of redemptive acceptance (the church) where, along with others, that value can be affirmed and celebrated.

Second, scraps from the woodworker's pile don't turn themselves into bowls on their own. Two things are necessary before that transition from scrap to art becomes a reality. The first is that the woodworker must see the potential that lies in wood scraps. Then they must make a conscious decision to redeem the fragments from the pile and transform them into objects of beauty and value.

Again, the analogy holds. The biblical message is that a good God created a good environment, placed good people in it, and gave them good instructions regarding how to live good lives in relation to one another and their environment. Human beings chose to go their own way, fell from their original place and purpose, and took their created environment along with them into finitude and fallenness. The God who created them said within God's self, "I am not willing to settle for that." And the unfolding biblical narrative is the story of God's choice to reach into a broken creation and restore it to its original place and purpose in the Divine economy. Christians believe that same Creator God chose to come and live in the scrap pile of fallen humanity in the person of Jesus of Nazareth. God did this in order to gather up the ugly fragments of sin, suffering, and social alienation so they might be transformed into a "new creation," which is the same "old creation" redeemed and restored to its original place and purpose in relation to its Creator (Rom 8:16-23).

At this point, a few words need to be said about the use of analogies in theological reflection. Analogies are comparisons that take something familiar in common human experience and use it to clarify and/or illuminate our understanding of some other reality that may not be as clear in our consciousness. They are particularly useful when talking about God and God's activity in the world for they help us to grasp, within the limits of our finite humanity, something of the limitless infinitude of God as revealed to us in Scripture, history, the natural order, and our own experience. They help us as we struggle, as the Apostle Paul did, with the reality that "now we see through a glass darkly . . ." (1 Cor 13:12). Analogies are never absolute; at best they can only point in the direction of significant truth. Some do so better than others.

Here the caveat must be made that human beings are not scraps of discarded wood. While the wood scraps have no choice in whether they will participate in the redemptive plan of the wood turner, human beings do have a choice regarding their participation in God's loving, redemptive purpose in and through Jesus Christ. While some live in hopeful anticipation of the completion of this redemptive purpose in their lives, others elect to remain on the scrap heap of fallenness, despair, and alienation. Unlike the woodworker who searches the scrap pile for fragments that may be redeemed, there is a double-search quality to God's redemptive purpose for human beings. The New Testament belief in incarnation is the story of God's search for us; the psalmist's "This poor man cried, and the LORD heard him, and saved him out of all his troubles . . ." (Ps 34:6) is the confession of our search for God.

There is a third commonality between the turned wooden bowls I make and any understanding of the nature of the church as the people of God in the world. Before the bowl can be turned, I must take the diverse pieces of wood and glue them to one another, both sides and bottom, with a particularly adhesive glue that unites them together into a single entity. This glue binds the bowl so firmly that it can withstand the stresses of the high-speed revolutions of the lathe and the buffeting of the turning tools as I cut and shape the rough corners, joints, and flat surfaces into a round and smooth vessel that is both beautiful and useful. Initially this process places great stress on the substance of the wood, and sometimes I fear the whole rough glue-up is going to fragment into pieces and fly about the shop, injuring me and breaking other things. That's why the glue is so important; it's what keeps the rough bowl from degenerating back into scrap.

In the life of the church, whether all Christians everywhere or a local congregation, our shared experience of Jesus Christ as Savior and Lord bonds us together in a common unity that is infinitely stronger than any simple human willingness we may have for community, self-interest, social identity, or cultural expression. In the midst of the Corinthian believers' tendency toward fragmentation under stress, Paul emphasized that it is "by the name of our Lord Jesus Christ . . . that ye be perfectly joined together . . ." (1 Cor 1:10).

However, this perfect joining in Jesus Christ does not erase the distinctive personhood and giftedness of each individual believer. This leads to yet another commonality between my turned bowls and the community of believers. My bowls are ordinarily carved from different species of hardwood: oak, maple, hickory, ash, mahogany, black walnut, cherry, etc. Each type of wood has a distinctive density, texture, grain pattern, and responsiveness to the application of turning tools. While this diversity of characteristics often presents challenges as one seeks to mold them together, the result is always worth the time and effort the process requires. In addition, as the various pieces of wood yield to the turning tools, the unique colors and grain patterns of each species are revealed. The result is, in my opinion, a much more beautiful bowl than one turned from a single, uniform block of wood.

The community of Christian believers is not, nor has it ever been, a uniform, monolithic entity. While we share the reality of "One Lord, one faith, one baptism, one God and Father of all . . ." (Eph 4:5-6), it is also true that "as we have many members in one body" (Rom 12:4), those members have "gifts differing according to the grace that is given to us . . ." (Rom 12:6). It is imperative to remember that the only way we are called to be exactly alike is in the commonality of our Christ-likeness. As this diversity of gifts is identified and enabled, we are, both individually and collectively, able to increasingly become more and more the people whom God has always intended us to be.

It is inevitable, as God's indwelling Holy Spirit pares away at our propensity to sinful self-centeredness, that stresses will emerge threatening to fragment the community of faith into pieces and causing us to fear that we will degenerate once again into the scrap pile of isolated lostness from which we are being redeemed. Have no fear! The God who has reached out to redeem us in the person and work of Jesus Christ assures us that Jesus is both "the author and finisher of our faith" (Heb 12:2). Paul assured the Philippians that "he which hath begun a good work in you will perform it until the day of Jesus Christ" (Phil 1:6).

On the other hand, as we yield ourselves to the molding will and purpose of the God who created us, the most beautiful aspects of our individual and collective personhood are revealed in all their wonderous glory. Our diverse gifts complement one another, and collectively we are infinitely more together than any one of us could hope to be individually. Because "every one of us is given grace according to the measure of the gift of Christ" (Eph 4:7), it is possible for us all to achieve "the unity of the faith, and of the knowledge of the Son of God, unto a perfect (person), unto the measure of the stature of the fullness of Christ" (Eph 4:13).

One last thought occurs to me regarding the characteristics shared by my wooden bowls and the church of Jesus Christ. There must be a means for me to attach my roughly cut and glued-up bowl to the lathe so it can be turned. I do so by gluing a block of wood to the bottom center of the bowl and then running screws through the faceplate of the lathe and the wooden block into the bottom of the bowl. Thus, the bowl is held securely to the faceplate while I turn it on the lathe. When the bowl is finished, I remove the screws and wooden block so I can sand and finish the bottom of the bowl. Inevitably, the marks of screw holes are left in the underside of the bowl's bottom. These scars are continual reminders of how the bowl was transformed from cast-off scrap into an object of beauty and usefulness.

It is worth reminding ourselves that this side of heaven, even in the process of being redeemed and transformed by the grace of God, telltale scars will accompany us for the remainder of our lives, reminding us of the suffering, trauma, bad choices, and just plain sin from which we are being redeemed. Some might ask, "Why doesn't God take all that away when we trust Jesus as our Savior?" I remind you that the resurrected Jesus invited Thomas to examine the scars left behind by his suffering on the cross for sinful humanity. Having seen them, Thomas humbly confessed, "My Lord and my God" (John 20:28). Our individual scars, and the collective scars of the community of faith, serve to remind us of what God has done for us in Jesus Christ that we could not possibly have done for ourselves. And they call us, in our innermost hearts and in the community of faith, to humbly confess, "My Lord and my God."

If You Want to Walk in the Sunshine, You've Got to Expect Some Rain

My wife Peggy and I were visiting her sister in Panama City Beach. I began the morning fully expecting a nice walk in the sunshine along the Florida Gulf Coast. I had such a walk the day before, and the day before that as well. As I left the home of my sister-in-law, all indications were that the present day was simply going to repeat the previous two. After all, one of the reasons I go to the beach in the dead of winter is to spend uninterrupted hours in meditative reflection while walking along the beach with the sunshine bathing my face and shoulders.

Quickly I marched the three blocks from the house to Front Beach Road, ducked into McDonald's to purchase a large coffee, then made my way down to the water's edge. Once there I adjusted my stride to a more leisurely pace, instinctively finding the rhythm of the surge and ebb of the surf. Only barely aware of sandpipers tracking the wet sand and gulls scudding effortlessly in the breeze, I turned eastward in the direction of the mid-morning sun, and my thoughts meandered toward the long fishing pier about a mile and a half in the distance.

Half an hour later I emerged from my reverie only a few yards from the pier. Lost in thought, I had failed to note that the southwesterly breeze blowing off the Gulf had significantly intensified. Looking over my shoulder, I noted the line of a rainsquall moving rapidly across the water, heading directly for my section of the beach. I paused for a moment, estimating how long it would take for the rain to arrive. Deciding I had time to get back home only if I left the beach, I went back up to Front Beach Road to use the sidewalk for my return trip.

Soon I was walking briskly westward with the realization that I had badly underestimated how swiftly the storm front was moving. As the wind picked up, I watched the first droplets of rainfall splash on the sidewalk ahead of me. I knew I would never reach my destination in time to beat the storm, but I pushed on as rapidly as my gimpy knee would allow. It was evident that the droplets I had seen were only the precursors of what would be a cold, driving rain.

By this time, I was nearing one of the few remaining small, old, privately owned beachfront hotels along the shore. Deciding to take haven under its drive-thru awning, I quickened my pace and got there just before the bottom fell out. Unfortunately, the gusting wind blew the rain in horizontal sheets, making the shelter of the overhead awning totally inadequate. Noting my plight, the middle-aged woman behind the desk in the lobby came to the door and invited me inside. She pointed toward a comfortably furnished lounge just off the lobby where I found hot coffee and a warm place to dry out while waiting for the storm to pass. Smiling ruefully at my wet clothes and soggy shoes, I found myself thinking, "If you want to walk in the sunshine, I guess you've got to expect some rain."

During the last decade of the twentieth century, we all chuckled at the obvious truth of Forrest Gump's assertion, "Life is like a box of chocolates; you never know what you're going to get." Both Forrest's observation about "chocolates" and mine about "sunshine and rain" draw attention to the same reality: there is a basic unpredictability built into the foundational structures of human existence. And this openness, this contingency in life, makes many people tremendously uncomfortable. Some want chocolate cream in every bite of life and uninterrupted sunshine on every walk along the beach. Such people feel cheated, misused, and put upon whenever they don't get the results they desire. They set themselves up for disappointment and unhappiness because they have failed to discover, or refused to admit, that caramel nougat and rain, at certain times and places, are just as pleasant as chocolate cream and sunshine.

The generations of the late twentieth century were profoundly influenced, perhaps more so than young people of any other period of history, by the pervasive self-centered egoism of much commercial advertising. American society was told, "You only go around once in life, so you've got to grab for all the gusto you can get." Teens learned to imitate the adolescent who whined, "I want my MTV." Women were encouraged to demand the most luxuriously expensive hair care and cosmetic products because they were "worth it." One consequence of such focus on personal self-gratification to the exclusion of everything else is that now, on the threshold of the third decade of the twenty-first century, those same people, who have become middle-aged and senior adults, have created a society plagued by obesity, road rage, reality TV shows, ethical relativism, social/political extremism on both the left and the right, and feel-good religion. And John F. Kennedy's challenge to "Ask not what your country can do for you, but what you can do for your country" has given way to a pervasive attitude of "If there's nothing in it for me personally, to hell with it." Or, to go back to the original metaphor, "If the sun doesn't shine all the time on my personal beach of life, somebody's going to get an earful of dissatisfaction from me."

It has taken a while, and a certain amount of painful experience, but I've been forced to face reality about a number of things. First among them is the truth that I'm not going to get my way all the time, regardless of how determined I am to do so or how disappointed I am when I don't. The world just doesn't seem to care if I throw myself down kicking and screaming in petulant disappointment that I'm not the center of anyone's universe, not even my own.

Some years ago, Peggy and I were having lunch in a restaurant with our three elementary-aged grandchildren. Each one had been given the opportunity, within limits, to order whatever they wanted from the menu. Once the food was delivered to the table, one of the granddaughters decided she would prefer what her brother had ordered to her own meal. Her grandmother patiently explained that she had been given the opportunity to choose whatever she wanted, and now it was time to eat what she had originally chosen. Her brother's lunch wasn't available for her consumption. This loving firm-handedness evoked a flood of pitifully pathetic tears, all to no avail as it was explained once again, "You can't have your brother's lunch. Eat what you selected for yourself, or do without." While the rest of us enjoyed our meal, that granddaughter pouted in anguished disappointment. But you know what? She didn't get her brother's lunch that day, and she threw away the opportunity to eat her own. Needless to say, she was more than enthusiastic about eating her own dinner a few hours later, and she showed no interest in anyone else's.

While children are going to behave this way from time to time, parents and grandparents have a responsibility to nurture them, sometimes pointedly, toward the realization that such petty, antisocial behavior will not be rewarded by letting them have their way. When children are taught that "no" means "no," after a while they catch on that self-centered petulance will not get them what they want, and they learn to make better behavioral choices.

Sadly, it appears that substantial numbers of adults did not figure this out along the way. Our society is plagued by the manifestation of this childish "I've got to have my way all the time or I will have a public fit" behavior in families, churches, civic clubs, political and educational institutions, and neighborhoods. And the result is that when full-grown adults behave shamefully, the foundational societal structures that give meaning and purpose to our collective existence are threatened and damaged by people who wear their self-centered egotism like a vest. Shame on us, all of us, when we behave this way.

Second, lifelong experience has taught me that I don't need my way all the time. Have you noticed that most of us have our own driving paths along which we get from place to place? And we are always sure our particular way is the better. Most of the time that belief is harmless, but sometimes it manifests itself in backseat (or front passenger seat) driving that can be both annoying and dangerous. I can think of a number of ways to get from my house to Asheville, North Carolina, and they are all about the same distance and take about the same driving time. Therefore, when headed to Asheville for dinner with friends and one of them suggests he thinks his favorite route is better than mine, I'm likely to respond, "That's fine with me. I don't care which way we go, as long as we get to the restaurant for dinner." While privately I may not think much of his favorite path, the difference is not worth disputing. Frankly, I value the preciousness of friendships infinitely more highly than I do my need to have my way all the time. But for some, their compulsive need to have their way all the time, and their misbehaviors when they don't, drive them to spoil a perfectly good day on the beach of life because they got caught in a brief shower of unexpected rain.

Third, bitter experience has taught me that when I insist on having my way all the time, demanding what I *want* may cause me to ignore or reject what I *need*. You and I often do this when deciding what to eat for our next meal. More often than not, my first impulse is to scan the restaurant menu for items I particularly enjoy eating. When I do, I am invariably drawn to the carbohydrates, the fats, and the highly spiced. I have grieved for years that meat markets now trim most of the fat off a good ribeye or T-bone steak. And when I go to a local chicken emporium, I always order my strips or wings drenched in the Nuclear Sauce.

Sadly, I have reached a stage in life when there is a price to pay for such culinary self-indulgence; and slowly, painfully, I am working to develop the discipline to allow my dietary choices to be dictated more by my body's nutritional needs than by the passions of my taste buds. Acid reflux, high blood pressure, and coronary disease are too high a price to pay for consistently gratifying my wants while ignoring my needs.

This gastronomic analogy readily applies to other areas of life and relationships. No one should be preoccupied with getting what they want from a marriage, a career, a friendship, etc. to the exclusion of getting what they need from such vital human relationships. Even more important, no one should be so preoccupied with the gratification of their physical and emotional appetites that they fail to attend to the central spiritual needs of their lives. Remember the question of Jesus, "For what shall it profit a man, if he shall gain the whole world, and lose his own soul? Or what shall a man give in exchange for his soul?" (Mark 8:36-37).

Finally, I have learned that often, after having gotten my way, I lived to regret it. And conversely, at other times I have not gotten my way and been grateful I didn't. Looking back over the decades, I recall employment, financial, relational, and social opportunities that gave the appearance that if I could just acquire them life would be one uninterrupted stroll along the beach, basking in the sunshine of good fortune. But the passage of time revealed that in not getting the job or the raise or the recognition I wanted, I had missed being blown away by a rapidly approaching storm that had not yet appeared on the horizon.

I recall laboriously working my way through a complex analysis of human reality in the universe called *Einstein's Space & Van Gogh's Sky*. In it the authors seek to explore the relationship between determinism and free will in human experience. They conclude that, "so far as human experience and behavior go, the present can be seen as continuous with, and determined by, the past, but the future cannot be predicted as new observables appear whose existence is, in principle, not possible to predict."[1] Put more simply, they assert, "In the realms of inner experience and of meaningful behavior the past is determined, the future is not."[2] Put even more simply, in the words of Forrest Gump, "Life is like a box of chocolates; you never know what you're going to get." Or, as I found myself thinking, after having sought shelter from a sudden storm, "If you want to walk in the sunshine, I guess you've got to expect some rain."

---

1. Lawrence LeShan and Henry Margenau, *Einstein's Space & Van Gogh's Sky* (New York : Collier Books, 1983), 37–38.

2. Ibid., 37.

It's Not So Much My Faith in God as It Is God's Faith in Me

None of us are likely to forget how our lives were so profoundly altered by the Covid-19 pandemic. I watched and listened as medical experts, politicians, media pundits, religious leaders, and various and sundry crackpots explained and opined regarding how, as a society, we should respond to this unfolding crisis. It is remarkable how this microscopic, primitive life form undermined our confidence in medical technology, eroded our trust in political leaders and governing institutions, challenged the objectivity and reliability of our sources of information, questioned the central assumptions and values of our faith traditions, and seduced many into giving credence to every conspiracy theory and snake oil cure that slithered along the so-called information highway.

Initially I chose to quietly remain at home, make sawdust in my woodworking shop, read volumes of presidential history, and share a strangely muted fiftieth wedding anniversary with Peggy as she continued to convalesce from a stroke. Perhaps I would have continued this sedentary, passive response had I not begun to hear increasingly strident assertions that how one responds to this crisis is a test of the authenticity of one's faith in God. As a Christian minister for more than five decades, a trained theologian, a teacher of both biblical studies and world religions, and a careful observer of religious psychology and sociology, I felt compelled to argue that how one responds to this, or any other existential crisis, is at least as much a matter of "God's faith in me" as it is of "my faith in God." I further contend that this truth is deeply enshrined in an appropriate reading and interpretation of the biblical text, both Old and New Testaments. Regardless of the pervasive human tendency to fall short of God's highest intentions for us, the reality of divine revelation asserts the Creator's confidence that human beings are endowed with the capacity of trustworthiness regarding the world that has been placed in our stewardship.

Though limited by their humanity, the iconic figures of the biblical literature share one characteristic in common: God elected to trust each of them with a monumentally difficult yet achievable task. Adam and Eve were tasked with managing the environment. Abraham was tasked with founding a nation. Moses was tasked with liberating an enslaved people. David was tasked with securing the existence of the Israelite kingdom. The Hebrew prophets were tasked with speaking truth to power amid internal national corruption and external threat from surrounding empires. And the original followers of Jesus were tasked with declaring the "good news" of what God had accomplished in Jesus's death and resurrection. It matters not how successful these people were in carrying out the tasks entrusted to them; what matters is that God was willing to have faith in them regardless of their human limitations.

To God-conscious people, individually and collectively, God has said in the past and continues to say in the present, "I created you, I have called you, and I am trusting you." Whether you believe it about yourself or not, I choose to believe that God has faith in me and that I am called to be a good steward of that Divine faith. For the sake of brevity, I will discuss only four areas in which I believe God's faith in me is manifest.

First, I believe God has faith that I will use the divine gifts of a discerning mind and sound judgment in my decision-making. The writer of 2 Timothy assured his readers that "God has not given us the spirit of fear; but of power, and of love, and of a sound mind" (1:7). While others may elect to make their decisions predicated on emotions, hormones, political/social ideologies, ethnic/racial prejudices, or economic bottom lines, Christian believers are not free to allow such matters to muddle and obscure the clarity of their critical reflection and decision-making. On the contrary, to refuse to appropriately exercise the discipline of critical thought flies in the face of Jesus's assertion that the first and greatest of the Divine

Commandments is that one should "love the Lord thy God with all thy heart, and with all thy soul, and with all thy *mind*, and with all thy strength" (Mark 12:30, emphasis mine).

It is important to note that the Greek pronoun translated *thy/your* is singular, not plural. Jesus seems to assert in his reply regarding the greatest of the commandments that this is a matter of individual, not collective, choice. I cannot surrender to others the responsibility for the love for God that should fill my heart, ground my soul, and be expressed by my actions. Nor can I transfer to others the decisions of my intellect for which I alone am accountable. God has faith in me to employ a discerning mind and sound judgment in making decisions regarding keeping myself safe from infection. God has faith in me to employ a discerning mind and sound judgment to decide how I will cast my ballot in elections. God has faith in me to employ a discerning mind and sound judgment in assessing medical advice and the medications I take. For Christians to abandon personal critical decision-making to others who demand that they ought to be permitted to make our decisions is to declare that we do not trust ourselves as much as God trusts us. While I am sure I will be held accountable for many things when I stand before God's judgment, I fervently pray that intellectual laziness and sloppy thinking will not be among them.

Second, I believe that God has faith that I will be at least as concerned for the health and safety of others as I am for my personal freedom and gratification. Again, the biblical text grandly illuminates this point. The Apostle Paul felt strongly about Divine liberation from the ritualistic restraints of the ceremonial law accomplished through Jesus Christ. To the Galatians Paul wrote, "Stand fast therefore in the liberty wherewith Christ has made us free, and be not entangled again with the yoke of bondage" (Gal 5:1). However, he was willing to voluntarily place reasonable restraints on his personal exercise of these freedoms for the sake of others. Regarding the eating of meat that had not been ritually slaughtered according to Jewish custom and had been previously sacrificed to idols he observed, ". . . if meat make my brother to offend, I will eat no flesh while the world standeth . . ." (1 Cor 8:13). While Paul felt there was no longer any obstacle to eating such meat, he was willing to refrain from doing so for the sake of others.

While the media frequently repeats the truism, "We are all in this together," there appear to be many among us who assert with their voices and their behaviors, "While the rest of you may be in this together, I am free to do as I damn well please regardless of the consequences for the rest of you." And many who so vigorously proclaim this blatant disregard for the welfare of others do so while hiding behind a screen of triumphant religiosity.

If I drive recklessly and kill someone in an avoidable automobile wreck, am I likely to be charged with vehicular homicide? Very likely! While I may protest that it was just a tragic accident, the truth is that this was no accident. I deliberately made a wrong choice and someone died as a consequence. Now, if I behave recklessly regarding reasonable infection precautions and someone dies because my ego's need for unlimited freedom was more important to me than the life of another, is this not a form of homicide as well? And the fact that I may likely never know who I killed through my self-centered refusal to limit my personal freedom for the sake of others does not make my behavior any less reprehensible.

Third, I believe God has faith that I can distinguish the difference between the tenets and values of my Christian faith and any political ideology I may espouse. It was Jesus who enjoined his hearers to "Render therefore unto Caesar the things which are Caesar's; and unto God the things that are God's" (Matt 22:21). Nowhere did Jesus deny our accountability to the temporal political structures of society, nor did he assert that his followers should not participate in the political system. What he did do was clearly delineate that some things distinctly belong to Caesar while others are exclusively reserved to the purview of God. It is hard to believe that Jesus would have emphasized such distinctions if he did not think that people were capable of recognizing them and striving to avoid allowing them to become entangled.

Many are willing to assert that Christians, and particularly ministers, should stay out of politics. Absolutely not! As citizens, Christians have a responsibility to assume the obligations and exercise the rights of citizenship. However, Christians hold dual citizenship in both the City of Man and the City of God. Our challenge is to insist that the values of the City of God influence and shape our participation in the City of Man. The history of the last two thousand years demonstrates that we are always endangered when we permit the values of the City of Man to define our identity in the City of God.

The second half of the twentieth century witnessed, and the first two decades of the twenty-first have perpetuated, a conflation of Christian identity and political affiliation. The result is that Christian orthodoxy is often judged and found wanting by the test of political identity and agenda. The City of Man asserts that "What belongs to Caesar belongs to Caesar; and that what used to belong to God now belongs to Caesar as well." Whenever and wherever this attitude has manifested itself, certain characteristic words describe it: Persecution, Slavery, Inquisition, Imperialism, Final Solution. Across the centuries God has had faith that people who know better will do better. Just because we haven't done better in the past is no justification for not attempting to do so in the present and for the future. Let's not betray God's faith in us again.

Finally, I believe God has faith that my ultimate hope does not rest in the promises of men and women, regardless of their wealth, charisma, power, or pedigree. The psalmist sang, "Do not put your trust in princes, in mortal men, who cannot save. When their spirit departs, they return to the ground: on that very day their plans come to nothing" (Ps 146:3-4, NIV). History cries out in agony occasioned by the pseudo-messiahs who rise up like dragon's teeth sown in the fields of misplaced hope. They have names, and most of us can recite many of them. They have come from every corner of the earth, every station in life, and every cultural and ethnic heritage. Yet they all share one thing in common: their favorite word is "I."

In one of the darkest chapters of Judah's history, Jeremiah looked out over the impending final destruction of Jerusalem and the exile of thousands to Babylon. Seventy years would pass before a remnant descended from those carried off into exile would return to the ruins of the city of David and Solomon. As the pestilential gloom of despair enveloped them, God spoke through Jeremiah and said, "'For I know the plans I have for you,' declares the LORD, 'plans to prosper you and not to harm you, plans to give you hope and a future'" (Jer 29:11, NIV). Paul reflected on the agony and suffering of fallen humanity living in a fallen environment. While not ignoring the groaning and travail of life, he was able to look beyond the pain and assert that "we are saved by hope" (Rom 8:24).

While I have had grave reservations about the consequences of attempting to return to pre-pandemic normalcy too quickly, I understand the deep-seated yearning of people to do so. It is a sign that one of the factors that defines humanity is that we are creatures of hope or, as Alexander Pope put it, "Hope springs eternal in the human breast."[1] However, a desire to recover the past is not authentic Christian hope. Christian hope does not look backward to recover the past. Christian hope looks upward and embraces the future. God has faith that through hope I can learn from the past and live for the future.

---

1. "An Essay on Man: Epistle I," III.ii.5, Poetry Foundation, poetryfoundation.org/poems/44899/an-essay-on-man-epistle-I, accessed April 13, 2023.

They Give You Cash, Which Is Just as Good as Money

My favorite television commercial of all time featured former New York Yankees' catcher Yogi Berra and the AFLAC duck. You may recall the scene. Yogi is sitting in the barber's chair and complains about a nick on the back of his head. This leads to a discussion of insurance between Yogi and the man in the chair next to him and then to Yogi's wonderful line, "They give you cash, which is just as good as money."

Unquestionably, this quip has joined the list of classic Yogi-isms. Some of them may be familiar to you. Of golf he once said, "Ninety percent of the putts that fall short don't go in." Yogi showed keen insight into human psychology when he said, "Always go to other people's funerals, otherwise they won't come to yours." Commenting on the falling attendance at professional baseball games, Yogi observed, "If people don't want to come out to the park, nobody's gonna stop them." Perhaps the most famous Yogi-ism of all time is his comment, "It's *déjà vu* all over again." As a writer and public speaker, my personal favorite of his is, "I didn't really say everything I said."

Some years ago, I found myself reflecting on Yogi's insight about the relationship of cash and money while making preparations for a trip to St. Anne's College at Oxford University. I had been invited to present a paper on the relationship of intentionally religious people and American public education. Several weeks before the departure date, I decided it would be a good idea to acquire some British currency, or pounds, prior to arriving so that, in an emergency, I would not get caught in the confusion of monetary exchange rates. Going to my local banking institution, I asked whether they could acquire British pounds for me. My banker replied that this was not a service his institution provided, but he helpfully suggested a couple of other financial institutions in the area that did provide such services. Thanking my banker, I headed for one of the other institutions and had a peculiar experience there.

It happened this way. I went inside the bank and told a receptionist what I wanted. She directed me to a vice president who listened patiently to my request and assured me that her institution both could and would acquire £250.00, or approximately $500.00, in British currency for me, explaining that it would take a couple of days to have the currency delivered. I assured her I did not mind waiting, and the discussion moved to how I would pay for the British pounds. From this positive point the conversation quickly spiraled downward.

She asked, "What account would you like us to debit to cover the cost of the British currency?" I explained that I did not have any accounts with her bank. Next she asked, "Would you like to open an account here?" I assured her I was perfectly satisfied with my current bank; I just needed to get some British pounds. Next she asked, "What credit card would you like to charge the pounds to?" Here I said that I had more than the necessary $500.00 in my pocket at the time and would be glad to pay the full amount of the pounds, and the bank's fee for the transaction, in cash and on the spot. Here her face clouded and she said, "We can't do that!"

"You can't do what?" I asked.

"We can't take cash for this transaction. We must debit directly from an account with our institution or charge the transaction against a major credit card."

Puzzled, I inquired, "You're telling me this bank will not accept money issued by the United States Treasury Department with the phrase *this note is legal tender for all debts, public and private* printed on it for a financial transaction in Rutherford County, North Carolina?"

"That's right," she said. "All currency exchanges made by this bank"—here she said the name of the bank—"must be done either by debit from an existing account or charged to a major credit card."

With this I couldn't restrain myself from quipping, in my best Yogi Berra voice, "But I want to give you cash, which is just as good as money!"

The bank VP didn't get the joke and proceeded to explain once again that she could open an account for me, or she could make a charge on my credit card; but she couldn't take the stack of perfectly good twenty-dollar bills I had extracted from an ATM machine only a few hours before.

Recognizing it was both a waste of my time and my breath to continue to argue, I thanked her and went home. From there I called the American Automobile Association, and their representative assured me that AAA could get me the British pounds I wanted, and they would be more than happy to accept payment for the service in cash. Apparently AAA, like Yogi Berra, thinks cash is just as good as money.

By now some of you are thinking, "While this story is mildly entertaining, does he have a point?"

I have several. First, that day I was reminded that regardless of how often a financial institution advertises its purpose to serve me, I need to recall that its primary purpose is to make money for the institution and its stockholders. If it can make money serving me, it will do so, but its primary purpose is not to serve me; its primary purpose is to make money. Therefore, the bank refused to accept my cash that day because the cash, unlike a debit from an account or a credit card, could not be electronically lumped together with all other such transactions that the mega-bank was making for thousands of other people on the global money market that day. Put simply, there was more money to be made through an electronic transaction of millions/billions than through a "cash-in-hand" transaction of a few hundred dollars, so my need for a financial service was rejected, not on the basis of the bank's desire to serve my need, but on the basis of the bank's need to make as much money as possible.

Second, I came away from my interview with the bank VP with the sense that she didn't think I was very bright. After all, she was a banker, and I was someone who walked in off the street looking for British pounds. Such a person should never be impertinent enough to question the vast wisdom of a major financial institution regarding its operational procedures. One should go along with the procedures because that's how we do it here.

Third, I found myself once again bemused by the assumption of some institutions that people have no alternative place to get their needs met—met just as well, and sometimes even better.

The next day, while driving to the AAA office in Hendersonville, North Carolina, to get my British pounds, I began to muse on the implications of my thoughts related to the banking institution when applied to the ministry of a local church. There are several parallels worth considering.

First, for the church it's not only a matter of advertising; the primary purpose of the church really is to meet the needs of people in the name and spirit of the God who created them. While banks may be in business for the purpose of multiplying the material investments of the institution and its stockholders, churches exist to minister to the spiritual, physical, psychological, and social needs of people—both those who are a part of the church, i.e., stockholders, and those who simply walk in off the street seeking help. Everybody knows it is mostly advertising hype when the bank says, "We're here to serve you." But when a church signals, "We're here to serve you," and then doesn't do so, it ought to be ashamed of itself for it is doing more than false advertising. Such a church is betraying the reason for its existence in the world.

Second, churches often alienate people they are seeking to reach by relating to them as though they are not smart. We do so in a variety of ways. Often we are condescending in our response to questions people outside the church raise about our diverse doctrinal, procedural, and sectarian issues. This is compounded by the fact that some insist on replying only in the language of Zion instead of using ordinary, everyday language. Another way we signal to people outside the church that we don't think they're smart is in our tendency to define "faith" as the uncritical embracing of a prepackaged set of abstract truths that can only be believed, never questioned. Again, people are not fooled when it is obvious that a church's primary goal for attempting to reach them has more to do with dollars in the offering plate and *derrieres* in the pews than with healing their hurts, renewing their hopes, and assuaging their spiritual emptiness and longing. Yet another way of signaling we don't think the people outside the church are smart is our insistence that we are entitled to challenge and critique the secular culture to our heart's content, but that secular culture has no corresponding entitlement to challenge and critique what it considers to be the shortcomings of organized religion. Yogi might have said in this instance, "What's sauce for the goose oughta be gravy for the other gooses too."

Finally, as surely as the banking institution failed to understand that I had other alternatives in my quest for £250, and would turn to one of those other alternatives in the space of a heartbeat, churches often assume that people have no other alternative places to get their perceived needs met—met just as well, and sometimes better.

Now, hear me clearly. I am not advocating that churches adopt a pandering posture of "Let's find out what people want and give it to them." Churches all over the country are doing this very thing and are in the process of converting themselves into nothing more than yet another entertainment venue. The result is that, in the desire to achieve statistical success in terms of income, attendance, and new stockholders (members), such churches are in danger of selling their souls into slavery to the hedonistic appetites of a secular culture. There are some things people perceive to be needs in their lives that the church has absolutely no business attempting to meet. Not only are those perceived needs not a part of the church's mission in the world, but they often run completely contrary to the church's mission and to the best interests of the people in question.

It remains true that people outside the church have many perceived needs that the church, if it genuinely is to be the Body of Christ in the world, is under a profound obligation and responsibility to meet. And the church has no right complaining when, after neglecting or refusing to meet those needs, it finds that searching and hungry people turn somewhere else and embrace something else. While I would have done business with the bank I first approached about acquiring British pounds for me, I did not have to do business with them. And people do not have to interact with churches they perceive to be disinterested in or unwilling to attempt to meet legitimate needs in the spirit of Jesus Christ, needs the Scripture makes clear are genuinely a part of the church's ongoing mission in the world.

Yogi Berra understood that "cash is just as good as money." Jesus wanted his disciples to understand that ministering to human needs is the same as ministering directly to him. Listen to his words:

> For I was an hungered, and ye gave me meat: I was thirsty, and ye gave me drink: I was a stranger, and ye took me in: Naked, and ye clothed me: I was sick, and ye visited me: I was in prison, and ye came unto me. Then shall the righteous answer him saying, Lord, when saw we thee an hungered, and fed thee? Or thirsty, and gave thee drink? When saw we thee a stranger, and took thee in? or naked, and clothed thee? Or when saw we thee sick, or in prison, and came unto thee? And the King shall answer and say unto them, Verily I say unto you, Inasmuch as ye have done it unto one of the least of these my brethren, ye have done it unto me. (Matt 25:35-40)

Jesus is clear here; what we do for others, we do for God.

Just Musing Along with My Mind Out of Gear

The week between Christmas and New Year's provided an opportunity to visit one of my favorite writing places on the shoreline of Panama City Beach. For decades I have come to this place once, sometimes twice, each year. While Peggy and her sister talk and shop, I spend my hours walking the beach, just musing along with my mind out of gear. The experience is always relaxing, frequently amusing, and sometimes creative. When the creative times come, I always end up at the same place, feverishly writing to get thoughts and images fixed in my consciousness before they fade. I visited my place on December 26, and not much happened. But I came back the next day, and boy, what a difference a day made. It all began when I took note of how much my place had changed over the years.

The first time I visited my spot on the beach, it was a simple walking path providing public access across the dunes to the sand and surf. Late one summer evening Peggy and I stood on the path and watched Fourth of July fireworks shooting skyward from a pier jutting out into the Gulf of Mexico. But, with the cycle of years, my place has dramatically changed. Some of the changes are simple matters of circumstance and were necessary responses to the need to preserve the shoreline. First, the sandy path through the sea oats and sand spurs gave way to a wooden ramp made from pressure-treated timbers, equipped with guardrails and a staircase permitting access to the beach. Eventually erosion from the annual hurricane season necessitated the construction of a vertical concrete drainage shaft with a steel grating on top that extends several feet above the level of the sand. The shaft permits floodwaters to recede back into the Gulf without taking away as much beach sand as before. Since my last visit, several feet back from the storm drain and beneath the beach access ramp, an eighteen-inch-wide concrete retaining wall has been constructed to prevent the sand from washing out from around the wooden posts supporting the access ramp. It is there to prevent the structure from collapsing in future hurricane seasons.

While these changes all detract somewhat from the attractiveness of my favorite place, I approve and will adjust to them, for, unattractive as they are, these modifications are intended to enhance the opportunity for me, and for many thousands of others, to continue to enjoy the spot for decades into the future. They do not impair my ability to sit in the morning sun with a gentle breeze at my back. They take nothing away from my ability to hear waves breaking on the shore or the shrill cries of delighted children playing in the sand while parents, grandparents, and lovers stroll the edge of the surf looking for unbroken seashells and sharks' teeth. But, sitting atop the new concrete retaining wall with my back resting against one of the sun-warmed posts of the access ramp on a breezy late December day, I found other changes more difficult to accept.

First, there is the massive increase in the number of high-rise condominiums. They have progressively walled off the ocean view from those who drive along Front Beach Road. Senior adults who stroll the sidewalks, because the shifting sands and sloping beach are hard on people with arthritic joints and unstable balance, now walk in shadows, shielded by the towering buildings from both sunshine and surf.

Second, while my favorite public access spot remains where it has always been, I note that these places are becoming fewer and farther between, making it more difficult for those who cannot afford to vacation in expensive beachfront condos. They have to walk farther and endure more inconvenience to gain access to public property. Furthermore, some condos and hotels are attempting to limit beach access directly in front of their property to their guests exclusively. Again, while they may hold title to the property on which their buildings stand, the shoreline is public property held in trust for the enjoyment of all.

Now, I know the high-rise condos significantly multiply the available housing in the area, and I know the people who own and rent them pump lots of money into the local economy. But the less financially endowed who come to visit, and the locals who live in the area year-round, pump substantial sums into the local economy as well, perhaps even more than the condo owners and their guests. Most high-rise condominiums are owned by gigantic corporate holding companies based in New York, Los Angeles, Houston, Miami, Las Vegas, London, Tokyo, etc. Profits from such ventures are used to pay dividends to stockholders, megabucks in salaries and perks to senior corporate executives, and the retainers of lawyers and lobbyists who influence legislation regarding tax shelters, zoning regulations, and the use of public lands and resources. That money does not stay in places like Panama City.

But the locals who work the tourism jobs (and all the jobs that make a community run) and those with limited budgets who visit such places and rent old, privately owned houses blocks from the beach are the ones who frequent the local diners and fast food establishments, shop in the mom-and-pop stores, and buy the inexpensive trinkets, beach supplies, and T-shirts their children think they must have. These are the people who fuel the local economy; and these are the people who should not, must not, be sealed off from America's great leisure places because they don't arrive in luxury automobiles or can't leave $50.00 tips in trendy restaurants.

Many of the tourists live in a real, albeit ordinary world, and after a few days of rest and relaxation they are going back to it. Meanwhile, they are as entitled to feel the sea breeze, bask in the sunshine, play in the water, fish in the surf, and daydream as anyone else. The truth is that while the real estate developers, construction companies, and condo owners put a lot into the local economy, they also take a lot out, and they take it with them somewhere else. But the locals and tourists put a lot in as well; and all they take out is, hopefully, a decent living for the locals and a few seashells, pieces of driftwood, cheap souvenirs, and enduring memories.

Musing along with my mind out of gear, I walked to my favorite oyster bar for a hot cup of coffee and a fried oyster po'boy; it ain't

South Louisiana, but it's close. Here I began to think about the implications of my earlier musing for my role as pastoral leader of a Christian community. Several thoughts came to mind. First, change cannot be prevented; it is one of the inevitabilities of life. Powerful natural forces work through human relationships that are analogous to the wind, rain, and cold of seasonal change on the Gulf Coast. Some of these forces are emotional, others are physical, and yet others are social and economic. Like a hurricane's storm surge, these natural human interactions are both creative and destructive; they are the sources of both suffering and joy.

In the Christian community, those who are determined to prevent change doom themselves to frustrating failure and make everyone around them miserable in the process. The refusal to adapt to changing circumstances is often the refusal to be open to the unfolding revelation of God's redemptive purposes in the world. It is Jesus Christ who is the same "yesterday, today, and forever" (Heb 11:8), not one single person or group's understanding of him.

Second, in the Christian community, while change cannot be prevented, it can be managed by people who elect to be proactive, not reactive. But this means one is not likely ever to be completely satisfied with the results. This is one of the most difficult lessons for Christian leaders to learn. Because we are passionately idealistic about our commitments, and we really are concerned to make the world a better place, we tend to forget that absolute perfection is not an available option this side of heaven. This leads to the conclusion that compromise, in and of itself, is automatically a bad thing. Such thinking is a mistake. While I regret the concrete retaining wall and drainage system that have intruded on the pristine simplicity of the beach, it remains true that these technological and engineering compromises have made it possible for me still to have my favorite musing place. While I can't have everything, I still, within limits, prefer something to nothing at all.

The same is true among the people I serve as pastoral leader. I gave up a long time ago on the idealistic expectation that I will get them to believe and think and do all I wish they would believe and think and do. I suspect many of them have faced the reality that it is unlikely I will ever believe, think, and do all they would like either. Fortunately, for almost everyone involved, we have worked at the fine art of compromise from a genuinely Christian perspective. We have learned to adjust our expectations in ways that make it possible for all to receive, learn, and grow while minimizing the amount of disappointment and frustration such accommodation always evokes. We remind one another that while no one is likely to get everything they want, something, within limits, is preferable to nothing at all.

A third thought is that while all are not able to contribute in the same way, or to the same degree, all have something to contribute to the life of any vital and active community, whether political, economic, social, educational, or religious. This truth presents a particularly complex set of challenges to the Christian leader who primarily accomplishes goals for the group with the cooperative assistance of volunteers. Therefore, the Christian leader must evoke the gifts, skills, and resources of those who have much to contribute while valuing and guarding those with fewer abilities and resources against being completely overwhelmed and walled out of decision-making by those who are stronger and more powerful. Yes, Jesus frequently kept company with the leper and the lame, the blind and the bigoted, the weak and the wanton. But he also was regularly in the company of religious leaders like Jairus of Capernaum, members of the social elite and political establishment like Nicodemus and Joseph of Arimathea, and the brashly materialistic and self-righteous man known to us only as a rich young ruler. One has only to read the Gospels to sense the tensions created by Jesus's comprehensive inclusiveness; but God's redemptive purpose being made known in and through him was a work of grace on behalf of all.

Like the beachfront, it seems to me, the contemporary church is succumbing to the temptation of believing that the contributions of the rich, the powerful, the talented, the well-connected are of more value than those of the average and the ordinary. Thus our flagship churches relocate their buildings along thoroughfares leading to affluent bedroom communities and surround them with vast parking lots so those who drive $60,000 automobiles can get in and out with ease. Meanwhile, the neighborhoods that have been abandoned by upscale Christians deteriorate into crime and violence, where the poor and the aged live their days and nights in fear. Combine this with altar areas designed like sound stages, auditioned choirs, soloists who behave like rock stars making music videos, and ministers with all the moves of slick game-show hosts, and the result is obscenely expensive "religiotainment" for the affluent, without mission, without mercy, and without any enduring meaning.

Now remember, I've recently been on vacation, just musing along with my mind out of gear, observing and commenting on the phenomenon of change in two of my favorite places—a stretch of beach along the Florida Gulf Coast and any place where those who claim identity with Jesus Christ gather to worship and minister. In both places change is inevitable. It is not the change to which I object. What raises my ire is the sense that the poor, the weak, and those who are least able to voice their concerns in ways that will be heard are slowly being walled out of both places as the most beautiful views and the most influential roles are monopolized by the people most adept at grasping the brass ring of American obsession with materialist ego gratification. Christian leaders should never forget that we are followers of the one whose life was threatened when he announced, "The Spirit of the Lord is upon me, because he hath anointed me to preach the gospel to the poor; he hath sent me to heal the brokenhearted, to preach deliverance to the captives, and recovering of sight to the blind, to set at liberty them that are bruised, to preach the acceptable year of the Lord" (Luke 4:18-19).

Light the Candles and Push Back the Darkness

It was the first Christmas following our marriage. Peggy and I met in early February, had a whirlwind courtship that lasted about two weeks before we became engaged, and we were married in mid-May. Everyone in her family and mine, as well as our friends and acquaintances, held their collective breath wondering if we would make it. After more than half a century together, I think everyone can exhale; I'm pretty sure we're going to be OK. And it has been a great deal more than just OK; it has been "a wonderful life," if I may borrow the title of the beloved Jimmy Stewart Christmas movie.

Still, 1970 was our first Christmas together, and there had been little opportunity to become acquainted with the long-standing holiday traditions of our respective families. Only recently had I become pastor of a church in suburban Birmingham, Alabama. We had hardly moved into the parsonage before it became time to put up our first Christmas tree, shop for presents, and share the Advent season with our new church family.

The weeks of Advent flew by, and suddenly it was Christmas Eve. Arriving home following a candlelight church service, I settled into my favorite chair in the living room while Peggy changed clothes prior to joining me there. I waited, somewhat impatiently, and, when she finally arrived, I asked, "Are you ready?"

"Ready to what?" she questioned.

"Ready to open the presents," I replied.

"Oh, we can't open them tonight," she said with astonishment. "We have to wait until Christmas morning."

"Why?"

"My family has always opened presents early on Christmas morning," she said, a look on her face that suggested I ought to know the obvious.

"Well, my family always opened Christmas presents on Christmas Eve," I said, imitating her tone and look. And here we were, about to have an argument—not our first one mind you, just our first one on Christmas Eve.

Suffice it to say that we worked through the problem, found a compromise, and began a new tradition of our own that respected the family traditions both of us brought to our marriage. Still, at this season every year, I find myself remembering that evening, smiling at the brief distress our cultural collision caused, and musing on how the experience set the tone for the way we have resolved most of the succeeding crises of life.

During Advent, in churches and private homes around the world, candles are lighted and the stages of the journey to Bethlehem are observed. It is the time when we sing familiar hymns commemorating the birth of the Christ child; attend gatherings of family and friends to celebrate the season; decorate our homes, buy presents, and wait anxiously for the time when we tear open the packages and discover what has been awaiting us under the tree. But the season has a dark side as well. As surely as the threatening figure of Herod the Great lurks in the background of the biblical narratives of the birth of Jesus, waiting for the opportunity to harm the newborn child, there are people and circumstances lurking malevolently in the darkness of each Christmas season. Immediately we think of the predatory personalities who steal credit cards, burglarize homes, bilk unsuspecting senior adults with seasonal scams, and mug shoppers in parking lots.

But other dark realities intrude from the shadowy fringes of the season as well: illness, grief, divorce, accidents, depression, and spiritual emptiness. Recent Advent seasons have been overshadowed by the grim reality of the Covid-19 pandemic that prevented us from engaging in so many of the customary worship, fellowship, and family gatherings we cherished while we mourned the deaths of millions in our own country and worldwide. Further, even after taking all the recommended precautions, we still wondered if this invisible menace would penetrate our efforts to protect ourselves and our loved ones and leave us remembering that our family was included among the thousands who observed Advent in mourning. For millions and millions, the choruses of "Peace on Earth" and "Joy to the World" rang with tinny hollowness as their lives were characterized by strife, despair, grief, and shock.

What can we do, in our own lives and in our interactions with others, to keep at bay these lurking dangers while at the same time we embrace the wondrous story of God's choice to become like us in order that we might become like God? Well, I have no magic formulas, but I do have suggestions to offer. Interestingly enough, they are drawn from how Peggy and I resolved the minor distress over when we should open our presents—on Christmas Eve or Christmas morning.

First, one begins with love—deep, abiding, sustaining, transforming love. Some of you are saying, "Here comes the mushy part." Not from me. It's the mushy part I wish to challenge, because the "mushy emotionalism" that passes itself off today for authentic Christian love is inadequate to meet the real needs of our lives. The New Testament writers, and the early Christian community, understood that the most common words in the ordinary Greek of their day failed to express the depth and richness of the love they had found in God's redemptive grace. Words like *phileo* and *eros* were too emotionally and hormonally oriented to express what they wanted to say, so they reached into the language for another word, *agape*, to express their understanding of how God had elected to relate to them in and through Jesus Christ, and for how they should relate to one another as the expression of their Christian identity.

They filled the word *agape* with content that moved beyond passion-driven instinct and sentiment-laden feeling. They understood that the most fully authentic expression of love in our lives is not that of hormones and feelings but that of choice—the choice to relate to those around us in ways that foster the fullest expressions of goodwill, grace, and godliness. Further, it is the choice to relate to others in these ways regardless of whether they relate to us in the same way. *Agape* is love given in the hope that such selfless love will evoke, but not demand, a corresponding response from the other. *Agape* love is about giving; it is not about getting, or winning, or possessing. It is the richest, the greatest, the most precious gift one person can bestow upon another; and when people choose to love one another in this way, there are no crises they cannot resolve together.

Next, find the humor that underlies the stresses of the holiday season, even during unprecedentedly difficult Advent seasons. Every married couple has a story similar to that of the Greggs' first Christmas together. And the memory of them always evokes a smile, because once we laugh together about life's circumstances, we can then begin to work together toward resolution of the stresses. Now, listen carefully. I'm not talking about putting on a false face and having a "Holly Jolly Christmas." Current circumstances are too serious for such superficiality. All I'm saying is that laughing together is one of life's best stress relievers, and while we use the phrase from time to time, I've never really known of anyone who died laughing. But people die all the time while they are shouting, swearing, shaming, shunning, or slandering one another. Humor reminds us that even the deepest darkness of despair cannot be allowed to be victorious. We must embrace the angelic announcement, despite the darkness surrounding us: "Fear not: for, behold, I bring you good tidings of great joy . . ." (Luke 2:10).

Third, remember that the only thing that never changes in life is the reality that everything changes in life. We can treasure the moments of the past, but we cannot infinitely perpetuate them. Children grow up, relationships flourish or dissolve, bodies age, minds fade, communities and churches are transformed by economics, demographics, technology, and the whims of fashion and taste. The Advent season is a time for recalling past experience and the richness of our religious and cultural heritage. But do not allow nostalgia for bygone days to prevent you from experiencing the timeless blessings of the present and future seasons. Doing so may require some concessions and compromises on your part, but stubbornly refusing to adapt is permitting our recalcitrant denial that the past is past to destroy the possibility of our having a joy-filled future. Frankly, I can make it through each future Advent season without celebrating the season in the same ways I have in the past. I would prefer to adapt to the demands of the present than die clinging to the past. There are too many future Advents I hope to celebrate with family, friends, church families, etc. for me to risk my life, and the lives of others, simply because I insist on observing Christmas during a time of crisis the same way I always have in the past.

Finally, as you journey along the road toward Bethlehem this Advent season, light the candles, and thereby keep pushing back the encroaching darkness with its Herod-like malevolence that would slaughter our innocence.

Early in the development of Christian worship, much attention came to be paid to the images of light reflected in both the Old Testament and the New Testament. From the Genesis announcement that God said, "Let there be light," to the words of Jesus, "I am the light of the world," this image of light has profoundly influenced Christian thought and witness. For many decades congregations have made use of the Advent wreath, with its progressively lighted candles, to mark the stages of the journey toward the birth of the Christ child. Some, in their family worship at home, make use of the Advent wreath as a part of their more personal observance of the Christmas season. This is a practice I encourage, for I think it is of immeasurable value in helping people to keep their focus amid the stresses of this time of year.

While there are no absolutely uniform traditions regarding the color of the candles or the order of their lighting, there are two sets of interpretive symbols I think are particularly meaningful. For some, the candles represent the central Christian attributes of faith, hope, love, and joy. Others, with emphasis on the unfolding progression of God's revelation, call the first candle the Prophecy Candle, the second the Bethlehem Candle, the third the Shepherd's Candle, and the fourth the Angel's Candle.

For me, I find these sets of interpretive symbols most meaningful as they intersect. For when we merge the images of faith and prophecy, we are reminded that Christians do not have faith in faith;

our faith rests in the faithfulness of the God who made promises to the patriarchs and matriarchs and prophets.

Bethlehem and hope symbolize the nurturing power of God that sustains us through the most difficult times. The word Bethlehem is a compound of two Hebrew words *beth* (= house) and *lehem* (= bread), so the name of the village of Jesus's birth is literally "the house of bread." Bread nurtures us, bread sustains us, bread keeps body and soul united, bread keeps us alive. The Apostle Paul told the Roman believers, "we are saved by hope . . ." (Rom 8:24). In 1 Timothy 1:1 the author rooted his entire Christian identity in "our Savior and Lord Jesus Christ, which is our hope." As surely as bread nurtures our bodies and keeps us alive, hope nourishes the soul and enlivens the human spirit.

The Shepherd's Candle, seen as the Candle of Love, is especially meaningful. Tradition has idealized the role of the shepherd in biblical times through association with the shepherd boy David and the shepherds in the fields outside Bethlehem the night of Jesus's birth. But in truth, the image of shepherd was not revered and respected in the first century; shepherds were often viewed as dishonest, undependable, lazy, and immoral. The wonderful irony of the shepherds' witness to the birth of the Christ child is that these men were the outcasts of their society. Not respected and admired, not loved and trusted, they were viewed as the unlovely, the least. But God valued them so highly that they were among the first to hear for themselves, and then announce to others, the good news of God's redemptive love.

Last, the fourth candle combines the symbols of joy and the angelic hosts' triumphant song: "Glory to God in the highest and on earth peace toward [people] of goodwill" (Luke 2:14).

And so I say again, light the candles and keep pushing back the encroaching darkness. Light them in your churches and light them in your homes. But most of all, light them in your heart. Light the candles to keep yourself reminded that the hope that saves us in Jesus Christ will nurture us with the bread of life as we journey through the dark wilderness of life's circumstances. Light the candles to keep yourself reminded that God's redemptive love encompasses the sinner as well as the saint, the down and out as well as the up and out, the broken, the bruised, the misunderstood, and the lonely. Light the candles to keep yourself reminded that joy is not reserved for the angels; one of the signs of the Spirit of God in our lives is joy (Gal 5:22).

The Night I Killed the Christmas Tree

Peggy prides herself on the beauty of the Gregg family Christmas tree. While I know little of these things, I understand it is called a "memory" or "keepsake" Christmas tree. Since our first Christmas together in 1970, she has been collecting ornaments—dozens, perhaps hundreds, of ornaments. Some are the gifts of friends. Others memorialize special times in the life of the family. Yet others contain pictures of grandchildren and family pets, articles of memorabilia we have picked up along the way in our travels, and mementos passed along from our parents when we were younger and they were still with us. There are delicate ceramic and crystal pieces that she cradles as carefully as if she were handling nitroglycerine as they are transferred from box to tree.

One of my favorite Christmas memories over the years is sitting comfortably on the living room sofa, coffee cup in hand, while watching Peggy, and the boys when they were small, decorate the tree. The years have passed and much has changed, but I can still bet on the fact that the day after Thanksgiving the boxes will come out, I will assemble the sections of the tree and settle it on its base, and Peggy, one or both of our now adult sons, and the grandchildren will decorate the tree. It is one of the rituals that holds the Gregg family together across the generations. I can wait a few years while grandchildren finish college and find mates, but I look forward to the Christmases when great-grandchildren join the tradition.

Many may think that Ebenezer Scrooge has cornered the market on Christmas Eve nightmares, but I beg to differ. It happened this way: Peggy and I had come home after a 10:00 p.m. Christmas Eve Communion service to finish loading the car and begin our almost annual trek to Panama City Beach to spend a few days between Christmas and New Year's. The extended family had gathered earlier on Christmas Eve to exchange gifts, feast on all the traditional goodies, and worship together at the Christmas Eve Communion. Now grandchildren were napping in cars while parents drove them home for the much-anticipated visit of Santa Claus.

As we were doing various things to close up the house for several days, it occurred to me that it would be a good idea to slide the Christmas tree away from the double windows in our living room, making it possible to close the drapes and perhaps reduce the temptation of unwanted visitors looking in on our home while we were away. I stooped down to grab the base of the Tree so I could slide it across the hardwood floor to the corner of the living room. Unfortunately, one leg of the base caught on some imperfection in the floor, and a moment later I gasped in horror as the Christmas tree tipped over and fell flat on the living room floor. The din of shattering ceramic, crystal, and glass lights was nothing compared to the wail of despair as Peggy watched her prized "keepsake" Christmas tree die under the hands of a husband who meant well but who had created a Christmas Eve nightmare that would have made Tiny Tim laugh out loud in its tragic ludicrousness. That was the night I killed the Christmas tree.

Many years have passed since that night, but I still shudder when the images of the falling tree, the shattering ornaments, and the heartbroken cry of my wife come to mind. Have you ever driven for more than five hundred miles, through the darkness, in almost total silence?

Well, enough self-pity. We got over it, some of the ornaments were undamaged, others were salvageable, and, regrettably, some had to be thrown in the trash. But at the foundational level of our relationship, Peggy and I love one another, and we have made our way through experiences more traumatic than this one. So, while my well-meaning mistake could not be undone, it also has not defined the nature of our relationship in the years that followed. We have finally reached a point where we can chuckle about what happened, even though I remain careful about how much and how loudly I chuckle.

Are there lessons to be learned from "The Night I Killed the Christmas Tree"? I think there are, the first one being the realization that some things are more important to others than they are to you. All of us have the tendency to assume that the emotional depth that others have invested in certain things is the same as our own. That is a big mistake! While I enjoyed the keepsake quality of our Christmas tree, because I had not been involved in collecting the ornaments, making them, carefully preserving them from one year to the next, my level of emotional involvement with them was not nearly as deep as Peggy's. I thought they were pretty; she thought they were among the symbols that defined our marriage and the Greggs' identity as a family. To see some of them irrevocably destroyed was an experience of loss and an occasion for grief for Peggy, while for me it was simply a mess that needed to be cleaned off the living room floor. This is not an expression of callousness on my part; it is simply the acknowledgment of a difference of perspective.

This is probably a good thing to remember in all of our interpersonal relationships—in families, in the church, in our workplaces, and in our larger communities. People's perspectives, their emotional investments, their sensibilities are not all the same. If we insist on using our personal perspectives, emotional investments, and sensibilities as the standard for valuing everything else, we are careening toward a social collision from which everyone will go away damaged and with reservations regarding whether we care about anyone except our own selves.

A second lesson worth learning is the reality that saying "I hear you" is much better than having to say "I'm sorry." You see, even as I was insisting on moving the Christmas tree, Peggy was cautioning that it might be top heavy and that I needed to be more careful. Instead, in my preoccupation with getting on the road and covering the miles between me and a warm, sunny beach, I probably growled, as I am wont to do, "I know what I'm doing." Moments later, while ruefully contemplating the material and emotional carnage I had caused, my meek "I'm sorry, sweetheart" seemed inadequate. It still does.

While it is certainly important that we apologize and say "I'm sorry" when we injure others, literally, psychically, or spiritually, it is more important that we think carefully and behave appropriately so that saying "I'm sorry" becomes unnecessary. It is true that "All the king's horses and all the king's men can't put Humpty Dumpty together again." Once the old boy is broken, he's broken. And all the "I'm sorries" in the world can't undo the damage we have done.

One sadness of contemporary experience is the notion so many of us have that our behaviors, regardless of how selfish, insensitive, careless, and downright malicious they are, can be plastered over with a grudgingly contrite "I'm sorry," freeing us to blunder on to our next expression of at best childish and at worst purely egregious behavior. It is not acceptable to say "I'm sorry" with our voices while in our consciousness we are thinking, "I really don't give a damn."

A third lesson that might be learned is the reality that some broken things can be put back together, but not all of them. After returning from our trip to the beach, Peggy and I sat down with the fragments of the broken Christmas ornaments. Some were only partially damaged, and, once we identified the missing pieces, we were able to glue them back together and return them to Peggy's "keepsake" ornament collection. Others were so badly damaged that, while she would keep them in their boxes because of their sentimental value, they could never be used on the tree again. Regrettably, several were completely destroyed and had to be consigned to the trash.

Every loving parent knows the anguish of having a child bring them a treasured broken toy accompanied by the words "Fix it, Daddy" or "Fix it, Mom." Sometimes all we can say is, "Sweetheart, I love you dearly, but I can't fix this; it is broken beyond repair." Often as adults we go to God with the shattered fragments of marriages, friendships, family relationships, church fellowships, etc. We hold them up to God and say, "Fix it, Heavenly Father." Sometimes, if we are cooperative, God is able to guide us toward mending the brokenness and restoring meaningful relationships so effectively that one would hardly know the relationship was ever damaged. In other instances, the damage is so great that, while forgiveness and sociability are possible, the intimacy of the original relationship can never be restored. And, sadly, with some the damage is so profound and traumatic that God has to reply, "My beloved child, I love you and the other dearly, but between yourselves, the two of you have broken this relationship beyond repair."

The final lesson, for the sake of this reflection, is the truth that mistakes don't have to destroy precious relationships. The bottom line is the question of how precious the relationships are to those involved. The relationship between Peggy and me is such that, while from time to time each of us does something stupid, the commitment we have made to one another transcends the occasional poor judgment, insensitivity, and pure idiocy of either of us. We stood before God, our personal families, our church families, and our friends and we pledged ourselves to one another "till death do us part." The tragedy of a hedonistic, self-centered culture is that so many of us pledge ourselves to others "till we hit a bump in the road of life, or till it becomes inconvenient, or till we decide we would like to be superficially pledged to someone else."

Hear me! I know things that happen, things people do to one another, things people say to one another, often eventuate in the reality that some relationships are simply dead and there is nothing to do but face the truth and move on. No amount of wishing and hand wringing can make them alive again.

Before you despair, let me remind you of Advent. I know the Bible begins with the story of how human choices resulted in brokenness, suffering, estrangement, and death. But the Bible doesn't end with Genesis 1–3. The birth narratives of the Gospels of Matthew and Luke tell the story of God's refusal to accept the notion that the existential brokenness of the universe could not be fixed. God did not wait for us to initiate the process of renewal; God elected to make the first move by intervening on our behalf in the person of the "only begotten Son," who chose to become like us in order that we might begin the journey of becoming like him. The key to accomplishing God's aim has to do with "preciousness." Creation is so precious to God that our Creator was willing to make the ultimate sacrifice to redeem and renew the broken relationship between Creator and created. The question that must be answered is, "How precious is a right relationship with God, creation, others, and your innermost self to you?" Dumb mistakes don't have to destroy a precious human relationship if all parties believe the relationship is precious enough to redeem. Radical human sinfulness doesn't have to eternally alienate us from God if the people for whom God has already demonstrated how precious they are will simply reach out to receive the redemption that is offered. We can choose to pray with the hymn writer:

> Precious Lord, take my hand, lead me on, help me stand,
> I am tired, I am weak, I am worn;
> Through the storm, through the night, lead me on to the light,
> Take my hand, precious Lord, lead me home.[1]

---

1. Thomas A. Dorsey, "Take My Hand, Precious Lord," *Celebrating Grace Hymnal,* 2010, #400.

Any Good First Read Deserves a Second

I don't recall the first time I read the following quotation from Francis Bacon's *Of Studies* (1625): "Some books are to be tasted, others to be swallowed, and some few to be chewed and digested; that is, some books are to be read only in parts; others to be read, but not curiously; and some few are to be read wholly, and with diligence and attention."

However, I was so captivated by Bacon's observation that I committed it to memory and have made use of it, to the chagrin of students, church members, and innocent bystanders, many times over the years. I will not consume time and space by cataloging the many volumes I have been enticed to read, reread, and read yet again across a lifetime of pursuing my favorite hobby, which is at the same time such an important aspect of my academic and local church ministry.

Confined to home by weather at the end of one January, I had some time to browse my personal library and ran across my English translation of Dante's *Divine Comedy*. I recall being required to make my way through *Inferno*, *Purgatory*, and *Paradise* in a graduate-level course titled Psychology of Religious Experience way back in the previous millennium. My recollection of the event suggests that, at the time, I experienced more *Inferno* and *Purgatory* than I did *Paradise*. Still, either under the inspiration of Bacon's quote, or perhaps out of sheer boredom, I drew the *Inferno* volume from the shelf to give it a second cursory look. Hours later, completely enthralled, I found myself twelve cantos into Dante's poem and eager to read more. Truly, one of the blessings of senior adulthood is the acquisition of more time to consume at leisure books that, at an earlier time, one had to gobble quickly before moving to the next dish on the literary smorgasbord. One day of reading led to a second as, with Virgil as my guide and Dante as my inspiration, I followed these two ancient worthies into the depths of hell, convinced that volume 1 of *The Divine Comedy* deserved to be "read wholly, and with diligence and attention."

Circle by spiraling circle we made our way deeper and deeper into the anguished suffering of the human soul spiritually separated from God, environmentally separated from creation, socially separated from others, and psychologically separated from self. At each level I renewed my conviction that hell is not a geographic location somewhere in the cosmos; hell is a state of being in which a person, by his or her own choices, has decided to abide despite everything God has done to prevent our own self-condemnation. Many spend so much time worrying about eventually "going to hell" or conversely "escaping going to hell" that they fail to recognize how, in obsessive preoccupation with self, they have created living hells to which they condemn themselves and force others to suffer along with them the anguish of their existential lostness—what Dante called "the suffering race of souls who lost the good of intellect" (Canto 3:18). By "good of intellect," Dante does not mean the exercise of intellectual achievement; he means the loss of that greatest reality the human mind can conceive, Aristotle's *Summum Bonum*, which in the medieval thought of Thomas Aquinas, the most influential Christian thinker of Dante's day, meant "God." Whatever may be believed about hell as an ultimate state of existence after death and final judgment, the present hells to which people condemn themselves are, from Dante's perspective, a precursor of that eventual state of utter and ultimate separation from the Divine presence and beatific bliss that is generally understood as Heaven.

This reflective essay is no place to plumb the depths of Dante's description of existential hell in *Inferno*. However, it seems to me that in the opening cantos the poet identifies four characteristics that define the living hells in which so many choose to live. Perhaps by identifying them we can open ourselves up to the Divine grace that is the only reality that can possibly overcome them. These hellish characteristics are (1) fear, (2) indecision, (3) nakedness, and (4) violence. Each may be reflected on in turn.

Fear

In Canto 2 the Dante of the poem pleads his fear and unworthiness to make the journey with Virgil through the depths of Hell in order to return to the material world. Sternly, Virgil rebukes Dante for his fear with the chiding words,

> Your soul is burdened with that cowardice
> which often weighs so heavily on man
> it turns him from a noble enterprise
> like a frightened beast that shies at its own shadow.
> (Canto 2.45-48)

Dante himself acknowledges "the color of coward on my face" (Canto 9.1).

Understand that fear in and of itself is not the problem. It is giving way to the fears that threaten our being that creates an environment within which we then begin to construct our own personal hell. At the beginning of the poem, Dante is confronted by the terrors of failure in the form of a Leopard, a Lion, and a She-wolf. While there are many interpretations of these symbolic beasts, the most traditional are fraud, ambition, and incontinence. These may be the greatest of human fears: (1) Fraud—the fear that others will discover the true person lying behind the façade we show the world; (2) Ambition—the consuming fear that we will not be perceived as superior to others; and (3) Incontinence—the fear that we may not be able to control our drives and appetites and thus will become objects of public scorn and ridicule. Such overweening fears drive us to continual preoccupation with ourselves and our need for security. The result is that in our desire to secure ourselves from the threats of life in a dangerous world, we imprison ourselves in an impenetrable chrysalis of emotional, relational, and spiritual isolation.

Mature Christians understand that verses of Scripture are not magic talismans and should never be used as such. However, both

Jesus and the Apostle Paul offered words of encouragement as we struggle with our fears. In the context of Jesus's promise that he would send a Comforter to be with them always, he said, "Let not your heart be troubled, neither let it be afraid" (John 14:27). Young Timothy was assured, "God hath not given us the spirit of fear; but of power, and of love, and of a sound mind" (2 Tim 1:7).

Indecision

As Virgil leads the poet into the vestibule of Hell, Dante's ears are assailed by the piteous voices of a multitude of souls crying out in anguish and grief. When he questions Virgil as to who these souls might be, the ancient guide replies,

> This wretched state of being is the fate of those sad souls
> who lived a life,
> but lived it with no blame and with no praise.
> They are mixed with that repulsive choir of angels
> neither faithful nor unfaithful to their God,
> who undecided stood but for themselves. (Canto 3.34-39)

How many in this present life have condemned themselves to a private hell because, when faced with life's most ultimate choices, they choose not to make a choice. The biblical literature is replete with stories of personalities, confronted with life's ultimate challenges, who were called upon to make choices: Abraham, Moses, Israel entering Canaan, Elijah in the contest with the prophets of Baal, Esther, those preached to by John the Baptizer, those called by Jesus, etc. Experience reveals that the choice not to make a choice is a decision in and of itself that, more often than not, ends in regret, disappointment, and despair.

Nakedness

In the early Cantos of *Inferno*, the poet repeatedly surfaces the theme of nakedness as he describes the awful plight of those destined to suffer in the depths of Hell (Canto 3.65, 92; 13.116). While Dante perceives these various sufferers as physically naked, such nakedness is also a symbol of the human failure to cover our vulnerabilities despite our efforts to clothe ourselves in the protective garb of self-righteousness.

In the stories of Adam and Eve's attempt to cover themselves with fig leaves, Noah's sons covering his drunken nakedness following the flood, Lot's daughters revealing their nakedness to their aged father, Samson's nakedness in the Philistine temple, and David's lustful observation of the nakedness of Bathsheba, the theme of the vulnerability of the observed, the observer, or both is repeatedly found in ancient Hebrew/Jewish religious literature, both canonical and non-canonical. Beginning with Adam's insipid attempt to shift the blame to Eve and Eve's equally insipid attempt to blame the serpent, throughout the biblical literature there is the figurative nakedness of both victim and victimizer. And always there is some attempt at self-justification, to say, "It wasn't my fault!" Please do not hear me blaming the victim; that is not my intent. My intention is to suggest that our repeated failures to admit and confront our vulnerabilities, our nakedness of judgment, pride, ego, runaway ambition, greed, lust, and vanity, end in a self-inflicted hellishness where our attempts to cover ourselves reveal the futility of our attempting to do so. In the words of one of Dante's condemned, "pride, envy, avarice are the three sparks that kindle in men's hearts and set them burning" (Canto 6.74-75). We are better served when we become willing to cry with the prophet, "Woe is me, for I am undone" (Isa 6:5).

Violence

Finally, I suggest that the last characteristic of Dante's Hell in which so many of us choose to live is that of violence. As Virgil continues to instruct the poet he asserts, "All malice has injustice as its end, an end achieved by violence or by fraud . . ." (Canto 11.22-23). He goes on to say that "violence can be used against three persons . . . violence can be done to God, to self, or to one's neighbor" (Canto 11.29-32). Sadly, many wish to confine the term "violence" only to the physical attack of one person upon another. But violence takes many other forms: verbal, nonverbal, psychological, relational, social, economic, etc. Violence is the choice to harm the other simply because one has the power to do so. It matters little whether the violence is perpetrated by the raised fist or the raised voice; the crushing heel of a domineering boot or the crushing boot of economic deprivation; the silent ostracism of a trusting lover or the refusal to speak up for the racially or ethnically or gender marginalized and despised. To stand by in feigned ignorance or helplessness or inability is to become complicit in the violence even if the acts of violence are performed by others.

In his poem "No Man Is an Island," John Donne says, "any man's death diminishes me, / Because I am involved in mankind." The same could be said of violence. Violence done to anyone diminishes me because I, too, am involved in humankind. I have one of two choices in relation to the hellish violence that is so pervasive in our world; I can participate in inflicting the violence even while decrying it, or I can make common cause with the victims of violence, myself included, by choosing to act in ways that deny violence the power to perpetuate its hellishness. If and when I do so, I can sing with the poet, even in the darkness of the hells we mortals create for ourselves and inflict on others,

> As little flowers from the frosty night
> are closed and limp, and when the sun shines down
> on them, they rise to open on their stem,
> my wilted strength began to bloom within me,
> and such warm courage flowed into my heart
> that I spoke like a man set free of fear.[1] (Canto 2.126-132)

Of the ultimate I cannot judge, but in the proximate I am determined to push back on the "gates of hell," believing that the present hells created by fear, indecision, vulnerability, and violence are not invincible because I have been preceded by One who has "harrowed" hell on my behalf (1 Pet 3:19-20; 4:6; also see the Apostle's Creed).

---

1. Quotations taken from *The Divine Comedy: Vol. 1: Inferno*, trans. Mark Musa (New York: Penguin Books, 1986).

The Consumer and the Consumed—A BBQ Road Trip

We were three full weeks past our second Covid-19 shot. I had recently completed a seven-month interim pastorate. Spring yardwork that needed attention had been attended to, and Peggy and I were ready for an extended road trip. Prepared to take all sensible pandemic precautions, we discussed various options that might be interesting. I have family in Oklahoma whom I hadn't seen in years. Some personal business was taking me to Memphis, Tennessee. Peggy has a sister in Panama City Beach, so we decided to make our way to Oklahoma, via Memphis, to see my nephew and his family, and then drive to Panama City Beach before returning to North Carolina through Alabama, Georgia, and South Carolina.

The fact that Nephew Jeff owns a thriving BBQ restaurant in Oklahoma led to speculation about making the trip a BBQ adventure across several southeastern states. Having grown up in a serious BBQ culture in west Alabama, I had always dreamed of enjoying the regional specialties across the Deep South.

Our first stop was a place in Memphis made famous by Guy Fieri on *Diners, Drive-ins and Dives*. Sadly, the baby backs were dry, and the fried okra was only semi-fried. The best thing in the meal was the onion rings, but I wouldn't drive four hundred miles to eat them again. Guy needs to return and remind those folks what made them outstanding so many years ago. You can't sustain a great BBQ place simply by covering it with "Elvis Ate Here" signs.

Business finished in Memphis, we drove on to Clayton, Oklahoma, for the long-anticipated family reunion. There the quality of the renewed family time was matched only by that of the food. Jeff's pulled pork was outstanding, his baby back ribs equally fine, and his brisket was the best I have ever tasted. After surviving a particularly nasty overnight thunderstorm, it was time to pass out the hugs and move on to the next leg of the trip.

That next leg, passing through Texas and Louisiana, ended in Vicksburg, Mississippi. Without specific plans, after getting settled into our hotel room we returned to the car and began to cruise. Soon we came upon a take-out-only place run by two women who really know their stuff. They specialize in BBQ and soul food. Instead of baby backs, they serve full-sized spare ribs, the kind I grew up on and still prefer. The ribs plus black-eyed peas, mustard greens, and mac and cheese were "slap yo' momma" good. From Vicksburg we headed on, crossing southern Mississippi and Alabama, to Panama City Beach, Florida.

Jesus said, "Man does not live by bread alone." He also does not live by BBQ alone. There is an oyster bar in PC Beach that I frequent every chance I get. It specializes in oysters on the half-shell, hot wings, and po'boys. I arrive early for lunch and sit at the bar so I can watch the bartenders shuck oysters. These Redneck Riviera philosophers, with their nonstop banter, have tongues as sharp as their shucking knives. While not always sharing their views, one can't help being amused by them. I never consume fewer than a dozen raw oysters and as many naked wings covered with a blistering wing sauce and blue cheese dressing.

After a few days of walking the beach and eating seafood, we resumed our search for great regional BBQ as we made our way homeward. I know a couple of places in PC Beach and one in Opelika, Alabama, that will never disappoint; there is another in Bessemer, Alabama. Now I am home, walking off the accumulated pounds and reflecting on what I may have learned on the trip.

What makes regional BBQ wonderful is that it is so diverse. Conditioned by the protein available (pork, beef, chicken, etc.), the species of hardwood for slow fire cooking, any brine, rub, or seasoning used, sustained low temperature, and time in the pit, good

BBQ taste can be as diverse and subtle as the range of flavors in good wines. If you've had BBQ in one region, you haven't had it in all.

This is a good thing to remember about human beings as well. While we share a common humanity, there are so many variables in our genetic makeup, social/cultural conditioning, ethnic heritage, education or lack thereof, etc., that demonstrate by interacting with one fellow human being they have not interacted with them all. To assume that all people are alike, or that everyone in a particular sub-group is the same, is a horrible mistake that only exacerbates racial and ethnic prejudice, economic and social inequity, and religious and political extremism. It is not our "sameness" that gives flavor and texture and depth of meaning to our human interactions; it is the diversity within our shared humanity that overcomes the blandness and accentuates the zest of life with others.

A second thought that occurs to me is that almost everyone is sure the BBQ they grew up with is the best. I confess my own guilt here. I grew up on full-sized spare ribs roasted over a slow hickory fire with a basting sauce composed of cooking oil, water, lemon juice, garlic powder, liquid smoke, Worcestershire sauce, Dale's Steak Sauce, black pepper, and salt. Only at the end did we slather the ribs with the rich, thick, sweet, tangy, tomato-based Alabama red sauce that transformed smoked ribs into the gourmet delicacy of the rural poor of Tuscaloosa County, Alabama. Both Joe Scarborough and I will testify that this regional BBQ masterpiece has been elevated to perfection by the Dreamland folks on Tuscaloosa's south side and imitated by many others far and wide.

There is nothing essentially wrong with being comfortable with the familiar whether it has to do with food, social/cultural interactions, forms of entertainment, or religious convictions and observance. The problem emerges only when we refuse to expand the circle of that with which we are familiar and open ourselves up to the possibility that there is more to life than the part of it we know well. And we don't have to travel the world, or even the Deep South, to enlarge our circles of familiarity.

For almost three decades Peggy and I have lived in the foothills of the Blue Ridge Mountains in western North Carolina. You don't have to live in the Carolinas for long to discover that its BBQ culture is decidedly different from that of west Alabama. The Carolinas are primarily a pulled-pork region with sauces ranging from the thin, watery red sauces of the west to the vinegar and mustard-based varieties of the Down East and Low Country. Exploring this diversity does not require that one traverse both states; sometimes all that is necessary is to visit the next county.

My point is that cultural, religious, political, or social insularity is a choice, not a condition. They all emerge from the fear that the enlargement of one's circle of familiarity risks the possibility that one may be required to change one's mind about those who differ in one way or another. This inordinate fear of "losing" something keeps many from "gaining" something. The ultimate truth is that we human beings are more alike than we are different, and to spend all our time focused on maintaining our chauvinistic and/or xenophobic differences prevents us from being enriched and renewed by what others have to offer.

Science and experience both demonstrate that excessively close inbreeding of any species or sub-species ultimately eventuates in genetic deterioration, sterility, and neurological disease as the gene pool becomes so concentrated it collapses on itself. An analogous reality is true with human social/cultural interactions. Without periodic infusions of new ideas, new experiences, and new relationships, the social/cultural/intellectual "gene pool" of any group will become distorted, sterile, and diseased because of collective group-think and the refusal to entertain the possibility that there is more that we need than what we already have.

To return to my BBQ analogy, though I am exceedingly fond of this particular culinary delight, for my own good health I need more in my diet than smoked meat. And people who gain their news from only one source, or express their religion in only one way, or interact socially with only one ethnicity, or listen to the political values espoused by only one party are willfully and consciously choosing to deny themselves the intellectual diversity they need to maintain good emotional, social, and cultural health. As surely as you can die from malnutrition, not because you don't have enough to eat but because of the lack of nutritional diversity in what you consume, you can die from intellectual malnutrition by restricting your mind to an informational/experiential diet that will not sustain you in a world that is infinitely more diverse than your small existential corner.

By now you may be growing weary of playing this "BBQ Road Trip" game with me, but I am not quite finished reflecting on the implications of the trip for me and possibly for you as well. Back in graduate school days I read an important treatise in Cultural Anthropology by Claude Levi-Strauss titled *The Raw and the Cooked*. Inspired by Levi-Strauss's title, I have elected to call this little reflection "The Consumer and the Consumed." When it comes to BBQ, one can spend a lot of time and energy concentrating on the meat that will ultimately be consumed. The type, quality, cut, and age of the meat to be smoked and consumed is not unimportant; neither is the rub, wood, temperature, and cooking time. Whether the result is poor, good, superior, or outstanding is significantly conditioned by the personal tastes of the consumer. This subjectivity can be both a blessing and a curse. One's preference for what is most familiar at least gives the BBQ consumer a standard by which to gauge their enjoyment of BBQ from other regions, smoked with other woods, and sauced with other sauces; this is the blessing and also the curse. You see, any refusal to think openly and critically about the BBQ, or about the really important things of life, prevents one from moving beyond complacent contentment with the *status quo* to the place where we can not only say what we like but can articulate why we like what we like.

Archimedes (287–212 BCE) is reported to have said, "Give me a place to stand, and I will move the world." I have been quoted as saying, "If you ain't somewhere doin' somethin' you ain't nowhere doin' nothin'." The two aphorisms are essentially the same. Everybody's got to stand somewhere, and everybody's got to be somewhere. But this does not require that we always stand in the same place and/or do the same thing all the time. Life is too rich and dynamic to allow static sameness to rob us of the vitality and joyfulness of all of God's blessings.

One of the primary faults of religious people is having the habitual preference for a particular flavor of religious identity without taking the time to investigate whether there are other flavors as well. The result is that the religious identity is much more about the not-reflected-on personal preferences of the religious "consumer" than it is about the content and depth of meaning within the religious tradition being "consumed." Consequently, God is forced into the subjectively narrow mold of "what I want God to be like" as opposed to the issue of the more expansive question, "What does God want me to be like?" Such people embrace an attitude like this: "If the BBQ [insert religion, political view, etc.] doesn't taste like the BBQ I grew up with then something must be wrong with the BBQ, 'cause there couldn't possibly be anything wrong with me and my preferences, prejudices, predilections, and piousness." And this is no way to relate to God, or to others, or to good BBQ!

Does It Hurt When You Jump Up and Down?

It was a tough day. I had taught two classes that morning while dealing with a periodic intense pain in my lower right side. While I was driving home the pain became sharp enough that I decided to call my doctor's office to see if I could be worked into the late afternoon schedule. Reaching for my cell phone, I dialed the number and the phone was answered with a cheerful identification of the name of the medical practice followed by the question, "How may I help you?"

Briefly I identified myself and my physician and then described the symptoms I was experiencing. The receptionist promised to refer my call to my doctor's nurse, and, after a wait of several painful minutes and miles, the nurse came on the line. Once again I described the pain in my side. The nurse asked a number of diagnostic questions including, "Does it hurt when you jump up and down?" Under the impression that she was looking at a computer monitor containing my electronic medical records, I replied with some exasperation, "Lady, as you can probably see on your screen, I'm sixty-five years old. I haven't jumped up and down in years."

The nurse laughed, we talked for a few more minutes, and she set me up with an appointment for the next day. It is obvious that after many tests and much spending of my own and my insurance company's money, followed by a painful surgical procedure, I survived the excruciating pain I was suffering that day.

It is not the purpose of this little reflective exercise to bewail the limitations, despite all the sophisticated technological testing procedures, of American medical care. I wish to explore the nuances of the nurse's question, "Does it hurt when you jump up and down?" and my somewhat testy response, "Lady, I'm sixty-five years old. I haven't jumped up and down in years."

Frequently I hear questions posed in ways that suggest diverse motivations on the part of the questioner. In this instance, without much thought about the question, the nurse appeared to have been simply going through a routine litany of diagnostic questions always asked when someone called in complaining of stabbing pain in the side. I understood the question even though I thought, given the circumstances and the information I knew she could see on her computer monitor (my age, weight, previous medical issues, etc.), the question was irrelevant. No harm was intended on her part and no real offense was taken on mine. However, there are other questions that seem to have senseless, inappropriate, and often even dark motives behind them.

For instance, during my college teaching days I could count on some young person in a class appointing themselves as the person to ask the "rabbit chasing" questions. You know about "rabbit chasing," don't you? A hand is raised and acknowledged. The questioner, in a most sincere voice, poses a question tangentially related to the subject matter with the intent of getting the professor to engage in a lengthy excursus about something everyone knows will not show up later on a test. Sometimes this is useful in the learning experience, but often it is only a means of avoiding work.

When "rabbit chasing" questions threatened to get out of hand, I always reminded the questioner and the class that they had been given a study guide for the unit we were covering and that the upcoming test would be drawn from the content of the study guide regardless of whether I had the opportunity to deal with the material in classroom lectures. I then asked, "Do you folks want to chase this 'rabbit' today, or would you rather have me provide you with information about which you will be held accountable on the next test?" Inevitably the "rabbit chasing" questioner would get harsh looks from other class members and the rabbit would collapse and die on the spot.

Truth to tell, I didn't mind these classroom hijinks; I found them amusing. It didn't take students long to figure out that, after decades of experience, I was much better at the "chasing rabbits" game than they were. And from time to time we would chase an interesting rabbit if it served the purpose of enabling a healthy learning experience.

Other questions are neither harmless nor amusing. In the course of my abovementioned medical testing, I went to the local hospital for a procedure that had been scheduled. In the waiting room I found the spouse of a good friend and we began to catch up on family, health, church life, etc. while we waited to be called for our tests. In the course of the conversation, it was mentioned that I was a minister. Immediately another person in the waiting room inserted himself into the conversation and posed what he thought was a significant biblical question. I gave him the best answer I knew based on decades of careful study of the biblical text and reflection on the topic. However, it wasn't the answer he wanted to hear because it didn't jibe with what he had already concluded was the correct answer.

The individual turned out to be one of those self-appointed checkers of the theological orthodoxy of ministers. As he pursued the discussion in order to prove how wrong I was, he became thoroughly irritating to everyone in the waiting room. When I indicated, while nursing the pain in my side, that I really didn't wish to pursue the discussion further he insisted, heatedly and loudly, "You're a minister aren't you? Isn't it your job to answer the questions people ask you?" Finally, to prevent him from disturbing anyone further, I asked the receptionist if I could be seated elsewhere while I waited for my test. I had no need, simply because I was a minister, to allow myself to be subjected to the poor biblical exegesis, bad manners, and faulty judgment of an out-of-control ego who was sure he had a straight line to God. No effective Christian witness ever emerges from a posture of being obnoxious for Jesus. And people who pose questions in order to take cheap shots at ministers because they're pretty sure the minister won't shoot back are high on the list of the most obnoxious people I know. No one should have to put up with verbal bullying simply because they are a Christian minister.

There's another type of question that is both dark and disturbing. It is the question asked in a public setting deliberately intended to embarrass or put on the spot the person to whom it is addressed. I've heard this kind of question posed in town hall meetings, faculty meetings, church conferences, political forums, and various other settings. The questioner feigns the need for more information about a topic in order to pose a question intended to create an awkward situation for the person being questioned. Often the information is readily available or could have been acquired by asking in some other more private setting. Frequently the questioner already knows the answer to the question before asking it. However, the questioner is not really interested in the answer. This person is interested in publicly humiliating another person while promoting their own personal sense of self-importance in front of an audience they wish to impress.

Jesus experienced this in his encounters with the religiously self-righteous scribes and Pharisees of his day. His usual response was to answer the question with a counter-question that exposed the motivation of those seeking to publicly humiliate him (Matt 12:1-5, 10-13; 22:1-46). The model Jesus provides is that of "holding accountable" the people who appoint themselves to hold everyone else accountable to them. I can almost see the smile on the biblical writer's face when he concluded by saying, "No one could say a word in reply, and from that day on no one dared to ask him any more questions" (Matt 22:46 NIV). My mother would have said, "That's how you cure a 'yaller dog' of suckin' eggs!"

Yet another type of question deserves consideration. A young minister, Titus by name, had been sent to be the pastor of the Christian community on the Mediterranean island of Crete. Apparently, troubled by the convoluted arguments some of the Cretians were engaging in, Titus had appealed to the Apostle Paul for advice. Paul replied, "Avoid foolish questions, and genealogies, and contentions, and striving about the law; for they are unprofitable and vain" (Titus 3:9). From the first century CE to the present there have always been people the Christian community who wanted to engage in the wildest speculation for the sake of hearing themselves talk. While we should not avoid challenging questions simply because they are challenging, life contains some unanswerable conundrums that cannot be resolved no matter how much time we devote to speculating about them. Excessive preoccupation with arguing with one another about theological "Which came first, the chicken or the egg?" questions only leads to divisiveness and diverts us from devoting appropriate time, energy, and resources to effectively communicating the "good news" of the gospel.

Listen to me carefully. Anyone who knows me knows I am no proponent of Christian intellectual laziness. However, I staunchly resist any attempt to revive the medieval scholastic speculation regarding "How many angels can stand on the point of a needle?" in any of its contemporary manifestations. In another place the Apostle Paul warned against those who are always striving to explore the novel, the esoteric, and the speculative to the extent that they refuse to hear sound Christian teaching when it is offered to them. "For the time will come when [they] will not put up with sound doctrine. Instead, to suit their own desires, they will gather around them a great number of teachers to say what their itching ears want to hear. They will turn their ears away from the truth and turn aside to myths" (2 Tim 4:3-4 NIV). This is the danger of endlessly pursuing questions that have no answer this side of eternity. I don't know the answer to "Do those who have died observe what is going on in our lives?" I don't know the answer to "Why do bad things happen to good people and good things happen to bad people?" I don't know the calendar answer to "When will Jesus return?" And you don't either.

Finally, there is what I call the "trick question once removed." Here's how this works. Person A, wanting to remain anonymous, entices Person B to pose some obscure, unanswerable, or stress-inducing question. Lacking the moral courage to speak for himself or herself, Person A simply uses others as the instruments of anonymous mischief making. If problems eventuate from the manipulative question, Person A simply leaves Person B out there flapping in the breeze of the negative response the loaded question elicited. Person B ends up feeling badly used while Person A sails breezily along as though oblivious to the personal and institutional mayhem they have caused. However, Person A is not oblivious; they have achieved exactly what they intended while avoiding any responsibility for the stress they have caused. Shame on them, and pity on the Persons B of the world who allow themselves to be exploited in this way.

Sometimes a question is just a question, innocently asked whether it makes sense or not. Usually this is harmless. But other questions are relational IEDs (improvised explosive devices), wielded by people who wish to cause confusion, hurt, and distress within the communities in which they are posed. Mature Christian believers need to be able to tell one from the other so they do not become the victims of dangerous questions and divisive questioners.

And no, I still don't know whether it would have hurt if I had jumped up and down. As I said, "I haven't jumped up and down in years." Well, not physically. Occasionally, as in this essay, I have been known to jump up and down verbally.

Give Your Minister a Break, and You Won't Break Your Minister

Once people have been in vocational Christian ministry as long as I have, they presume they have paid enough dues to get by with saying some things even if saying them causes stress. After more than five decades, it is pretty evident that I'm not one of those ministers who bailed out or dropped out when the romance wore off and it came time to get down to the nitty-gritty of ministry. However, more than fifty years of observation have given me some insight into why some ministers, many of them fine, godly, committed people, decide to pursue a vocation other than as pastor or staff member of a local congregation. I've come to the conclusion that, while there aren't any perfect ministers and all of us make our fair share of mistakes and poor judgments, if more people were willing to give their ministers a "break," there would be fewer "broken" ministers.

I shall always recall several years ago when, as a local church pastor, I sat in a hospital waiting room with a family awaiting news regarding a complex surgical procedure being performed on a loved one. If you've been in these places, you know the waiting areas can become pretty crowded, making it impossible not to overhear the conversations of others.

Near where I sat, another family talked together about their pastor while they waited for news from the surgical suite. Some people have never learned the art of verbal volume control, so everyone in the waiting area heard the young woman as she announced, "I don't know where that preacher is. You'd think he'd be here when one of his members was havin' surgery. I'll bet he's not even out of bed yet."

Over the next several minutes, various others joined in the game of "Let's Beat Up on the Preacher." It was the usual stuff. He didn't visit enough. His sermons were too long and boring. He didn't speak to me at Walmart. That wife of his is stuck up. If he can afford to drive the car he drives, the church must be payin' him too much money. You know, the usual drivel that comes out of people's mouths when they have nothing to say but insist on saying it anyway.

As the interminable minutes passed, a member of the family I was with, distressed that I might be offended by what was being said, tried to be helpful by intervening. "Well, all preachers are not that way. Dr. Gregg here is our pastor, and we think the world of him." I knew what was coming next. I was about to be bombarded with questions regarding whether the Bible really teaches this or that, what I believed about the second coming of Christ, and if I preached out of anything but the good old King James Version.

My parishioner was correct; I was annoyed by what we were being forced to overhear, and I didn't intend to defend my views on eschatology or biblical translations to total strangers, so I decided to mix things up. Before someone else could ask me a question, I began asking some pointed questions myself:

"Does your pastor know your father is having surgery today?" Silence.

"I suppose one of you made a point of calling him to make sure he knew what was going on today?" More silence.

"Let me make sure I understand. You people are ticked off at your pastor for not being somewhere he doesn't know he needs to be and for not doing something he doesn't know he needs to do because you didn't have enough initiative to make sure your pastor knew your dad was having surgery today?" Absolute silence. Wriggling in chairs and sullen looks.

"Do you people think God sends ministers emails about the hospital's surgery schedule or that we find out about these things through osmosis?"

A moment later one of the men said, "I'm goin' outside for a smoke." Most everyone else in the group thought they needed to go for a smoke too. I thought I saw smoke coming out of the ears of some as they hurried down the hall. As they disappeared around the corner, now with two ministers to be ticked off at, I thought, "There goes another family who won't give their minister a break, and so they'll probably break their minister. They ought to be ashamed."

Allow me to answer some of the questions you've always had about ministers. Yes, we pay federal and state income taxes at the same percentage rates as everyone else. And, as self-employed people, we pay both sides of our Social Security. No, those who live in parsonages don't live in them for free; they are taxed on the fair rental value of the house, and unlike homeowners, ministers who live in parsonages don't build equity they can use later to send their kids to college. And if a minister dies, the family has to find somewhere else to live while still processing their grief. Yes, ministers' children are conceived in the same way other people's children are conceived; and surely ministers and their spouses enjoy the process of conceiving them as much as other people. No, ministers are not all partial to fried chicken. No, ministers aren't people who are too lazy to really work for a living. While some ministers may be lazy, I challenge anyone to take every step the typical minister makes in the course of an ordinary week. Yes, ministers are as offended as anyone else when people make bad jokes about their profession or take cheap shots at them or their family members because it is presumed ministers aren't going to shoot back. No, there's not something wrong or unspiritual about a minister who doesn't agree with you regarding your politics, views on eschatology, or position on certain social issues. And to seek to deprive a minister of their means of earning a livelihood simply because they don't see eye to eye with you about everything is spiteful. Yes, ministers do like some people in their congregations more than others. It's a simple fact that some people are more likeable than others, and it's also a fact that friendship is much easier to bestow when it is reciprocated.

Now, for those who haven't stopped reading, let me suggest some ways you can give your minister a "break" so your minister is not as likely to become "broken." First, be sociable. Hang out with your minister. Things like a Sunday night cup of coffee, taking your spouses to see a movie together, bumming around in flea markets on

Saturday morning, or going to a baseball game go a long way toward keeping your minister whole. Most ministers know hundreds, if not thousands, of people, but many can count their real friends on the fingers of one hand.

Some are thinking, "But we have all kinds of social activities at the church." Sure you do. But at church social functions everyone else is there voluntarily; the minister is at work. While such functions are less formally structured than Sunday morning worship, they are still not places where the minister can simply relax and be comfortable. If something goes wrong or gets confused, everyone is still going to look to the minister to solve the problem. Most of your interpersonal social interaction doesn't happen at your workplace, and your minister's shouldn't either. Social isolation and loneliness will break your minister.

Second, be helpful before the fact instead of critical after the failure, and you won't break your minister. Any minister would prefer to be told half a dozen times something they need to know instead of everyone assuming someone else is going to do it and ending up with no one telling them about it. The difference between a successful, effective minister and one who fails is usually measured by the willingness of others to be helpful. Things like "You may already know, but I thought I'd call just to make sure" and "Can I take care of that for you today?" are among the most blessed words a minister can hear from a thoughtful church member. Give your minister a "heads up" and they will be grateful. And it's a whole lot more helpful than stepping on your minister's head after they have stumbled over something you could have warned them about.

Third, remember that your minister is your minister, not the church's groundskeeper, custodian, or secretary. The minister is also not the referee at your family quarrels or your psychiatrist. Your minister is your minister. Ministers end up doing too many things around the church that detract from the time and energy needed to do real ministry. An attitude of "I can take care of that" as opposed to one of "That's what we pay the preacher to do" goes a long way toward keeping a minister from becoming broken.

Fourth, avoid dumping "cold water" on your minister by insisting on dealing with things right before a worship time is about to begin when those things could wait until later. The minister can pray and prepare all week to lead a significant worship experience only to be ambushed by someone about trivial things prior to morning worship. On Sunday morning the minister's mind should be focused on leading a meaningful worship experience; it should not be focused on stopped-up commodes, thermostats not set to your satisfaction, typographical errors in the bulletin, questions regarding why the lights in the sanctuary haven't been turned on yet, or an announcement you want them to make but didn't take the time to write down legibly.

Fifth, take care of your minister's financial needs through your church's budget, and don't do it grudgingly. Ministers pay the same prices at the gas pump and grocery store that you pay. If you insist on keeping your minister "broke," you can count on your minister becoming "broken" financially. I've heard laypeople tell stories about broken, failed ministers who "couldn't manage their money." But I also know the stories of ministers who, in terms of compensation, were never given sufficient money to manage. You expect your employer to pay you justly for the work you do. Ministers have every right to expect congregations to pay them justly for the work they do as well. Every congregation ought to have responsible people who will fairly represent the minister's financial needs so the minister doesn't have to. You don't want to go into your employer's office, hat in hand, to beg; your minister shouldn't have to do that either.

Sixth, keep your ministers from breaking themselves by getting caught up in a messiah complex. Saying "We don't know what we would do without you" too often can become destructively seductive. Insist that your minister take scheduled days off or make them up on other days if an emergency interferes with the scheduled day off. And then leave your minister alone on off days. Prior to my retirement, I received many phone calls that began with "I know this is your day off, but . . ." that could easily have waited until the next day. Ministers need vacations as much as others. Ministers need interests and hobbies apart from their work. Regardless of how well educated your minister is, they still need continuing education and refresher experiences. Care enough to lovingly ask your minister, "How are you taking care of yourself?" If you don't get a sensible answer, keep probing until you do get one. An overworked, clinically depressed minister, or one in intensive care with a coronary or stroke, can't be there for you when you need them. It is in your own best interest to be concerned that your minister is healthy physically, emotionally, and spiritually.

Seventh, and finally, if it becomes evident that your minister or someone in their family is broken, make a conscious effort to contribute to healing the brokenness instead of disposing of them and getting a new one. Ministers and their family members are subject to the same struggles and difficulties as everyone else. Physical illness, depression, marital misunderstandings, conflicts in the workplace, children with special learning needs or behavioral issues, too much month left over at the end of the money—the list is endless for everyone.

And from time to time your minister, regardless of the depth of their spirituality, will stumble under the load. When it happens, church members need to remember that the person who has so frequently helped them to bear their burdens is now a burdened person who needs the same compassionate assistance. While sometimes the brokenness is so thorough it cannot be healed, you don't know this is true until you have made the effort. People who expect their ministers to "be there" for them in the dark brokenness of life ought to be willing to "be there" for their ministers when they walk through the same dark brokenness.

Remember, if more people would give their ministers a "break," there would be fewer "broken" ministers.

God Trims My Trees, But God Expects Me to Clean Up the Mess

It was one of those wonderful pre-spring, late February days in the foothills of Western North Carolina. The sky was classic Carolina blue streaked with high-altitude contrails streaming from the exhausts of jet liners carrying cargo and passengers toward destinations near and far. Bright sunlight promised to warm the brisk morning air and I thought about getting something out of the freezer to incinerate later in the day on the gas grill. While I was savoring my third cup of morning coffee, Peggy asked, "What are you going to do today?"

"Well," I replied, "the grapes need to be pruned, brush fallen from the trees in the backyard needs to be collected and moved to the brush pile, and the trash and recyclables need to be hauled to the service center. That should keep me busy for a while." With this I drained the coffee cup, dressed in worn jeans and a sweatshirt, pulled on my work boots, and headed to my basement shop to get out the yard tools I would need for the outdoor tasks the morning demanded.

An hour or so later the grapes were pruned and I had raked the vines down to where I maintain a brush pile. That was pretty easy. Breaking out the old riding lawn mower I use for a tractor, I attached my trailer and headed deep into the backyard to clean up fallen limbs that had accumulated over the winter season. The lower quarter of the Greggs' acre and a quarter is populated by dogwood, hickory, poplar, cedar, and oak trees. In addition, it contains the only living natural-growth chestnut tree I know anything about. Every year the wind, rain, and occasional snow of winter deposit dead limbs on the ground that must be cleaned up so I can periodically mow and weed-eat the area to keep it from becoming too rustic to be of any use for family BBQs and fish fries. This was tougher going. Some of the limbs were too large to fit into my small trailer, so they had to be manually dragged up the hill to the brush pile. Others had to be picked up off the ground, sometimes broken into smaller sections, and piled into the trailer. At age forty-two this was no big deal for me; in my early seventies it is more of a challenge. At one point, taking a break to huff and puff a bit, I found myself musing, "It is good of God to trim my trees, but God still expects me to clean up the mess."

By now those of you who know me well know it doesn't take much to set me exploring the implications of pretty insignificant thoughts for various aspects of Christian living and growing amid the ordinary business of daily living. I think I am in good company here. When I explore the Bible, I find that the psalmist regularly drew inspiration from his natural surroundings; so did the author of Proverbs. Jeremiah listened while God spoke to his heart as he watched a potter's wheel, and the Apostle Paul drew illustrations from the athletic pursuits of his day. So perhaps you will cut me some slack if I find inspiration in the course of cleaning up a backyard mess.

It occurs to me that there are some things around my house that I cannot or should not do for myself, particularly at this stage in life. A number of years ago I gave up climbing the ladder, walking out to the edge of the roof, and cleaning out the gutters and flushing the downspouts. I let someone younger and more agile do that now. I have probably scraped, primed, and painted the soffit and facia on my house, particularly on the back where it is two stories high, for the last time. I know a reliable painting contractor who can do that for me when necessary. There was a time when I thought nothing of leaning a ladder against the trunk of a tree and, armed with my bow saw, proceeding to cut away and drop to the ground dead limbs before they had time to rot out and fall. Peggy says I shouldn't do that anymore either. As an independent and self-reliant person who is also pretty handy with tools, it has taken much effort to acclimate to the notion that I must rely on others to do things for me that I have been accustomed to doing for myself. On the other hand, it is probably not good for me to surrender all responsibility for attending to matters that inevitably demand attention in the course of life. Thus it seems sensible to depend on others to do some things for me while I continue to manage the things that remain within the range of my competence.

Every winter eventuates, with its rainstorms, winds, snow and ice, and the natural aging of the trees, in a good deal of debris ending up on the ground in the Greggs' backyard. Since most of this is the result of naturally occurring phenomena, for years I have jokingly referred to the fact that God trims my trees for me every winter, but God always leaves the mess for me to clean up myself. Given the circumstances, this seems a fair enough arrangement; God does the God stuff and leaves the Larry stuff to Larry.

In the spiritual and relational realms of life, there are some things we cannot do for ourselves. At the core of our being there is an existential alienation from our Creator that, despite all the attempts we may make, cannot be overcome by our own effort. The biblical message is that human estrangement from God is so radical that it can be overcome only by God's choice to intervene on our behalf to do for us what we cannot possibly do for ourselves. Christians believe that God has intervened in the person and work, the death and resurrection, of Jesus of Nazareth to bridge the void created by human sin and open the way for reconciliation with the One who has caused us to be and who sustains our being.

Christians further believe that, through this act of Divine grace, God has made it possible for broken relationships to be healed, prejudices to be overcome, hatreds to be laid aside, addictions to be broken, and every form of sin, personal and collective, individual and institutional, private and social, to be forgiven. For those who place their faith in the redemptive work of Jesus Christ, all that is destructive and death dealing can be pruned away and left lying on the hard ground of human finitude. Only God can do this. However, that's not the end of the matter. In Divine grace, God is willing to forgive and renew, but God leaves it to us to clean up the mess resulting from our need to be pruned and renewed. God doesn't say "I'm sorry" to those whom we have injured by our self-centered egoism; we must do that ourselves. God does not purge our minds of racial and ethnic prejudices; we must do that ourselves. God does not prevent us from abusing our bodies and minds with addictive substances and behaviors; we must learn to say "No" to those things ourselves. God does not make it impossible for us to engage in personal, institutional, and social immorality and sin; God expects us to engage in behaviors that close the door to such destructive patterns of living and behaving.

Am I saying that after we trust God's saving grace in Jesus Christ, God abandons us to our own devices for the future? Certainly not! In the Gospel of John (14:15-18), Jesus promised his followers that he would send a *Paraclete*, an Advocate, a Comforter, One to go along with them and help them. Christians understand this One to be the Holy Spirit of God indwelling the life of the believer. However, the role of this One is not to miraculously do for us what we can do for ourselves. The work of the Spirit is to inspire, guide, enliven, comfort, and reassure us as we assume responsibility for appropriately living our lives. The Holy Spirit works in our lives to keep us reminded of the intimate relationship we share with God (Rom 8:16). The Spirit is there to help us when we are having difficulty finding our way (Rom 8:26). The Spirit is there to assure us that, despite our deepest fears, there is not one single reality in the universe that can separate the believer from the loving grace of God made known in Jesus Christ (Rom 8:35-39).

What I am saying is that, while God does not abandon us to our own devices after we are redeemed in Jesus Christ, God does expect us to grow in mental maturity, spiritual insight, moral integrity, and behavioral discipline. God expects us to become increasingly able to assume appropriate responsibility for the injuries we have inflicted on ourselves and others in the past, plead for forgiveness when we need it, be willing to forgive others when they need it, make restitution when possible, and learn new ways of living when necessary. Put simply, we made the mess and God expects us to clean up its consequences as much as it is possible for us to do so.

Earlier I mentioned that there are some things I don't do for myself anymore; I call on others to help me with them. I also observed that there are some things I remain perfectly capable of doing for myself and should have no expectation that someone else will intervene on my behalf to do them for me. I don't climb trees anymore to cut out dying or dead limbs. However, I remain competent to prune my grapevines by myself; I don't need the help of others. I have the tools and the skills to manage on my own, and I know what needs to be done.

It seems to me that, by analogy, the same is true in living my life as a responsible person. While there are aspects of my living that would go seriously awry without the presence and guidance of God, there are other aspects of living that I have the tools to handle on my own. God gave me a brain and expects me to use it. God gave me the ability to learn and grow, and God expects me to be learning and growing. God gave me the capacity to think about my behavior and the consequences of that behavior for myself and others, and God expects me, as a reflective, intelligent, and morally responsible person, to think my way through to the appropriate answers and actions for which I am responsible.

The Bible doesn't say, "God helps them that help themselves." That was Benjamin Franklin in *Poor Richard's Almanac*, 1736 Edition. It is worth noting that this insight is also contained in the thought of such worthy ancients as Sophocles, Euripides, and Aesop as well as in Franklin's near contemporary Algernon Sidney. It is a classic illustration of the notion that "When better thoughts are thought, I'll think them." But while the explicit quote is not in the Bible, the biblical literature is replete with examples of this principle of faith-filled self-reliance in action. God announced the coming of a flood and the need to prepare; Noah built the ark. Pharaoh dreamed; Joseph organized Egypt to deal with the famine. Boaz observed Ruth's need and provided; Ruth gleaned the wheat from which she made bread. Jesus healed the paralytic; the man picked up his bed and made his way home. James said, "Show me your faith without your works, and I will show you my faith by my works" (Jas 2:18). This list could go on and on, but it boils down to this: I trust God to take care of the God stuff. I trust God's Holy Spirit to be there for me when I need Divine help with the Larry stuff. And God trusts me to take care of the Larry stuff that I am perfectly capable of taking care of on my own. God doesn't think I'm pathetically helpless, and God doesn't want me to think I am either. God says, "Larry, I'll keep trimming your trees, but I expect you to clean up the mess." I reply, "God, we've got a deal."

You Can't Catch No Fish if You Don't Go Near the Water

During one of my many visits to Panama City Beach I had an opportunity to indulge in one of my favorite pastimes—people watching. In an earlier chapter I mentioned a pleasant day spent in an oyster bar sipping coffee and eating a fried oyster po'boy. Sitting on a barstool with my back against the wall, with nowhere I needed to go and nothing in particular to do, I was presented with the ideal opportunity to watch and wonder.

One has to be careful regarding the impressions one forms of the people found in such a place. Some readers may have already concluded that, as a Christian minister, I should never have been in an oyster bar to begin with because alcoholic beverages are served in such places. It is my opinion that such an attitude is a major detriment to effective Christian witness on the part of ministers.

One of the sad truths of contemporary Christian witness is that most ministers don't know many lost people and spend little time with the ones they do know. The minister's days and nights are taken up with staff and committee meetings, leading worship and participating in church activities, visiting hospitals and nursing homes, and attending an unending series of denominational events. We spend so much time oiling squeaking institutional wheels, mollifying the sensibilities of the easily offended, promoting denominational "horse and pony" shows, and attending meetings that we have little time left over for being sensitive and responsive to the needs of the least, the loneliest, the longing, and the lost. While we fervently preach that our mission is to "seek and save" those who are lost, we spend little time in the places where the lost are to be found. After all, some of those places aren't "respectable," and good Christian ministers shouldn't risk sullying their reputations by being seen frequenting them. Those commissioned by Jesus to become "fishers of men" seem to have lost the truth that "you can't catch no fish if you don't go near the water."

The problem isn't new—it's as old as the ministry of Jesus. The religiously self-righteous of his day couldn't understand how Jesus could be a holy person sent from God and yet spend large amounts of his time with the non-religious, the immoral, and the socially marginalized. In response to the carping question of the scribes and Pharisees, "Why do you eat and drink with publicans and sinners?" (Luke 5:30), Jesus answered, "They that are whole need not a physician; but they that are sick. I came not to call the righteous, but sinners to repentance" (5:31-32).

Somehow, I have the impression that Jesus spent a good deal of his time in the equivalent of today's oyster bar, pub, and all-night coffee shop. And I suggest that those who wish to declare the "good news" of God's redemptive love in and through Jesus Christ should spend time in those places as well. Furthermore, it would behoove us all to be more careful about rushing to judgment regarding the sanctity of people simply on the basis of the company they keep. Experience demonstrates that within the church there are entirely too many "wolves in sheep's clothing" and in the outside world there are entirely too many "saints" for casual complacency in either place. Those who minister in the name of Jesus Christ, if I may borrow an analogy from Augustine of Hippo, have a calling to live faithfully both in the "City of God" and in the "City of Man."

Now, let's return to my afternoon at the oyster bar in Panama City Beach. An interesting collage of people had gathered for lunch that day. Nearest to me was a young couple in their early twenties with an approximately eighteen-month-old little boy. They sat in a booth near enough for me to hear their voices as they discussed what they could afford to eat. When the waitress came the young man ordered appetizers and soft drinks instead of a full lunch. I suspect the cost of the appetizers was still a strain on their budget. However, their apparently limited financial resources failed to inhibit their playful banter with the laughing child or their simple enjoyment of being together as a young family. They reminded me of another young couple and child I knew decades ago who scrimped and scraped to make economic ends meet while in college and graduate school, but were richly blessed in the love they shared together. I hope that young family had a wonderful time together making memories that will endure for decades in the future.

At a table in the center of the bar sat a "yuppie" couple eating grouper sandwiches and drinking beer while middle age crept up on them. The woman was wearing a hooded sweater and low-slung jeans—slung so low that I could see the tattoo at the base of the small of her back. The man, with cheap sunglasses perched on top of his head, griped to the waitress about the quality of the food. From their demeanor it was clear that both the man and the woman wanted to be "cool," but I suspect they were as average as everyone else in the place.

Then there was the senior adult couple, apparently lifelong partners who had scrimped and saved for decades, like my wife's sister and her husband, in order to buy a modest house several blocks from the beach as a place to live out their retirement years together. They talked in low voices about children and grandchildren who had visited for Christmas and then gone on their busy way, leaving the old couple both saddened and relieved by their departure.

Across the room sat a family of three: a forty-something man and woman who apparently had come to the beach during their high school aged daughter's Christmas break. I surmised that he was a modestly successful self-employed businessman. Mother and daughter were dressed in matching pastel blue jogging suits, and while both were attractive, neither seemed compelled to offer everyone else in the oyster bar a public display of her anatomy.

Finally, there was the brash, strong-voiced waitress who was probably there late the night before and among the first to return the next morning. Deftly she dealt with the fading "yuppie" complaining about his food, played with the eighteen-month-old, brewed fresh coffee for me, and kept up a steady banter with others. Coarse voiced and earthy, she "honeyed" and "sweethearted" and "babied" everyone in the place. I suspect that had she known she was being eavesdropped on by a Baptist minister and college teacher with a string of degrees listed behind his name, she could not have cared less. She had a job to do and she did it competently, pleasantly, and with enthusiasm. I hope everyone she served that day left her a generous tip. I did.

It was a late lunch crowd of ordinary people, the kind of people who keep places alive and vital and making a positive contribution in the world, whether those places are eating establishments and watering holes in tourist retreats or local churches in county-seat towns.

Strange as it may seem, as I departed I felt as though I had been in church that day. One of the reasons I like places like the oyster bar is that the people in such places remind me so much of the people I share life with, and worship with, in western North Carolina. I can reach into my memory and apply the name of someone I know to almost everyone I observed that day dining or working in the oyster bar. My suppositions about the people in the restaurant may or may not match up with the realities of their lives. It does not matter. What does matter is the fact that I can imagine things about them points out that each of them has a personal story regardless of whether their story matches my imaginings. Each one is a unique human being with hopes and dreams, sufferings and disappointments, longings and needs. Each one has something to give to the rest of us, and each one needs to be given to by the rest of us. And all are people for whom Christ died and rose victoriously over death that they "might have life, and have it more abundantly" (John 10:10).

This particular experience took place at the dawn of a new year, a time when many make lists of resolutions and set goals for the future. I am one of them, for I have resolved that, in order as a Christian minister to be a more effective "fisher of men," I'm going to have to spend more time near the water. Thus, there are some things I am determined to do more faithfully in the future than I have in the past.

First, I am going to deliberately cultivate more friendships with the least, the loneliest, the longing, and the lost. I am going to seek them out in the places they frequent and offer them my friendship, regardless of whether they are open to the gospel or not. Having spent some time with such people, I must confess that many of them are more likeable than some of the more consciously religious people with whom I spend so much of my time. They laugh more, posture less, and are more tolerant of my humanity than many of my fellow Christians.

Second, I plan to make more forays into the "City of Man" in order to help others find their way to the "City of God." Too often in the life of the church, we simply issue directions regarding how someone may find us if they are interested. This is not enough. Therefore, be fairly warned. You may see me frequenting places where ministers aren't ordinarily seen, you may find me keeping company with people who are frowned upon by the "respectable" of the community, and you may discover that I am less amenable to simply oiling the machinery, placating the ill-tempered, and promoting the programs than I have been in the past. And if on occasion you find me hard to find, assume that I've gone down to the water to fish for people.

Third, I'm going to assume the possibility that there is as much "gospel" out there in the world as there is within the confines of our church buildings. With my imagination I have given lives and personalities to the ordinary people I found in the oyster bar. Who knows if there is any accuracy in my imaginary descriptions? And who knows whether, in that mundane place among those ordinary people, there was not infinitely more than my mind was capable of imagining?

I wonder, could it be true that the young man and woman eating meager appetizers and playing with their infant son were really Mary, Joseph, and the baby Jesus on their way to Egypt to shield the Christ child from the wrath of mad old King Herod? Maybe the middle-aged couple with the teenaged daughter were really the tent-making missionaries Aquila and Priscilla on their way to meet the Apostle Paul at some new Corinth. Were the "yuppie" couple with the sunglasses and tattoos really a former "Rich Young Ruler" and "A Woman Taken in Adultery" struggling with the implications of their encounter with Jesus for how they would live in the future? Could the senior adults have been the aged Roman Christian Phoebe and her husband talking together about how to be "deacon" and "deaconess" in that persecuted community of faith? And is it possible that the brash and harried waitress was Lazarus's sister Martha, devoted to freely lavishing hospitality on all who passed through her dwelling?

Was it an oyster bar in Panama City Beach, or was it Beth-el, the place where one meets God? Truly, it was both, for if one cannot recognize the presence of God in the faces and stories of the people with whom one shares life, one will not recognize the presence of God in the pages of Scripture or the walls of a cathedral. So why not resolve today to spend more time out there in the world in the presence of God among ordinary people? Remember, "you can't catch no fish if you don't go near the water."

God Sees Stuff the Rest of Us Don't See

The people who know me well, and even many of those who don't, know that at the core of my personality I am a scavenger. I mean that not in the sense of being a buzzard, wolf, or some other animal that feeds off the carrion and refuse of another animal. By the term "scavenger" I mean one who is continually bringing home something found at the local service center, an item from a yard sale, or even something abandoned on the side of the road. I find great satisfaction in taking what others have discarded as useless and turning it into something that is useful and sometimes even beautiful.

This propensity for collecting the cast-off junk of others has often been a source of exasperation to my wife, but she never complains about the result of some of my most unlikely acquisitions. Thus our house is furnished with, among other things, bookcases and afghan holders made from old forklift pallets as well as an entertainment center/gas log fireplace, bed headboard and side tables, and a deacon's bench made from cast-off oak and pine barnwood. The toolbox on my pickup truck was found at the local service center where we haul our household trash. The coffee table and a couple of paintings in our living room came from the same place, as did the small drop-leaf table and prep table next to the gas grill on our deck. Once I took the console and keyboard of an abandoned organ and turned it into a rolltop computer desk. On another occasion, with the significant help of a friend, I took a beat-up, rusted out 1973 Datsun 240Z and made it look like it just rolled off the showroom floor. This could go on *ad infinitum*, or perhaps *ad nauseum*, but what can I say? I've already told you, at the core I'm a scavenger.

Even the house we live in has something of this "reclamation project" quality to it. In the early 1990s, shortly after I joined the faculty of Gardner-Webb University, Peggy and I were looking to buy a house. In a process that can only be attributed to God's grace, we found a 1960s-style red-brick house on an acre and a quarter in the Blue Ridge foothills. The house was well worn and needed lots of loving attention, but its floor space, location, and possibilities suited us. I even noted to Peggy as we looked at it one rainy Sunday afternoon, "This looks like a great place for us to grow old and die."

In the process of purchasing the house and property, I brought an attorney friend who specialized in real estate to take a look and tell me what he thought. He was not impressed and pointedly said so. We bought the house anyway. A couple of years later he and his wife came out one evening for dinner. We toured them through the house so they could see what we had done with it. At the end of the tour my friend said, "I can hardly believe it. That day we came out to look, you obviously saw things in this house I just didn't see."

My latest find is an old, beaten up, and badly used rocking chair I spotted discarded on the side of the state road about a mile from our house. As I slowed the car to take a look, I couldn't help but envision its possibilities. I hurried home, exchanged Peggy's car for my pickup truck, and headed back for the chair, hoping someone else had not gotten to it first. They hadn't, so I loaded it up, brought it home to my shop, and took a few minutes to analyze my find. It is in bad shape. One of the spacers separating the legs is broken. Tenons have worked loose, and the undercarriage and rockers are about to separate from the seat. Dirt, dust, and whatever are all over it; the paint is peeling in places and scratched in others. In short, the old rocking chair is a mess, and I love it.

So here is my plan. I am going to repair, restore, and refinish the rocking chair. As I do so I will reflect, as a craftsperson, on the various steps in the rocking chair's restoration and rehabilitation and, by analogy, reflect theologically and spiritually on God's "reclamation project" that includes the restoration and rehabilitation of those who are willing to trust in Divine mercy and grace. This process will take a while, but I have no need to hurry. With the other demands being made on my time and energy, I plan to take my time, if for no other reason than that I need to think carefully about both the restoration of the chair and what that process has to say about God's restoration of people, and all of creation, to wholeness and usefulness within the Divine economy.

I begin with one basic presupposition: I refuse to believe that the chair, badly damaged though it is, is beyond redemption and restoration, and that no human being is beyond the redeeming and restoring power of God made known to us through the "good news" of what God has done and continues to do in Jesus Christ. I also begin with one basic assertion: the chair has no choice. It can only be a passive participant in my attempt to renew its original purpose and beauty. If the project fails, it will be due to my lack of skill and/or persistence.

On the other hand, human beings are not passive objects; we are active, dynamic someones who make decisions about whether we will respond to God's redemptive and restorative overtures. The rocking chair did not abuse, mar, and break itself and thus bears no responsibility for the condition it is in. However, we abused, marred, broken human beings share some measure of responsibility for the condition in which we find ourselves. While things happen to all of us over which we have no control, there are other matters in our lives for which we are simply deluding ourselves when we attempt to absolve ourselves of responsibility. We made bad choices and the results of those choices have had negative consequences for our lives. If we want to take a measure of credit for the positive in our lives, we must also be willing to be held accountable, in some measure, for the negative. If the rocking chair is never restored to usefulness, it bears no responsibility for the failure; the fault belongs to me and the limitations of my skill. On the other hand, people who refuse to permit the Divine craftsman to repair and heal, redeem and restore, must bear the responsibility for the failure. Despite the self-pitying protestations of those wishing to deny their own accountability, it is not God's fault. We must all confess along with the psalmist, "Against thee, thee only, have I sinned, and done this evil in thy sight . . ." (Ps 51:4).

Now, let me return to my attorney friend's observation that I saw something in the house Peggy and I bought that he didn't see. Possibly he was correct, for we brought different perspectives to the matter. I was seeing from the point of view of a person in his early forties who knew that if we were ever going to buy a house, it had to be soon. My friend was seeing from the perspective of an experienced and successful professional who already owned the house he would live in for the remainder of his life. He was thinking in terms of a real estate transaction; I was thinking from the perspective of a husband and wife approaching middle age, with the nest about to empty, who needed a home to share with adult offspring, hopefully future in-laws and grandchildren, and our trove of treasured friends.

I submit that God also sees differently than we do because the Divine perspective is infinitely wider ranging and more comprehensive than yours or mine. The fifth-century BCE philosopher Plato argued that lying behind the objects we perceive and interact with in the world are ultimate, perfect, eternal, non-perishable *ideas* or *forms*. Thus a "chair" is real to us because it participates in and expresses the ultimate *form/idea* of chair-ness. This is not the place to argue for or against Plato's theory of how and why things exist. However, from the perspective of Christian thought it can be posited that, as Creator/Sustainer of all that is, God sees not only our brokenness, finitude, and frustration; God also sees the original Divine intent and purpose for human existence, collectively and individually. The Christian doctrine of redemption is not just about being rescued from the destructive consequences of fallenness and sin; it is about being ultimately restored to being the people, individually and collectively, whom God always intended us to be. Sometimes we become so preoccupied with being saved from "original sin" that we forget there is an "original goodness" that God intends to restore. Even in my finite knowing, I know enough about chairs to see what needs to be done to my broken rocker to restore it to some semblance of its original beauty and utility. And we can be sure that the infinite knowledge of God comprehends the original Divine intent, the depths of our brokenness, and the means whereby we may be restored to the original "goodness" of our creation. While we may have difficulty seeing so comprehensively, God, in Divine grace and loving-kindness, sees it all.

I further suggest that because God sees more than we do, God looks beyond the broken, marred, scarred reality of our present existence and has elected to act in the present to overcome the consequences of our past and open us up to the glorious vision of the future in store for us as we trust in God's redemptive grace. But the glory of God's vision for our future requires our willingness to cooperate. Like the young and selfish and vindictive Eustace in C. S. Lewis's *Voyage of the Dawn Treader*, we must be set free by another, for we are ultimately unable to free ourselves. We must cooperate with God as the encrusting carapace of ego, selfishness, greed, and pride is peeled away, liberating us so that, in the words of the Apostle Paul, we may "press toward the mark for the prize of the high calling of God in Christ Jesus" (Phil 3:14).

Finally, because God sees stuff the rest of us don't see, God can envision the possibilities for our future that are yet to be realized. Paul wrote that "eye hath not seen, nor ear heard, neither have entered into the heart of man, the things which God hath prepared for them that love him" (1 Cor 2:9). It is relatively easy for us to see ourselves and others as we used to be or as we are at present. It takes a remarkably insightful consciousness to see the positive potential within another, despite their liabilities, that may be evoked, nurtured, and assisted to flower from the ugliness of the present into the blossoming beauty of the future.

A special friend gifted Peggy with an amaryllis bulb before the Advent season. I must admit that when she took it out of the box, the misshapen, turnip-like bulb showed no sign of the potential beauty that lay within. Still, following the directions, Peggy planted the bulb, watered it, placed it in appropriate light, and waited for days to see what would happen. By Christmas Eve the stalks were over two feet tall and the plant had blossomed into a beautiful harbinger of the coming of the Christ child. The potential beauty was there all along, but had it not been unboxed, planted, watered, and allowed to experience the light, it would never have bloomed. The exquisite beauty of its blossoms would never have emerged had someone not had faith in its possibilities.

Peggy had faith that the condition in which she first acquired the amaryllis did not have to dictate the conditions of its ultimate destiny, so she did the things necessary to allow the plant to achieve its glorious potential. The Genesis narrative relates the story of God's strolling through the original goodness of creation only to find the man and the woman hiding in guilty shame, naked in the truth of their disobedience, seeking a scapegoat to blame for the consequences of their bad choices. God could have abandoned them to their fate. Instead God chose to cover their nakedness, renew the Divine/human community, and hold at bay the destructive selfishness inherent in the freedom they had been given. And the balance of the biblical narrative, both Old Testament and New Testament, is the unfolding story of God's determined faith that deep in the darkness of human fallenness there remains that original "goodness" that may be evoked, nurtured, and loved so that it blossoms into the fullness of the Creator's original intent. Why is this true? It is true because God sees stuff the rest of us don't see!

Sanity Ain't Necessarily All It's Cracked Up to Be

People who know me well know I'm a hard-nosed realist who insists that those who want to enlist me in something they think important, or have me subscribe to a belief or opinion they hold dear, don't have a chance of getting my sympathetic attention unless they can provide me with rational, sensible reasons why. Appeals to emotion, sentimental attachment, popular opinion, or age-old habit don't motivate me unless they are also supportable by objective, logical analysis that will stand up under careful examination in the marketplace of ideas and human interactions. I am convinced that the truly biblical concept of "faith" (*pistis*) has nothing to do with blindly embracing anything without first responsibly examining the data available. From my perspective, this is an imminently sane and sensible way to conduct one's life.

When I look about me, I observe that some people approach life and its challenges much the same way I do and others are highly motivated by the influences of emotion, sentimental attachment, popular opinion, and age-old habit. When talking about issues of religious identity, they define "faith" precisely as a blind leap of commitment predicated upon no more than the subjective belief that a particular action is the right thing for them to do. And, from their perspective, this is an imminently sane and sensible way to conduct their lives.

Such a reality is open to a series of possible explanations. It may be that my way is right and everyone else is wrong, perhaps even insane. It may be that my way is wrong or insane and everyone else is right. And it may be that this business of sanity ain't necessarily all it's cracked up to be.

Over decades of teaching World Religions classes, one of the first things I told students was how important it was to recognize that we were examining various religious traditions (Hinduism, Buddhism, Judaism, Islam, etc.) from the outside in; that is, most of us had been raised in, or significantly influenced by, the dominant Christian religion of American culture. In addition, our perception of authentic Christianity had been colored by whether we were primarily exposed to Christianity's Roman Catholic, Orthodox, or Protestant traditions, not to mention the bias that came along with whether our exposure to Christian belief and culture was a positive or negative experience. Furthermore, if our background was Protestant, our understandings were influenced by which flavors of Protestant tradition we had been exposed to (Methodist, Presbyterian, Baptist, Pentecostal, etc.). Finally, our subjective assessment of value in other religions is shaped by whether our own Christian identity is nominal, superficial, and uncritical or is the product of thoughtful reflection and deep commitment. Because we do not convert to these other religions, we always stand on the outside looking in; we can never look at another religious tradition from the inside out. And even if we convert, we will still bring the psychological and cultural baggage of our prior religious heritage, or lack thereof, with us into our new religious environment. As much as we might wish to do so, we cannot erase our past and its influence on our present and future.

Why is it important to understand this fact? It is important because it helps us guard against dismissing other understandings as illogical, primitive, silly, ignorant, and perhaps even crazy simply because they are somewhat, or even radically, different from our own. It also contributes to the understanding that if we want others to take us and what we think and believe seriously, we must take them and what they think and believe seriously as well. Such mutual respect does not require acceptance or agreement with others' point of view, but it does require that we not use words like "crazy," "stupid," and "insane" when referring to their value systems and decision-making processes. The main reason why sanity ain't necessarily all it's cracked up to be is that what is considered "sane" as opposed to "insane" is often no more than a matter of who is defining the terms, particularly when "sane" means to be like me and my group and "insane" means to not be like me and my group.

While I have used an analogy from World Religions, the analogy could be drawn equally well from diverse political systems, economic models, literary types, and sporting events. Unless one is an initiate of a particular worldview (*Weltanschauung*) to a greater or lesser degree, one does not understand what is taking place within it. As an American, I assess all forms of government through my experience with representative democracy, all economic systems through my knowledge of capitalism, all literature through my training in English/American literary studies, and all competitive athletics through my grasp of the fundamentals of American baseball, football, and basketball. Thus, while I may have opinions about dictatorships, Marxist economics, Japanese haiku, and cricket, they are always from the perspective of an outsider. Any value judgments I make about them, and I will make such value judgments, must be qualified by the fact that I have never lived in a dictatorship, worked in a Marxist society, written poetry in Japanese, or played the English national game. While they all seem a little "crazy" to me, I must remember that "sanity" ain't necessarily all it's cracked up to be.

Many decades ago, I was introduced to four questions I have since considered essential to making critical decisions about my own ideas or those of others. While I don't set these questions forth as an absolutely infallible guide, I do think they provide an objective, non-emotional, and fair-minded means of exchanging insight and understanding, particularly in the realm of religious beliefs and the values for living derived from such beliefs.

The first question: *Is this concept or belief coherent?* To paraphrase, can this concept be readily understood by most anyone who makes an honest attempt at understanding it? To conclude that something is coherent does not require my agreement, acceptance, or endorsement of the point of view; all it requires is that it be understandable using the common tools of human reason and reflection.

Frequently I hear someone say, "I don't understand how Hindus can refuse to eat beef when millions of cattle roam India, and the protein content of the food supply would be significantly increased if they did so." Another will say, "I can't understand why Muslims place so much emphasis on the words of an illiterate orphan who earned a living following caravans on the trade routes of the Middle East in the seventh century CE." These same people would likely become intensely indignant if someone said to them, "I don't understand how anyone could believe that the death of one man on a Roman cross two thousand years ago can provide a means of salvation for all who confess that Jesus of Nazareth was/is the Christ of God." Yet, when one takes the time to become acquainted with the foundational assumptions of Hinduism, Islam, and Christianity, one discovers that each of these belief systems is coherent; it can be understood by those who make the effort, even if one does not embrace the belief system.

Second question: *Is that belief or idea non-contradictory?* Like matter and antimatter, some things cannot occupy the same place at the same time. In my Philosophy classes the students and I discussed the Principle of Non-Contradiction, which asserts that a statement and its opposite cannot both be true at the same time in the same way. The propositions "The glass is full" and "The glass is empty" are in contradiction when used to refer to the same glass in the same place at the same time.

Many people do not carefully nuance the distinction between contradiction and paradox. Life has much in it that is paradoxical; so does religious belief. Paradox (like the Christian assertion that Jesus of Nazareth was/is both fully God and fully human) focuses on the stress created by the need to affirm two essential truths even though they are in tension with one another. Every conscientious parent knows the paradoxical stress of loving our children so much that we do not want to see them suffer in any way and the knowledge that one of the ways they learn to fend for themselves in the world is through painful experience.

Contradiction, however, is not paradoxical tension; contradiction is head-on collision. While balancing paradoxes is often difficult, the maintenance of mutually exclusive contradictions is ultimately impossible. As Augustine of Hippo pointed out many centuries ago, the attempt to do so is to end in a skepticism that questions if we can be certain of the truth of anything.

Why is this important? Let me illustrate its importance by referring to a central truth of Christian faith. Christians affirm their belief that an infinitely good and loving God created the universe in which we live and placed human beings in it to live responsibly and participate with God in the Divine purpose. It is not possible to affirm this central proposition of the Christian faith and at the same time assert that the universe in which we exist is the product of meaningless happenstance, without origin, without goal, and without any ultimate meaning. These two propositions cannot be reconciled; they are in contradiction, and thus, from the perspective of Christian faith, the authentic believer cannot embrace them both at the same time. Furthermore, only one of the propositions is coherent within the framework of Christian belief about the nature of God and the world.

Question three: *Does this belief or point of view correspond to reality as reality is commonly perceived?* In an altered state of consciousness (i.e., drug induced, the product of sleep deprivation and/or torture, or the consequence of a brain tumor), I may believe that snakes are crawling all over my body, that I am impervious to bullet wounds, or that I am an alien life form living in secret on Planet Earth. Under the influence of such beliefs, I may behave in ways that others consider peculiar, outrageous, and even dangerously insane. But if I want them to take me seriously there must be some correspondence between their perception of reality and mine. Furthermore, to elect to act on beliefs that are radically out of sync with commonly perceived reality may cause me to do great injury to myself and to others.

Correspondence to commonly perceived reality keeps us reminded that all our beliefs are, ultimately, public beliefs. While they may be intensely personal, they are never private. Because what we believe has consequences for how we behave, and our behavior has consequences for others, we are not free to construct an exclusively private reality that does not correspond to reality as others perceive it. Authentic reality is shared reality.

Question four: *Is this understanding or belief comprehensive?* That is, does it take into consideration the broadest aspects of life, and does it offer an answer that satisfies most, if not all, of the issues related to it? The more comprehensive a belief system, the more effective it is in satisfying the needs of those who hold it and the greater its likelihood of being held by a substantial number of others.

While I may insist on maintaining that the planet on which we live is the center of the universe and that everything else revolves around it, such a position, once held by many, is not comprehensive enough to explain seasonal change, the motion perceived in other celestial bodies, and various other phenomena. I may insist that my position is a central article of the Christian faith and persecute others who dispute my assertion. This is precisely what happened to many during the Late Middle Ages as they challenged the Christian church's official understanding of the order of the universe. However, with the passage of time and the accumulation of the data of scientific observation, it had to be conceded that the hypothesis of an earth-centered universe was no longer supportable, and the search began for a more comprehensive explanation of the relationship between the earth and the sun, other stars, and other planets.

To this series of critical-thinking questions to which I was introduced decades ago, I have added a fifth: *Is this position, point of view, belief system corrigible; is it open to correction?* I do not fault people of an earlier time for not knowing what they could not possibly have known when they formulated and expressed their conclusions about the reality of the physical world, the structure and organization of human society, the cause and cure of diseases, the meaning of life, and religious belief. I do find fault with people who insist on continuing to embrace ideas, values, and beliefs that additional objective information has emptied of any meaningful content. As a believing Christian I embrace the conviction that all authentic truth, regardless of its origins or implications, is ultimately and finally God's truth. The corollary to this conviction is the obligation I have to be open to correction when it is apparent that, regardless of the depth and fervor of my sincerity, I was still mistaken.

Five questions about beliefs: *Is it coherent; can it be understood? Is it non-contradictory? Does it correspond to reality as commonly perceived? Is it comprehensive enough to take in all the data available, and is it the best explanation of the facts as commonly understood? Is it corrigible; is it open to correction when confronted with new and verifiable information that was not available at an earlier time?* These are the interrogatory tools I use to test my own values and those of others. When I use them properly, I never find myself stomping my feet, pounding my fists, shouting down others because I think they are crazy, and condemning to hell anyone who disagrees with me. Also, when I use them properly, I never shrug my shoulders and say, "It really doesn't matter all that much what you believe as long as you're sincere." This approach allows me to passionately embrace my carefully considered convictions while being able to explain to others why I hold them. It permits me to listen respectfully to the convictions of others, even though I may think they are wrong. And it challenges me to swallow my pride, acknowledge my own mistaken views, and make necessary corrections when they are appropriate.

The Challenges to Renewal Leave Questions to Be Answered

I finally found a Saturday to spend some time with the abandoned rocking chair I found on the side of the road. Making my way down to the shop shortly after breakfast, I turned on the heaters to ward off the cold and settled down to closely examine the chair. My aim was to develop a plan for its restoration. Earlier a little sanding had revealed that, underneath the worn-out finish and accumulated crud, the chair was made entirely of wonderful old red mahogany. As I sipped hot coffee and stared at the chair a number of questions began to surface in my consciousness: (1) Is this beaten-up old rocking chair worth the time, effort, materials, and elbow grease that will be required to restore it? (2) How do I reinforce the weak places in the chair without creating unsightly evidences of the necessary repairs? (3) Is removing all the scars and blemishes of the chair's past worth the risk of sanding away too much material? (4) Once the original wood is all exposed, what are the options for finishing it?

As usual, such questions turned my thinking toward their relevance for the process of individual personal and spiritual renewal or the restoration to vitality of a congregation that has become so battered and bruised by conflict and recrimination that many have abandoned it to whatever fate transpires.

The question of whether the old rocking chair is worth the time, effort, materials, and elbow grease required to restore it is a subjective question that may be answered positively or negatively with no significant consequence. After all, I found it abandoned on the side of the road and picked it up on a whim. The choice as to its value or lack thereof is purely mine. Whether I restore it or not is no more than a matter of my choice to do so; the chair has no voice in the decision. And if I choose to restore it, there is a high degree of likelihood that in a generation or two it will be junk once again.

So much for the old chair, but human beings and Christian congregations are an altogether different matter. As a Christian I cannot cavalierly conclude that a broken individual or congregation is not worth an investment of my resources in enabling the possibility of personal rehabilitation and/or congregational renewal. If, as a member of the "Body of Christ," I am called to participate with God in the Divine project of renewal and restoration through the atoning death and life-giving resurrection of Jesus Christ, I have no alternative but to invest the gifts entrusted to me in attempting to aid my broken sibling. It is equally incumbent upon me to work together with others in the "Body of Christ" to bring healing and renewal to a dysfunctional congregation.

One caveat must be made here. It is not a back-door excuse for me to avoid my responsibility as a Christian, but it is a recognition that my ability to help is limited by the other's willingness to permit me to help. While the chair has no choice as I apply my tools and skills to its restoration, individuals and congregations may choose to remain broken and dysfunctional despite all attempts to help them heal and move beyond the accumulated scars of individual and collective abuse and/or bad choices. I bear all the responsibility for success or failure with the rocking chair, but Christian maturity insists that, while I am called to do my best, I must not allow self-righteousness to lead me into a co-dependent posture that ends with my accepting responsibility for the behaviors/decisions of others over which I have no control.

The second question has its own challenges as well. Close examination reveals that wear, abuse, and time have taken their toll on the old chair. There are cracks in the seat, splits where dowels have swollen and broken through the material around their holes, and scratches and dents where excessive sanding would leave unevenness and the risk of creating new vulnerabilities in the excessively dry wood. It will take the careful insertion of screws and covering plugs, and the equally careful application of sanding and finish, to restore the integrity of the chair while leaving minimal evidences of the repairs I make.

Can I make less painstaking and time-consuming repairs to the chair and it still be strong enough to be useful? Sure I can. But no self-respecting woodworker can make such makeshift repairs and still consider themselves a craftsman. There is no place in fine woodworking for the question, "What's the least I can do and say I did it?"

And there's no place for "What's the least I can do and say I did it?" for those who are called to participate with God in what God is doing in the world. One sadness of contemporary Christianity is the individual and collective loss of a sense of calling to excellence in what we do. Many individual Christians and churches are characterized by intellectual laziness, biblical ignorance, lack of moral courage, missional ineptitude, power grasping, and spiritual immaturity. It's not that we don't know what we are supposed to do. It's that many don't care if we do it well as long as they get what they want with minimal involvement and personal sacrifice. Some demand special privilege and sneer at those they consider beneath them in righteousness or insight or pedigree. Some ally with others who at the core have un-Christian agendas and are willing to use non-critical-thinking Christians as tools to achieve their ends. The desire for easy, quick, uncomplicated, platitudinal fixes to the challenges of Christian living militate against our ability to be useful to God, ourselves, or others.

Question three is easier to deal with: "Is removing all the scars and blemishes of the chair worth the risk of sanding away too much of the original material?" The answer here is pretty straightforward. "No, it is not worth the risk!" Understand, I am not trying to make the chair perfect; I'm trying to make it better and restore it to meaningful usefulness. While I don't want to keep them all, some of the scars and blemishes remind me that the chair has a history. I don't know one single thing about that history, but knowing something about people and chairs, I can surmise some things. Was the old chair originally a wedding present or the shower gift for a couple's first pregnancy? How many babies were rocked to sleep, how many tears were shed or wiped away, how often was it occupied late at night by someone waiting for a teen to come home? Was it a favorite sitting place where small children climbed up into a parent or grandparent's lap to have stories told and books read to them? Did an aged widow or widower rock away lonely hours in the old chair, recalling the pleasures, heartaches, family celebrations, and griefs of a lifetime? Frankly, I don't know what the chair's history was, but I know it has a history; and I know that history deserves to be preserved in some, if not all, of the scars, discolorations, and evidences of wear that have become a part of the chair itself. The chair doesn't need to be made *new*; it needs to be carefully *renewed*.

And among people and congregations, it is nonsense to attempt to jettison individual or collective history in order to be made whole, useful, and happy again. Who we are and what we are is, in part but not wholly, defined by our past. Personally, I have no desire to recover the 120-pound, strongly muscled, jet-black-haired twenty-year-old I was when Peggy and I first married. Life has been too rich, filled with too much adventure, scratched and dented by too many challenges that had to be overcome, and blessed by too many wonderful people and too much laughter to abandon it all and be "new" again. I am not necessarily proud of all of my history, but it is *my* history. In some ways I am less than what I was five decades ago, and in others I am much more than I was then. Did life turn out as I wanted? Absolutely not, and in some instances, thank God it didn't. Are there regrets? Yes. Are there things that, if given the opportunity to do over, I would do differently? Some yes and some no.

Here's the point. It took a while, but I finally figured out that it is all I can do to live meaningfully in the present while oriented toward the future. My options for dealing with the past are limited. I can whine, weep, and wail; I can preen, posture, and pretend; but either way I risk making myself thoroughly obnoxious to others regardless of whether I spend my time mourning over or bragging about my past. Or I can treasure my successes, learn from my failures, smile at my foibles, and savor my memories trusting that collectively they have all contributed to helping me become more and more the person God always intended me to be. I haven't the remotest interest in returning to what I used to be; I am passionately interested in all that I have yet to become by God's grace. And while I'm not proud of all my psychic, spiritual, and physical scars and blemishes, I am not ashamed of them either. For collectively they keep me reminded that in a fallen world the pristine and perfect are not only impossible but also probably useless.

Everything I have said at the level of the personal is equally applicable to Christian congregations. Too many churches risk committing internecine suicide quarreling over how to recover an idealized past while squandering away opportunities to minister effectively into a glorious future. Thomas Wolfe was right: *You Can't Go Home Again*.[1] Churches can't relive their past; they can only work in the present to build on the positive and the negative of the past and, having learned from their scars and blemishes, re-vision a meaningful future.

Last question regarding the old rocking chair: "What are the options for finishing it?" I could simply seal the mahogany and allow the richness of the original wood to be seen even though this would heighten the visibility of the scars and blemishes. I could stain and then seal the chair; this would cover up most of the irregularities and dents. I could simply paint the old chair and cover up everything, but then the wonderful mahogany would be completely obscured and the chair's history would all be lost. I could elect to seal part of it and paint the rest. In this way I could probably cover up the ugliest of the chair's blemishes while allowing the richness of the original wood to be visible as well. By now some of you are saying he has drifted off into nonsense. Not necessarily.

Many times I have heard someone say that God has only one special will and purpose for our lives, individually and collectively, and that our job is to figure out what that will is and then do it. If we genuinely believe that God has given each of us a measure of autonomous freedom to make choices, then I contend that God's will for people and for churches may be multiple and open-ended. God may confront us personally with a number of options/behaviors/choices while saying, "Either one of these is perfectly acceptable to me. Select one and then follow it out to see where it takes you." The same may be true for congregations. Instead of pushing and shoving on one

---

1. *You Can't Go Home Again* (New York: Harper & Row, 1940).

another with sanctimonious assertions that person or group "A" has a better understanding of God's will than person or group "B," it seems to me that God's ultimate will for all of us is summed up in this verse: "What does the LORD require of you, but to do justice, and to love kindness, and to walk humbly with your God?" (Micah 6:8). It matters not how I choose to finish the old rocker as long as it fulfills its ultimate purpose as a rocking chair. Consistent with God's revelation of the Divine self in Jesus Christ, I think God's primary concern is that our finishing contributes to fulfilling our ultimate purpose to become people of justice, loving-kindness, and humility. We don't all have to be finished the same way, but unless we focus on justice, loving-kindness, and humility, we will never be beautifully finished.

There Are Some Things I Just Plain Hate

As much as possible I try to avoid using the word "hate." Given my Southern background and the tendency of Southerners to speak in superlatives, I must admit that avoiding the word is a challenge. Take the time to listen to yourself and others in everyday conversation. The pendulum of our verbal expressions swings radically from one extreme to the other. We "love" this and we "hate" that. We "can't stand this" and we "can't get by without that." We could "eat up" one person while we have "absolutely no use" for someone else. People "love" a particular sports team while "hating" another. This is the verbal environment in which we all live, and for the most part it is pretty harmless; it's the way people express themselves.

On the other hand, such extreme expressions may not be as harmless as we think. When the word "hate" is directed at people because of their ethnicity, sexual identity, nationality, political affiliations, or religious convictions, the word is not only harmful but tremendously dangerous.

If the above is true, and I believe it is, how do we determine from a Christian perspective when it is appropriate and when it is inappropriate to use the word "hate" in our private thoughts and public speech? When I turn to the biblical revelation, the Scripture seems to indicate that individually and collectively we should "love" what God loves and "hate" what God hates. This essay is not the place for an exhaustive search of Scripture, but the Bible is replete with texts pointing out what God loves and what God desires that we love. God loves the world (John 3:16). God loves all of us (1 John 4:19). God loves sound judgment (Isaiah 61:8). God loves humility on the part of those who worship (Psalm 51:17). God wants us to love God

(Matt 22:37). God wants us to love our neighbor (Lev 19:18, 34; Matt 19:19). God wants us to love one another (John 15:12). God wants us to love the stranger in our midst (Deut 10:19). God wants us to love our enemies (Matt 5:43-44). To save space I'll stop there.

Knowing what God loves and, consequently, what I should love is challenge enough. Knowing what I should hate because God hates the same thing is even more challenging. To simplify the process, let's turn our attention to "some things I just plain hate" because I am convinced from Scripture that God hates these things as well. Like the above, this list is not exhaustive, but I hope it is illuminating to all and even disturbing to some.

I hate religion without a social conscience, and God does too. The classic scriptural basis for this assertion is Amos 5:21-24 where, through the prophet, God castigates Israel for preoccupation with elaborate religious observances while ignoring the need for justice within the society. In Amos 2:6-8 these so-called "people of God" are rebuked for their greed, victimization of the poor, sexual immorality, and profaning of their worship. In his sermon in the synagogue at Nazareth, Jesus drew upon the words of Isaiah 6:1-2 to announce that his mission was to ". . . preach good tidings unto the meek . . . bind up the brokenhearted . . . proclaim liberty to the captives . . . opening of the prison to them that are bound . . . comfort all that mourn . . . ." In Matthew 25:31-46 Jesus spoke plainly to his disciples regarding the practice of social justice as a sign of true identification with him and the eternal negative consequences for those who wished to call him "Lord" while ignoring the needs of "the least of these."

Yet today many contemporary Christians seem primarily preoccupied with building costly venues for the staging of elaborate religio-entertainment productions, embracing their ethnic and cultural prejudices, and enriching manipulative religious media snake-oil purveyors willing to fill their "itching ears" (2 Tim 4:3) with whatever they want to hear. To the self-interested political and religious leaders and people of Judah, God said, "Thus saith the LORD of hosts, the God of Israel; drink ye, and be drunken, and spue, and fall, and rise no more, because of the sword which I will send among you" (Jer 25:27). God hates religion without social consciousness, and because God hates it I do too.

I hate the mixing of religious symbols and political symbols so that no distinction can be made between them, and I think God hates this as well. Remember, it was Jesus who said, "Render to Caesar the things that are Caesar's, and to God the things that are God's" (Mark 12:17). Paul, perhaps with this saying of Jesus in mind, spoke in reference to the believer's relationship to the secular power: "Render therefore to all their dues . . ." (Rom 13:7). He enjoined his readers to duly respect the secular authorities of their day (Rom 13:1-4). Paul placed great value on the privileges and responsibilities of his Roman citizenship, but at no point did he ever equate being Roman with being Christian or being Christian with being Roman.

A quick Google search will reveal that millions of dollars are being made through the marketing of "Cross and American Flag" lapel pins, posters, decals, bumper stickers, banners, framed photographs, and more all over the Internet. God repeatedly warned ancient Israel that the elevation of any object or person to divine status was an abomination (Exod 20:3-4; Deut 7:25-26). To equate being Christian with being American by merging such symbols is to elevate the nation to a status co-equal with the Divine and is thus a blatant expression of idolatry. My love for my nation is deep and profound, but I reserve my worship for God alone.

I hate being told by my fellow believers that I'm wrong simply because I hold an opinion that is different than theirs. Many of Paul's letters in the New Testament devote attention to matters of diversity of opinion among believers. Galatians addresses the Judaizing Christians who insisted all Gentiles must convert to Judaism before they could become followers of Jesus. The apostle used direct language to illustrate how strongly he felt about such legalism (Gal 5:11-12). He also challenged believers who refused to share table fellowship with others because, coming from Gentile backgrounds, they did not observe the Jewish ceremonial laws related to food (Gal 2:10-13). The Corinthian church was a mess of divisiveness with conflicting opinions regarding the role of women in worship, eating meat sacrificed to idols, speaking in tongues, the diversity of spiritual gifts, marriage, pursuing lawsuits in secular courts, resurrection, and the gluttonous abuse of the common worship meal that preceded the observance of Communion. The Thessalonian believers were consumed with speculation regarding bodily resurrection and the return of Christ.

This cacophony of dissonance was no more edifying than "sounding brass" and "tinkling cymbals" because of the absence of love on the part of people whose chief interest was proving they were right and others were wrong. The biblical injunction that we "be of one mind" (2 Cor 13:11; Phil 4:2) is not a license for individuals or groups to go to war with one another over whose mind is to be the "one." Within the believing community there is only one mind that should prevail in everything, and that is the "mind of Christ" (1 Cor 2:16; Phil 2:5). God's judgment is pronounced on those so devoted to maintaining their own opinions that they disrupt the fellowship and ministry of the community of faith (1 Tim 6:3-5). After more than fifty years of Christian ministry I have come to hate the spirit of divisiveness that possesses so many individuals and congregations, and I think God does too.

I hate the notion that if I'm not a Christian in the same way you're a Christian, then I'm not a good Christian and maybe not a Christian at all. Jesus had little patience with the niggling sectarianism of Pharisees, scribes, and Sadducees who insisted that those who did not identify with their brand of Judaism were unworthy of anything other than their contempt. I suspect that God, as revealed to us in Jesus Christ, continues to have as little patience with such self-righteous attitudes today as Jesus did with disciples who wanted to control who could and could not speak on his behalf (Mark 9:38-39; Luke 9:49-50).

Today's sectarian "you and me, God, and to hell with everyone else" people need to hear Jesus's words: "I am the good shepherd, and know my sheep, and am known of mine . . . . Other sheep I have, which are not of this fold . . ." (John 10:14, 16). Jesus pronounced stern judgment on those who would dare presume that they were entitled to decide who was his and who was not (Mark 9:42). I hate the notion that if I'm not a Christian just like you're a Christian, then I'm not a good Christian and maybe not a Christian at all. And I think God does too.

I hate the marginalization of people simply because they are not like others ethnically, socially, religiously, or by gender identification. God, speaking through Zechariah, said, "These are the things that ye shall do; speak ye every man the truth to his neighbor . . . . And let none of you imagine evil in your hearts against his neighbor . . . for all these are things that I hate, saith the LORD" (Zech 8:16-17). Paul was sure that because of what God had accomplished in Jesus Christ, "There is neither Jew nor Greek, there is neither bond nor free, there is neither male nor female: for ye are all one in Christ Jesus" (Gal 3:28).

Sadly, the first point of stress in the early church was ethnic and social discrimination against Greek Christian widows by people within the Jerusalem church from a Hebrew background (Acts 6:1). James found it necessary to enjoin his readers to demonstrate the authenticity of their religion by managing their tongues when they spoke of others and by caring for the orphaned and widowed (Jas 1:26-27). He also warned them not to discriminate against the poor or give preferential treatment to the financially well heeled (Jas 2:1-9). Simon Peter discovered, when confronted with the racial, ethnic, and social barriers of his day, that "I perceive that God is no respecter of persons . . ." (Acts 10:34).

The writer of Ephesians rejoiced that, through what God had done in Jesus Christ, "the middle wall of partition" dividing people from one another had been "broken down" (Eph 2:14). The allusion here is to the dividing wall in the temple that separated the Court of Israel from the Court of the Gentiles. The Jewish historian Josephus reported that there were thirteen evenly spaced placards along the wall, in Latin and in Greek, assuring any foreigner who crossed the barrier that he would be responsible for his own immediate death. As surely as that physical barrier between people no longer exists, from the Christian perspective there should no longer be any barrier between the believer and God or between the believer and others.

It angers me when I myself, and others, seek to nullify the consequences of God's ultimate expression of redemptive love by building walls that separate instead of working with others to ensure that such walls are never erected again. I hate the marginalization of people simply because they are not like others. And I think God does too.

One concluding word of caution. The hating of behaviors alienating us from God and others does not require that we hate the others. Instead, we are called to love other people as God loves them and us (1 John 4:7-8; Matt 5:43-48) despite the behaviors, theirs or ours. You may not agree with me regarding "some things I just plain hate," but I have no right to hate you for that reason. And, especially if you are a Christian, you have no right to hate me for that reason either.

Things I Want to Accomplish before I Die

Who would have thought inspiration would come in the Ingles parking lot in Landrum, South Carolina? But it did, and there I was reminded of one of life's most important lessons. It happened back in 2005. I was in the parking lot of the grocery store on that Friday evening because it was our regular meeting place to collect grandchildren for their weekend visits. Our eldest son and his family live in Travelers Rest, South Carolina, so Landrum is about halfway between our respective homes. Situated at the intersection of I-26 and SC-14, the Ingles parking lot was a convenient place to meet.

On this occasion Peggy had gone into the store to purchase treats for the grandchild who was coming for that weekend. I remained in the van so I could see the kids when they drove up. I often take such moments of uncommitted time to jot down thoughts and impressions or to work on something I am writing. As I worked on a message for the radio program I hosted back then, I caught a movement in the corner of my eye. Looking out the window of our van I saw an elderly man who appeared to be in his mid to late seventies, wearing a red windbreaker to protect him from the chill of the late February evening. Noting his feet, it registered with me that he was also wearing brown Hushpuppy shoes. My fascination with his feet was occasioned by the fact that they were vigorously pumping the pedals of a unicycle. Yes, I said *unicycle*. The senior adult in the red windbreaker was leisurely making his way up and down the parking lot, confidently perched atop a one-wheeled contraption I had never seen outside a circus act.

I watched in amused astonishment as the old codger expertly threaded his way between parked cars while waving at shoppers and their children stopped dead in their tracks all over the parking lot. A moment later he wheeled himself beside a nearby white Buick Century and stopped, balancing himself by resting his left hand on the fender of the car. After a brief pause to catch his breath, he began to roll back and forth on the single wheel. Then pushing off from the fender he was at it again, traversing the grey-black asphalt in the gathering twilight.

By this time, I had forgotten the message I was working on. Grabbing my note pad, I began to jot things down while my mental impressions were fresh: old man, white Buick, red windbreaker and brown Hushpuppies, unicycle. Even the possible title for a new message had begun to form in my mind, "If God Had Meant for Men to Have Wheels . . . ." You know, something like that.

Then the old man glided up to the Buick Century once again. This time he dismounted, folded up the unicycle, raised the trunk lid, and placed it inside. Closing the trunk, he moved toward the driver's door preparing to leave. I could contain myself no longer. Powering down my window I said, "That was wonderful. How long have you been riding?" With a smile of thanks he replied, "Just a few years. It was one of the many things I wanted to accomplish before I died." With these words he climbed into his car, started the engine, and drove away leaving me in open-mouthed admiration for both his skill on the unicycle and his profound insight into the meaning of human existence. In an instant I abandoned my half-formed essay title, for I knew this piece had to be called, "Things I Want to Accomplish before I Die."

It is my opinion that most people come to the end of life wishing they had been more intentional in their living instead of drifting along with the flow of circumstances. Here was a man who had, apparently many years before, chosen another path. At some point he had intentionally developed a mental, and perhaps written, list of life goals. Had the opportunity been afforded for us to talk longer, I suspect I would have learned that some of those goals were grandly ambitious, some pretty mundane, and at least one as whimsical as learning to ride a unicycle. From my perspective, what was on his list was not nearly as important as that he had a list, for such a list of life goals reflects an optimistic, proactive, positive attitude toward life.

Think with me about this for a few moments. Having goals for our lives says something about the quality of our personhood. In one sense, there are two kinds of people in the world: the ones who "let" things happen and the ones who "make" things happen. The "letters" of the world express a lack of hopefulness by passively permitting life to unfold around them without direction or intentionality. Sometimes this works out well, but at other times it doesn't. The "makers" of the world express hopefulness by actively engaging life and consciously seeking to give it shape, substance, and meaning. And sometimes this works out well, while at other times it doesn't. Hopefully, you are getting my point. The results, the consequences of our choice to live as "letters" or "makers," have no guarantees. We may come to the close of our lives being viewed by others and ourselves as successes or failures regardless of the path we take. The result says almost nothing about our personhood; it is the conscious choice to be one or the other that speaks volumes about the kind of people we are. We can summarize the difference as between "being alive" and "having a life." Sadly, entirely too many people go to their graves having "been alive" but never having "had a life."

By now you have probably figured out that, since from the perspective of the world one may be judged a success or a failure regardless of the path one takes, I favor those who take the active path of intentionality in living. While I am not sure it is the same as Robert Frost's road "less traveled by," I am convinced it is the road worth taking for at least two reasons.[1]

First, I think the proactive approach to living is the better path because here there is risk involved, and authentic faith, particularly the Christian kind, is about taking risks. How many times do you figure that old guy on the unicycle fell off the thing, bruising and scratching himself, before he got the hang of it? How often did his spouse or children or well-meaning friends tell him it was entirely too dangerous for someone his age? How often was he chided for

---

1. See "The Road Not Taken," Poetry Foundation, poetryfoundation.org/poems/44272/the-road-not-taken, accessed April 13, 2023.

making a foolish-looking spectacle of himself and urged to get a hobby more suited to his age and station in life? How many times, aching and sore, misunderstood and rebuked, did he consider giving up and quitting before he mastered the contraption? And yet there he was pedaling to his heart's content back and forth across the Ingles parking lot because he elected to exercise faith in what he could do if he tried.

Too often within the Christian community, we think faith is some kind of quantifiable commodity we can measure in terms of "more" or "less," the way we measure weight, length, or volume. But in the New Testament, faith always has a decisional quality about it; faith is not something we "have" but something we "do." Authentic Christian faith is not a possession; it is a choice to be proactive in the challenging circumstances of life, confident of the presence of God amid all we do. And such faith is what keeps us moving forward despite the pain, despite the fact that others may fail to support us, despite the fact that some may laugh or shake their heads in pity, despite the weariness and loneliness that makes us consider giving up and quitting.

Second, this proactive approach demonstrates that we are hopeful people who are open to the future. Having goals for ourselves is one of the ways Christians demonstrate that we are a people of hope open to the unfolding purposes of God in the world and in our own personal lives. I am convinced that all people, particularly Christian people, should have a list of the many things they wish to accomplish before they die. Doubtless it is true that most who strive will never accomplish everything they set out to do, but those who never set goals and strive to reach them will never accomplish anything. Thus it is better to die never having accomplished everything on one's list than to die never having had a list to begin with. Jesus's words, "well done, thou good and faithful servant . . . enter thou into the joy of thy lord" (Matt 25:21, 23), were uttered in commendation of those who took what they had been given and, with a spirit of openness to the future, did something useful with what was entrusted to their care. In contrast, the man who, out of fear for what might happen, refused to strive to achieve found himself rebuked as a "wicked and slothful servant" (Matt 25:26) who not only failed to accomplish anything but ultimately lost what he had been given as well.

If you agree with me that the path of having things we intend to accomplish before we die is the better path, it seems that some space should be devoted, particularly by the Christian personality, to reflecting on what to include on one's list. Without a doubt, there should be family and career goals, exploration of hobbies and interests, goals of altruism and sacrifice, and goals that are as serendipitously frivolous as learning to ride a unicycle. Everyone, believer or nonbeliever, should have these kinds of goals. But are there other goals that the Christian personality should commit to achieving? The Apostle Paul thought there were. Let me mention some of the uniquely Christian goals he included on his list.

In Ephesians 5:1-2, early Christian believers are challenged to be "followers of God, as dear children," and to "walk in love as Christ has loved us." While acknowledging that he had not achieved everything he set out to do, Paul told the Philippians that his most important personal goal was to "press toward the mark for the prize of the high calling of God in Christ Jesus" (Phil 3:14). The Romans were challenged to set as their goal the determination not to be "conformed to this world: but [to] be transformed by the renewing of [their] minds, that [they] might prove what is that good, and acceptable, and perfect will of God" (Rom 12:2). On the threshold of his own death the Apostle was able to look back on his life and conclude, "I am now ready to be offered, and the time of my departure is at hand. I have fought a good fight, I have finished my course, I have kept the faith . . ." (2 Tim 4:6-7).

Setting such goals for the living of our Christian lives is one thing; achieving them is another. Like the old man on the unicycle, we are going to fall down and get bruised and scratched along the way before we get the hang of consistent Christ-like living. Frequently the most important people in our lives will offer us more discouragement than encouragement. We will often hear carping voices accusing us of self-righteously making a spectacle of ourselves because we don't live by the same values as a self-centered and egotistic world. Many times, with aching hearts and spirits sorely tried, we will consider giving up and quitting. At such times, we should remind ourselves that if this business of Christ-like living was easy, anyone could do it. Furthermore, at our times of deepest trial, we have the assurance that we "can do all things through Christ [who] strengtheneth [us]" (Phil 4:13).

Frankly, I expect to die with many of the things I wanted to accomplish unfulfilled. They will be unfulfilled for a variety of reasons, some of which I could have managed better and others over which I had absolutely no control. However, I'm not nearly as concerned with worrying about what I will fail to accomplish as I am with being grateful for what, by God's grace, I am able to accomplish.

What's on your list of the many things you want to accomplish before you die? What's that you say? You "don't have a list"? Well, as long as you're still alive, it's not too late to start one. Reach out and grab paper and pen, think carefully about this business for a moment, place a #1 at the top of the page, and then start to write. Don't allow yourself to come to the end of your days having been alive but never having had a life. Surely you have some things you want to accomplish before you die.

Peggy Said, "Watch My Purse!" I Said, "Why? What's It Gonna Do?"

We sat together in the waiting room anticipating the time when someone would call my wife's name and lead her back to an exam room for an appointment with her optometrist. While Peggy leafed through an old magazine, I jotted down notes on my "things to do" list that I carry with me everywhere. Finally, the announcement came. A surgically garbed nurse with a file folder in her hand called out, "Peggy Gregg." Peggy immediately stood, and as she stepped toward the nurse she said, "Watch my purse!" I shot back, "Why? What's it gonna do?" She made the same face at me that she always makes when we play this game and followed the nurse down the hall into the exam room. She knows every time she says, "Watch my purse!" I'm going to respond, "Why? What's it gonna do?" She makes a face and sticks out her tongue. I grimace back with narrowed eyes and a wrinkled nose. Anybody within visual and/or hearing range concludes we're both a little weird, and life goes on.

We've been playing this silly, apparently meaningless game for decades, and it's too much fun to stop now. And underlying the silliness, something else is being affirmed that is infinitely important to us both. I know that "Watch my purse!" really means "Thanks for coming with me today." And she knows that "Why? What's it gonna do?" really means "There's nowhere else I would rather be today." You see, when properly translated, such seemingly meaningless verbal games aren't meaningless at all. Instead, they are filled to overflowing with the deepest, most profound meanings imaginable.

There is never a waking moment when we human beings are in the presence of one another that we are not communicating. Sometimes we are thoroughly confusing in our verbosity and magnificently eloquent in our silences, but whether "yakking our heads off" or "quiet as a church mouse," we are always sending and receiving information. One would think all this exchanging of information would enable better understandings of one another. But casual observation reveals this is often not the case; our communications, both verbal and nonverbal, are many times the sources of confusion and conflict rather than the instruments of understanding and communion.

Why is this the case? I think there are a number of reasons, which I am inclined to call gaps in our communication with one another—and for that matter, in our communication with God as well. These gaps, if not properly understood and accounted for, are the sources of the misinterpretation and misunderstanding that so often plague our existence. While there are many such gaps, the pointing out of only a couple will suffice to illustrate my point.

First, there is the gap between "what was said and what was meant. When one of our sons was quite small, he was frequently rewarded with the exclamation, "I'm impressed!" when he successfully avoided an accident in his potty training, did a good job putting away his toys, or dressed himself without getting a shirt on inside out. He came quickly to understand that the phrase "I'm impressed!" signaled approval and evoked good feelings. One day, in response to something that particularly pleased him, and desiring to make use of his growing vocabulary, he said, "I'm depressed!" when he really meant to say, "I'm impressed!" His mother and I chuckled, but we understood what he intended to convey because we understood the gap between what was said and what was meant. But, from that day forward, the word "depressed" took on an entirely new meaning in the Gregg household. Now, if you hear one family member say to another, "I'm depressed!" it has nothing to do with the depth of the speaker's personal sadness, despair, or moodiness. Among the members of the Gregg family, to say "I'm depressed!" really means "I'm impressed!"

While it may be acceptable to assign these personal, private meanings to words among people who understand how they're being used, it is not appropriate to attempt to universalize private meanings in public conversation. To do so is to create untold amounts of confusion among those who are not "in" on the private meanings we have assigned to the words. The use of privately assigned meanings is perfectly acceptable within the intimate interaction of a personal family, intimate friends, or some other small group where everyone is in on the game. However, in the marketplace of public ideas, including religious understandings, it is imperative that we use commonly shared definitions of our words and terms. We cannot insist on "what it means to me" to the exclusion of "what it means to everyone else" who is using the language as well.

This insight is particularly important in the matter of seeking to understand and communicate the message of God as made known in the pages of Scripture. The confusion is not in God but in you and me. Our tendency to want to personalize the definitions of words leads us to examine a biblical verse, passage, or even entire book of Scripture from the perspective of "what does it mean to me?" Unfortunately, the result is that it means whatever the individual interpreter wants it to mean because they are assigning it a meaning out of the context of personal experience and circumstances.

There is a public quality to the Divine revelation that insists our personal, private interpretations and applications must be able to stand up to the light of the public interpretations and applications of others. Phrases like "My Bible says . . ." are utterly useless and misleading because the Bible has never been, nor ever shall be, the personal, private domain of a single individual or closed confessional subgroup. The Bible is the believing community's book.

Because God has elected to reveal God's self in the believing community's book, my personal, private interpretations of the biblical message must stand the test of the public scrutiny of that believing community. This does not mean the believing community is automatically right; it means I am never justified in huffing off into a corner and attempting to do it all by myself. While the community may not always be right, it is right more consistently than the isolated individual, no matter how well intentioned they happened to be. We work together to close the gap between what was said and what was meant by sincerely engaging one another in the ongoing, mutually correcting conversation of the Christian community.

Second, there is the gap between what was said and what was heard. I'm reminded of the old story of the preacher who was invited to Sunday dinner in the home of an elderly couple. The gentleman of the house was somewhat hard of hearing and too vain to admit he did not always understand what others said. During the meal he lifted a platter of fried chicken and extended it toward the preacher, who politely said, "No thanks. I've had sufficient." The old man, somewhat puzzled, said, "You say you've been afishin'?" The preacher responded, "No. No. I said I've had plenty." To this the old man queried, "You say you caught twenty?" Clearly, between the elderly host and his ministerial guest there was a gap between what was said and what was heard.

Sometimes such gaps are the result of a deficiency in hearing. While troublesome and often amusing, most of the time deficiencies in hearing are not excessively harmful in human relationships. However, there are occasions when the "gap" is not the result of a deficiency in hearing but one of a deficiency in listening. Deficiencies in listening are tremendously disrupting to our ability to hear the voices of others and to hear the voice of God in Scripture, in human experience and history, and through the insights of the community of believers.

All parents know that children are notorious in their capacity to "hear" without "listening." Sadly, the achievement of physical maturity does not always overcome this problem. The reason is that hearing is a sensory function while listening is a behavioral choice. Sensorily, I may be able to hear "pins drop," or I may be "deaf as a post," but whatever the case, I have extremely limited control over this sensory function. I hear, with various levels of clarity, all the time; but while I am always hearing, I am not necessarily always listening.

Those of us who earn our livings by talking understand this clearly. In the classroom I frequently had students who heard my words, but they were not listening to anything I said; and inevitably their performance on tests demonstrated that while they were hearing they were not listening. The same is true in my role as pastor/preacher. Over the decades I have spoken to literally thousands upon thousands, many of whom, while hearing my words, were not listening at all. All hearing involves is the stimulation of the human body's auditory system; real listening expresses itself in conscious behavioral responses.

This distinction between "hearing" and "listening" is evident at various levels of human relationship. Marriages often founder upon the refusal of spouses to listen to one another. Conflicts between ethnic groups, among nations, and within churches and civic groups often go unresolved because, while there is often much talking and hearing, no one is listening. In recent months many thousands have died, families have been overwhelmed with grief, our healthcare system has been swamped, our nation's economy has been disrupted, and political decision-making has nearly halted. Why? Because so many have refused, while hearing repeatedly, to listen to the guidance of science and the healthcare community regarding the Covid-19 pandemic. This worldwide tragedy, while having many dimensions, seems to me to be primarily an expression of the refusal of people with perfect "hearing" to listen to reliable, trustworthy voices when they speak regarding the collective behaviors necessary to overcome the pandemic.

Likewise, when God speaks, there are many who while hearing the words neglect to listen to the message. The author of James challenged his readers to "be . . . doers of the word, and not hearers only . . ." (Jas 1:22). He understood that an authentic encounter with the claims of the gospel of Jesus Christ has direct behavioral consequences in the life of the believer. If your Christian identity does not express itself in how you live your life, you are a victim of the gap between what was said and what was heard, and the deficiency is not one of the inability to "hear" but one of the choice not to "listen." We work together to close the gap between what was said and what was heard by cultivating the capacity to listen—to listen to one another and to listen to God.

Where do we begin in bridging these and other communication gaps in human/human and Divine/human relationships? I suggest we begin by reminding ourselves of the game Peggy and I often play. She says, "Watch my purse!" and I say, "Why? What's it gonna do?" The reasons that intimate communication takes place between the two of us during this exchange are many. First, we are thoroughly invested in one another. You may make use of such words as love, goodwill, commitment, affection, loyalty, etc., but it all boils down to the truth that I care about her and she cares about me. People who do not care about one another cannot effectively communicate.

Second, caring leads to trusting, and trusting is one of those all-or-nothing realities in life. While we may say, "I trust Jane a whole lot" or "I don't trust Joe very much," in truth the phrases "whole lot" or "not very much" are irrelevant. We either "trust" or we "don't trust." While it is somewhat embarrassing to fall back on an overused and probably sexist truism, there is still truth in the observation that "Women cannot be a little bit pregnant; they are either pregnant or not pregnant." And others cannot be a little trusted; they are either trusted or not trusted. People who will not trust one another cannot communicate effectively.

Finally, people who care, and because they care they trust, are people who can reveal themselves to one another as they truly are. They can lay aside all pretense, all subterfuge, all hiddenness, and all other impediments to effective communication. They become what the Apostle Paul called "likeminded, having the same love, being of one accord, of one mind" (Phil 2:2). This mutuality of mindedness closes the "gap" between ourselves and others, between ourselves and God, making it possible for us to communicate with one another with understanding and communion.

What're Ya Huntin' For? Nothin', I'm Just Huntin'

The man strolled eastward along the beach, randomly swinging a metal detector before him as he walked along. I found myself somewhat amused by the half-hearted, disinterested way he swung the instrument back and forth. I had the impression he had recently been given a birthday present he didn't really want, but he felt some obligation to try it out in order to stay in the good graces of whoever had given it to him. Coming westward along the beach was another man. Evidently the two were acquainted, for both stopped, shook hands, and exchanged words of greeting within earshot of where I was sitting, writing pad in hand. A moment later the newcomer queried, "What're ya huntin' for?" The man with the metal detector laconically replied, "Nothin', I'm just huntin'." With these words the two parted, and the man with the metal detector continued down the beach, swinging the instrument back and forth, devoting a beautiful morning to "huntin' for nothin'." I suspect he found it.

The days of my life are consumed with going in and out of a lot of different places. I move back and forth between community organizations, local churches, both secular and religious professional communities, etc. I hang around with church members, students, nonreligious people, educators, woodworkers; you understand, the list goes on and on. Living in such a diverse environment provides me with the opportunity to observe substantial amounts of frenetic activity on the part of people who seem to be incessantly searching without any particularly clear idea of what they are looking for. Like the man with the metal detector, they seem to be continually scanning their environment out of some sense of obligation to do so. But, when pressed to describe the object for their search, all they can offer are vague, unfocused, ambiguous mumblings that sound a lot like, "Nothin'. I'm just huntin'."

Those who spend vast portions of their lives "huntin' for nothin'" have fascinating ways of diverting attention from the aimlessness of their pursuit. When asked, "What are you looking for?" some reply, "I don't know; but I'll recognize it when I find it." Others reply, "Well, I'm not looking for anything in particular; I just enjoy the process of looking." Now, please don't hear me being critical of these folks; quite often I'm one of them. But I'm convinced that the most valuable realities of life are rarely stumbled across in the act of random looking. These realities are apprehended by those who devote themselves to disciplined, deliberate searching. While a pleasant morning, or even an entire day, may be whiled away at the beach aimlessly "huntin' for nothin'," I doubt that this is a useful way to live one's life.

I have this sneaking suspicion that the man walking down the beach with the metal detector wasn't telling his friend the whole truth when he said, "Nothin', I'm just huntin'." I'm inclined to think he had heard stories about valuable items that have been found from time to time: old Spanish doubloons, lost pieces of jewelry, artifacts that occasionally wash ashore from shipwrecks, the treasure chests of pirates. Maybe he wasn't "huntin' for nothin'"; he was unwilling to articulate his thoughts out of fear that his friend would laugh, or begin to hunt himself, or tell others his innermost thoughts. And so he was playing it "cool," deliberately cultivating an air of casual disinterest, while hoping that the randomly swung metal detector would discover something that would totally change his life. Certainly, there was no harm in this. Who knows? Before the day was over he may have gotten lucky.

A casual stroll along the beach with a metal detector is hardly a useful model for the business of living one's life; yet this seems to be the preferred choice of many. Whether it has to do with choosing a career, managing their money, discovering a life partner, embracing the pivotal values of living, or determining the nature of their relationship to the deepest spiritual realities of living, they're hoping they'll get lucky. Rarely does this ever happen. Infinitely more often, such important life realities are the by-products of careful, deliberate, disciplined striving to experience and understand.

As a Christian minister, I'm particularly distressed by the "huntin' for nothin'" posture assumed by many in relation to the most important issues of human existence. Life confronts us with a challenging bundle of questions that cry out for meaningful answers: Is there any ultimate meaning and purpose in our existence; and, if so, what is it? How can we be sure of the soundness of the truth claims we are called to embrace? Are there any ultimate values on which we should base our relationships and decisions; and if so, what are they and what is the foundation on which they are based? Is there any hope for the future that transcends the apparently endless cycle of births and deaths; are we on our way to somewhere?

While the above list is short, I guarantee that careful exploration of these questions will make your head hurt. But they are as old as human collective memory and as fresh as this morning's news. It is the plaintive cry of the ancient psalmist, "What is man?" (Ps 8:4). What does it mean to be a human being? From the day of our birth till the day of our death, we make our way along the beach of life, waving our sensors and looking for the answer. Some hope they'll get lucky and stumble across it. Others, heeding the advice of Jesus of Nazareth, take to heart the words, "Ask, and it shall be given you; seek, and ye shall find; knock, and it shall be opened unto you: for every one that asketh receiveth; and he that seeketh findeth; and to him that knocketh it shall be opened" (Matt 7:7-8). Such words are reminiscent of those attributed to Socrates of Athens who reportedly said, "The unexamined life is not worth living."

Without jumping to the conclusion that I am putting Socrates on a par with Jesus, I challenge you to hear the deep wisdom in the words of both. When I reflect on the above quotations, three thoughts come to mind related to how to find the answers to life's most important questions. First, the quote from Socrates suggests the possibility that some, if not all, of the answers lie within us. Second, both Socrates and Jesus seem to caution that discovering the answers is the disciplined work of a lifetime. And third, Jesus certainly points to the truth that we are going to need some help from outside ourselves along the way. Let's take a look at each of these thoughts in turn.

Closely associated with Socrates's assertion that "the unexamined life is not worth living" is his insightful challenge, "Know thyself." Most people don't know themselves well. Oh, we know lots and lots of stuff about ourselves, but that's different from knowing our innermost self, i.e., what makes us tick. Those who have taken an MMPI (Minnesota Multiphasic Personality Inventory), or some similar battery of psychological tests, know that often there are vast differences between how we consciously perceive ourselves to be and how we are subconsciously. Some slight disparity between the actual self and the perceived self is pretty much universally normal and should not be particularly upsetting. But significant disparity may signal potentially disturbing psychological problems and, sometimes, serious mental/emotional illness.

Such failure to genuinely "know ourselves" often leads to the conclusion that the causes of most of our problems, disappointments, and hurts lie outside ourselves. If other people would see things our way, do things our way, follow our leadership, everything would be fine. In truth, sometimes the hardships and sufferings of life are occasioned by the choices and behaviors of others; but sometimes they are simply the consequences of our own failure to manage our lives responsibly. A regular, thorough self-examination of our drives and motives is one way to avoid a lifetime of "huntin' for nothin'." It's simply a matter of following the suggestion of the Apostle Paul that "if we would judge ourselves, we should not be judged" (1 Cor 11:31).

Socrates spoke of an "unexamined life." Jesus used the proactive terms "ask," "seek," "knock." In the language of the Greek New Testament, all three of these verbs are in the second person and are imperative in mood, present in tense, and active in voice. Imperative mood suggests urgency, present tense suggests current and continuously ongoing action, and active voice denotes something one does for one's self rather than expecting it to be done by another. Now, to get away from the technicalities of Greek grammar, what Jesus literally says in Matthew 7:7 is "You ask, and you keep on asking . . . , you seek, and you keep on seeking . . . , you knock, and you keep on knocking." Jesus wanted his followers to learn that this search for an understanding of God's will and purpose for human existence is an ongoing process that is never completed.

During my teaching years, I was exceedingly frustrating to students who took my classes expecting to be told the one, short, always applicable answer to their questions. The primary concern of these people was, "What is the least I can know and still make a good grade on the test?" Sadly, they had not yet learned, and may never have learned, that passing courses and getting an education, while related, are not the same thing. My aim was to help them develop their critical thinking skills for a lifetime, under the assumption that the questions of today are going to come up again in the future in other forms, and today's answers may not be adequate for tomorrow's circumstances. The person who has a bachelor's degree from a college or university and assumes they have an education is in for profound disappointment. Four years of college are capable of doing only two things: one, helping you to discover how much you don't know and, two, equipping you with the critical thinking tools to continue educating yourself for a lifetime. The process of grasping and holding meaningful answers to the challenging questions of life require "huntin' for somethin', not nothin'" and the persistence to "press toward the mark for the prize of the high calling of God in Christ Jesus" (Phil 3:14).

Finally, Jesus's injunctions regarding "asking," "seeking," and "knocking" imply the existence of One who will answer, One who will permit himself to be found, One who will respond to our knocking. From the Christian perspective, we must assert that we obtain the answers to life's most important questions through careful, disciplined searching on our part and through the merciful, gracious revelation of God from the side of the Divine. Such a realization brings into focus the truth that the Creator and Sustainer of the universe is "no thing"; God is Some One. God is person, not object, and the only way to obtain the answers to life's ultimate questions is through personal encounter and relationship with God. As surely as it is not sufficient simply to know "stuff" about ourselves, it is not sufficient simply to know "stuff" about God. God reveals God's self as trustworthy protector, guide, teacher, and friend. Jesus promised those who trusted him the presence of the *Parakaleo*, the Advocate, literally the "one who goes along with us to help us."

Those who go through life incessantly searching will never find the treasure for which they are looking until they discover they are not searching for "some thing"; they are searching for "Some One." And that One has, from the foundation of the universe, been throwing himself across the path of their search. If you keep looking for "nothin,'" "nothin'" is all you're ever going to find. But those who "seek . . . the LORD while he may be found" (Isa 55:6) testify, "I cried unto the LORD with my voice, and he heard me out of his holy hill. I laid me down and slept; I awaked; for the LORD sustained me" (Ps 3:4-5).

The Game Is Called *Shut-the-Box*

It is Christmas morning, and, while waiting for children and grandchildren to gather, I am afforded an opportunity before the bedlam begins to reflect on Christmases past and on life and living in the new year that is about to begin. Near at hand is the Greggs' game called *Shut-the-Box*. I was first introduced to this ancient game one late autumn while at a book signing, hosted by a local bookstore, for my little collection of reflective essays, *If You Ain't Somewhere Doin' Somethin' You Ain't Nowhere Doin' Nothin'*. Intrigued by the simplicity of the game where one throws dice and flips down corresponding mathematical combinations, I decided Peggy and I needed it for Christmas. After purchasing the game, I brought it home, wrapped it carefully, and placed a label on it saying "To Peggy and Larry from Larry and Peggy." Through the long December weeks, Peggy begged and pleaded to know what was in the package I had placed under the Christmas tree. I stoutly refused to reveal the secret until Christmas Day. As the years have passed, we have had great fun playing the game together and alone.

Shut-the-Box isn't difficult to play. You open the hinged lid of the wooden box to discover that inside, nine wooden blocks, numbered sequentially from 1–9, are suspended in such a way that they may be flipped up and down to hide or reveal the painted numbers. To play, you cast the wooden dice inside the box and read the number. Whatever the cast, from 1–12, you then flip down the number of wooden blocks that equal the sum of that number. For instance, suppose you cast a double 6. The sum of those two numbers is 12. Now you have several mathematical options. You may flip down the 9 and the 3; the 6, 4, and 2; the 1, 2, 3, and 6; the 5 and 7; the 8 and 4; or the 3,

4, and 5. You get the idea. Any combination of numbers that equal 12 may be flipped down. Having done so, you cast the dice again. Let's say this time you roll an 8. Again, you may use the wooden block with 8 on it or any combination of numbers that total 8, with this exception: if a number has already been used in a previous roll, it cannot be used a second time. You keep going until you roll the dice and lack sufficient numbers to continue. Your turn ends and your score, reading left to right, is the number represented by the blocks that have not been flipped down. Sometimes it is quite a small number; on other occasions it is astronomical. Whatever the case, what is left is your score.

Part of the fun of playing *Shut-the-Box* is that it requires the player to make choices and then live with the choices made. You may select any combination of numbers, but once the choice is made it cannot be revoked. Sometimes there is only one choice. For instance, if you roll "snake eyes" or double 1, the only option available is to flip down the number 2. But at the beginning of the game, in all other possible combinations of the throw of the dice, multiple options are available. Furthermore, your previous choices have consequences for all subsequent choices. Later, you have fewer choices to flip. For instance, suppose after several previous casts only the numbers 4, 5, and 8 remain. If on the next cast you roll a 9, you have only one option: the combination of 4 and 5.

Lucky is the player who flips down all the numbers and then shuts the box. More often than not, the player is caught with numbers that cannot be flipped down because the opportunity to use them has passed, and one has to accept whatever score is left. I played twice while writing this piece. The first time, I was left with a score of 4,578; the next time, my score was 248. As in golf, the lower the score the better the game. The optimum low score is 0, a score one rarely achieves.

If you've begun to wonder how long I'm going to drone on about this before I get to the point, relax; I'm almost there. This side of the Second Advent, there is an event out there in the future for us all. At some memorial service, a funeral home employee is going to close and seal the lid on our coffin. Once that person has *shut the box,* all that remains is the evidence of the multitude of choices we have made across the years. Sometimes we struggled with the number of options available and made the most careful, thoughtful choice we could make. At other times, we carelessly followed the least line of resistance and made the choices that seemed easiest at the moment. From time to time, we discovered there was only one option, so, like it or not, we took the only course of action that remained open. But, whatever the multitude of combinations, all our choices had consequences both for ourselves and for others; and life required that we live with the consequences of those choices. Now, listen carefully. I'm not suggesting that human existence is nothing more than a game of *Shut-the-Box*, but I am asserting that one cannot play the game, or live life, without making choices and living with their consequences. And often others must live with those consequences as well.

One of the most blatant illustrations of the confusion and lack of focus of contemporary culture is the vast number of people who don't get it when it comes to the relationship between choices and consequences. Millions upon millions wish to be free to make whatever choices they desire about their sexuality, finances, family relationships, educations, employment, friendships, responsibility to take sensible precautions to protect themselves and others from infectious diseases, etc., but are unwilling to accept the consequences that devolve from those choices. They have confused "freedom," which always has limitations, with the "license" to do as they please without regard for the consequences to themselves and others. And, for too many, the result is that someone *shuts the box* over the face of the substance abuser, the reckless driver, the workaholic, the criminal, the unvaccinated, or one of the many victims of their addictive, irresponsible, and antisocial behavior. And the tale of a life and its choices has been told. Unlike in the game *Shut-the-Box*, where we can take another turn or play the game again, in real life we often get only one chance to make choices.

Perhaps you're thinking, "Well, he's got me sufficiently depressed here." That may be true, but if it is true, your depression has more to do with you than it does with what I have said about the realities of life. Occasionally I run across someone who says, "I'm bored all the time."

I always find myself thinking, and sometimes I say, "If you don't have enough initiative and interest in life to keep yourself entertained, you deserve to be bored. Your boredom is a self-inflicted wound." And, if you are shallow enough as a person to refuse to face the reality of, and accept responsibility for, the relationship between your choices and their consequences, you ought to be depressed. In this instance, your depression, the consequence of legitimate guilt, is also a self-inflicted wound.

I could subtitle this piece "Thoughts on Decision-making for the New Year." I could as easily call it "Thoughts on Decision-making for Any Year." While there are similarities between the game *Shut-the-Box* and daily living, there are significant differences as well. Perhaps the most significant is that while the only factors that come to bear in *Shut-the-Box* are those of random chance and personal choice, I would argue that "real" life is lived at the intersection of random chance, personal choices—our own and those of others—and Divine Providence, or the purposes of God. This means that, unlike in *Shut-the-Box*, in life our options are never absolutely exhausted. Though it remains true that the consequences of our choices cannot be repealed, as long as life remains within us we have a variety of alternatives regarding how we may respond to the consequences of our choices. The key is not "where you are" as the consequence of chance and choice; the key is whether you elect to stay where you are when Divine Providence provides alternatives worth exploring. You see, as long as you are alive, only you can irrevocably "shut the box" on you.

You may decide that who you are and where you are is no more than the product of random chance. People who decide that tend to absolve themselves of responsibility for their behavior and its consequences. They wallow in their misfortune, whine about how unjust the world has been to them, and generally make excuses that let them off the accountability hook. For them life is nothing but a "crap shoot" and their theme song is "Que Sera, Sera."

You may decide that who you are and where you are is simply the product of inscrutable Divine Providence. Such people assert, "If it hadn't been God's will, it wouldn't have happened." Such a perspective leads to the conclusion that human beings are nothing more than puppets responding to Divine string pulling. And inevitably, God gets the blame and/or the devil gets the credit for things neither of them necessarily had anything to do with. Furthermore, this posture suggests that, out of nothing more than omnipotent whim, God elects to bless some and curse others because God can. This may apply to Luke Skywalker's the Force in *Star Wars*, the Q of *Star Trek: The Next Generation*, or even the generally misunderstood concept of Karma. But such an understanding of Divine Providence is not found in the biblical tradition, so I'm not buying this "cop-out" either.

You may decide that who you are and where you are is solely the product of personal choice. This approach ignores a multitude of factors including heredity, place of birth, environment, historical setting, etc. that have significant influence on us but about which we exercised no decisional choice. While some may arrogantly insist, along with the poet, "I am the Master of my fate, I am the Captain of My soul," such prideful expressions ring hollowly because when pushed, even the people who assert such things concede that they don't absolutely believe what they are saying.[1] And so the insistence that it is only a matter of personal choice doesn't wash either.

Where does this leave us? As suggested earlier, I maintain that "real" life is lived at the dynamic nexus of random chance (contingency and the choices of others), personal choice (conditioned by various nature/nurture and hereditary factors), and Divine Providence (the belief that there is positive meaning and purpose in the universe). While this position accepts the reality that the consequences of our choices cannot be repealed, it does open the opportunity to explore the possibility that we have more options at our disposal than simply whining at the unfairness of random chance, angrily asserting that if we had it to do all over again we would do exactly the same thing, or shrugging in resignation while mumbling about inexorable fate.

It is true that I can neither undo the choices of the past and their consequences nor ignore the consequences of random chance in a yet-to-be-perfected universe. Even so, through faith in the

---

1. William Ernest Henley, "Invictus," Poetry Foundation, poetryfoundation.org/poems/51642/Invictus, accessed April 11, 2023.

providential guidance of a good, loving, and redemptive God, and through the exercise of my ability to make responsible choices in the future, I can adjust to some aspects of my past, compensate for others, overcome much, learn from many of them, and, of utmost importance, be forgiven.

As a new year (or day or week or month) dawns, I challenge you to remember that for those who are willing to acknowledge the reality of their finitude and its limitations, accept responsibility for the consequences of their choices, and appeal in faith to the One who is unfolding Divine purpose in the universe and through our lives, God has set not a *shut box* but an *open door*. By God's grace, may we walk through that door into an open future where, while we cannot ignore or undo our past, we are also not held captive by it.

The Travelocity Gnome

One spring morning several years ago, I was on my way to Spindale, North Carolina, to teach my classes at Isothermal Community College. Not far from our house, the road descends steeply and a small rock ledge sticks out from the embankment. On this particular morning, the ledge was occupied by a squirrel busily munching on something found in the nearby woods. The animal was so intent on its breakfast that it was not startled when my pickup truck passed by only a few feet away. Smiling, I proceeded on my way but did not travel far before the germ of an idea began to formulate in my lopsided way of looking at life. This marked the beginning of a tale that contains many significant lessons regarding human life and behavior.

This was in the days when almost every other commercial on TV featured the "Travelocity Gnome" showing up at various locations and assuring the viewers that they could also visit such interesting and exotic vacation destinations. I found myself wondering, as I drove along, how our small rural community would react if the Travelocity Gnome were to intrude unexpectedly upon my neighbors' comings and goings. When I returned home, I shared with Peggy the story of the squirrel on the ledge and my musings about the gnome. One of the wonderful things about Peggy is her willingness to assist in facilitating my wild ideas regardless of how off the wall they may be. Going online, she found an inexpensive gnome figure made of durable plastic. Within minutes she had ordered it, and a few days later the gnome was delivered to our door. Getting out her acrylic paints, it took almost no time for Peggy to transform the gnome figure into an exact reproduction of the Travelocity Gnome. Once the paint had dried thoroughly, I took the figure down to the rock ledge and glued it in place with a durable glue from my woodworking shop. Then we listened intently upon every visit to the local country store, hoping to hear someone talking about the gnome on the ledge and wondering who put it there.

Day followed day, and we took great delight in driving up and down the hill and seeing the gnome perched atop the ledge. Then, about a week into this whimsical adventure, I passed by and the ledge was gnome-less. Supposing my glue had failed, I parked nearby and walked back to see if the figure had toppled off the ledge and into the ditch. It had not. A close inspection of the ledge revealed that someone had deliberately broken the seal between the rock and the base of the figure and appropriated our roadside gnome for themselves. Why? I can only speculate regarding someone who felt entitled to deprive the entire community of mild amusement out of their senseless need to possess exclusively what was intended for all to share. Though still mystified by what may have become of the purloined gnome, I think there are impressions regarding both its production and its loss that are worthy, at least for me, of exploration.

When I think of this "gnominal" adventure, I am reminded of the importance of humor in making life meaningful. Much of today's society seems either to seek out opportunities to be depressed or to define humor as slapstick, obscene hilarity. Neither is helpful. But that which can cause one to pause, smile inwardly, evoke the amused chuckle, and refresh one's attitude seems imminently healthy for one's self and for one's relations with others. The ancient sage of Proverbs observed, "A merry heart maketh a cheerful countenance: but by sorrow of the heart the spirit is broken. . . . All the days of the afflicted are evil: but he that is of a merry heart hath a continual feast" (Prov 15:13, 15). Do you regularly allow the minor happenstances of life to bring a twinkle to your eye and a bemused smile to your lips? When you do, you bless yourself and become a blessing to others.

The acquisition, painting, and placement of the gnome figure reminds me of the joy of sharing life with another who is deeply loved and who loves deeply in return. There is nothing quite as precious as the intimacy of two people whose minds think and whose hearts beat in unison. With all its joys and amusements, life also contains its hardships, sufferings, and bereavements. People who can laugh together, harmlessly plot together, comfort and protect one another in life's darkness, and rejoice and labor with one another in life's brightest moments are truly blessed. How sad for those who think the biblical notion of "two becoming one" (Gen 2:24; Matt 19:5; Mark 10:8; Eph 5:31) is only about sex.

It is easy to become so turned in on one's self, one's ambitions, one's career, one's possessions, one's successes and/or failures that one neglects the importance of turning outward to the external world. Our placing of the gnome figure on the rock ledge to be viewed by passersby was an expression, small though it was, of our desire to be open to the larger world. It would have been easy to hoard my harebrained idea for our own private amusement. We could have painted the gnome and placed it somewhere in our house or in the floral garden in the backyard, and it would have become only another ornamental object—and not an especially attractive one at that. Instead, we sought to give away some of our amusement and joy to anyone and everyone who happened to catch a glimpse of our oddly located gnome-shaped figurine. In a world pockmarked by obscene graffiti and offensive, politically motivated signage smeared almost everywhere for the gratification of the vulgar and vindictive, we wished only to bestow a fleeting gift that would lighten, not further darken, the consciousnesses of those who saw the painted gnome. I'm sorry someone missed our point, and I'm even sorrier if someone got the point and then obliterated the message for others because, preoccupied with self, they could not bear the thought of anyone else being happy and amused if they weren't.

When I think of the disappearance of the gnome figure, I am saddened by the reminder that at the core we human beings have a broken ugliness that estranges us from self, others, our environment, and our Creator and Sustainer. It is easy to assign negative human behavior into hierarchies of harmless, not too bad, bad enough, and terrible. This enables each of us to find excuses for our own negative behaviors while deploring the negative behaviors of others. The most pitiful piece of excuse-making ever expressed is found in the words, "I may not be perfect, but I'm better than you." To embrace such a notion is to miss the prophetic truth that "All we like sheep have gone astray; we have turned every one to his own way . . ." (Isa 53:6). As surely as human brokenness expresses itself in the most heinous act of the serial killer, that same brokenness expresses itself in the self-centered behavior of people who thoughtlessly and greedily appropriate to themselves that which is not theirs. Thus, while we cannot overcome the problem of our sinful brokenness by ourselves, it is incumbent upon each of us to recognize the problem and take what steps we can to mitigate its consequences for ourselves and others. The Bible teaches that the first step to overcoming the brokenness lies in embracing the truth that, in the person and work of Jesus Christ, God has done for us what we cannot do for ourselves. This is why the same one who declared "for all have sinned, and come short of the glory of God" (Rom 3:23) could also declare that "whosoever shall call upon the name of the Lord shall be saved" (Rom 10:13). The second step is in the commitment to consistently model one's behavior after that of Jesus Christ. "For even hereunto were ye called: because Christ also suffered for us, leaving us an example, that ye should follow in his steps" (1 Pet 2:21).

Our attempt to amuse ourselves and the community with our model of the Travelocity Gnome serves to remind me that our good intentions, while not realized, were still good intentions. Let's be careful here. Some wish to use the notion of "good intentions" as a justification for actions on their part that eventuated in harmful consequences for others. This is not what I am suggesting. I simply wish to point out that regardless of how well-meaning we are, we are naive to assume that every well-intentioned act on our part is going to yield positive results. Sadly, I can recall many times when I acted with the best of intentions for myself or others only to discover that my attempt at goodness resulted in less than I had hoped. A compliment or correction misspoken, an action misunderstood, a decision based on inadequate information and reflection, while well intended, did not yield the hoped-for positive results. In our human brokenness, there is much for which we should rightly feel guilt. But we are not guilty of everything, and we must learn that in a broken world our good intentions may go awry through no fault of our own. In these circumstances, we must remember that we sincerely intended well despite the consequences. Otherwise, we will never be willing to risk failure in order to achieve worthwhile goals. While there is no excuse for careless, thoughtless blundering in our own lives or in the lives of others, Burns was correct when he asserted,

> But Mousie, thou art no thy-lane,
> In proving foresight may be vain:
> The best laid schemes o' Mice an' Men
> Gang aft agley,
> An' lea'e us nought but grief an' pain,
> For promis'd joy![1]

However, I am willing to be unsuccessful from time to time with my "best laid schemes" despite occasional "grief and pain." I refuse to permit the thwarting of my good intentions in one instance to prevent me from having good intentions in future instances.

Finally, my reflection on the blocking of our mock Travelocity Gnome to achieve our intentions for it does not prevent me from recognizing the importance of moving beyond life's failures and disappointments. In 1967, at age seventeen, I graduated from high school in the spring and became an entering freshman at the University of Alabama in the fall. I was woefully unprepared for the academic demands of a sixteen-semester-hour class load while working a full-time job to make economic ends meet. The result was that, without going to the trouble to formally withdraw, I quit attending class, ended up with automatic "F's" in every subject, and was sentenced to academic probation. My second attempt in the spring of 1968 ended the same way. In May 1970, Peggy and I married and I attempted college again at the University of Alabama in Birmingham. Same result, but I did have the sense to formally withdraw. An attempt at Samford University ended similarly. This was in the days when there was no such thing as academic forgiveness. When I decided to try once again after the birth of our first son in 1973, I had a negative

---

1. Robert Burns, "To a Mouse," Poetry Foundation, poetryfoundation.org/poems/43816/to-a-mouse-56d222ab36e33, accessed April 11, 2023.

QPA. It took a couple of semesters to get me back to zero. If one judged my intelligence, discipline, and maturity on the basis of my early undergraduate transcripts, one would conclude that this particular young man was academically and intellectually hopeless. That would have been before I earned five academic degrees in less than sixteen years.

One of the sublime truths of living is that "It ain't over till it's over." And to the person who is willing to learn and grow, it is, "It ain't over till I say it's over." Thus I echo, in times of failure and disappointment great or small, the lyrics of that wonderful old Dorothy Fields/Jerome Kern tune: "Take a deep breath, pick yourself up, / Dust yourself off, and start all over again."[2]

Life is too sublime to permit the loss of a mock Travelocity Gnome, or any of life's missteps and failures, to rob me of a meaningful future.

---

2. "Pick Yourself Up," composed in 1936 for the film *Swing Time*, starring Frank Sinatra and Ginger Rogers.

You Can't Experience the "Power of God" and Worship the "god of Power"

All one has to do is adjust a TV set or radio to a religious broadcasting station to hear one of dozens of preachers declaiming upon the need for people to experience the "power of God" in their lives. Favorite texts include "ye shall receive power, after . . . the Holy Ghost is come upon you" (Acts 1:8); "be strong in the Lord, and in the power of his might" (Eph 6:10); and "for God hath not given us the spirit of fear; but of power . . ." (2 Tim 1:7). They preach about the "power of the Holy Spirit," "the power in the blood," "the power of prayer," and the "powerful name of Jesus." They remind us that Jesus called unto himself the Twelve and "gave them power against unclean spirits, to cast them out, and to heal all manner of sickness and all manner of disease . . ." (Matt 10:1).

The core of their message is the conviction that contemporary Christians, individually and collectively, need to experience the fullness of the "power of God" in their lives. With this I have absolutely no quarrel. What does trouble me, however, is that in the midst of all this talk about the "power of God," many seem to be in danger of succumbing to the temptation to bow down and worship the "god of power." I fear some have already done so. I wish to remind all those who are losing the ability to distinguish between the "power" of God and the "god" of power, "You cannot experience the 'power' of God and worship the 'god' of power at the same time."

That "power" has attained the status of a quasi-religion in the contemporary world is evident when one compares the current expressions of power with an inclusive definition of religion. I began my "World Religions" classes each semester by spending a few minutes with the students in the brainstorming exercise of defining the word "religion." Their suggestions were often insightful, frequently amusing, and always interesting. After hearing them out, I would suggest that, for the purposes of the class, we make use of the following textbook definition: "We define religion as a system of symbols, myths (stories), doctrines, ethics, and rituals (prescribed behaviors) for the expression of ultimate relevance."[1]

I am prepared to contend that the practice of the exercise of power in the modern world displays all the general characteristics of a religion mentioned in the above definition, i.e., a system of symbols, myths (stories), doctrines, ethics, and rituals (prescribed behaviors) for the expression of ultimate relevance. In the following pages I will defend this assertion.

First, let's explore the notion of ultimate relevance, or what twentieth-century theologian Paul Tillich called "ultimate concern."[2] Tillich argued that what concerns us ultimately is, for us, God. Now, here's the point.

Some time ago I had the opportunity to hear a well-known preacher speak on a number of occasions. As I listened, I became conscious of the frequency with which he made use of the personal pronoun "I" and the personal possessive "my" in the course of his sermons. Because of a preacher's personal commitment to the truths they proclaim, it is often necessary that one express oneself in first person singular. What troubled me was not that there was personal content in this man's messages; what was troubling was that there was almost nothing but personal content in his messages. It was easy to suspect that the central, centering personality in "his" religious life was "himself." This is disturbing in anyone, but it is particularly disturbing in one who exerts tremendous power and influence over the lives, resources, and conduct of others. Those who worship at the altar of power have an object of worship, and all they have to

---

1. Denise Carmody and T. L. Brink, *Ways to the Center: An Introduction to World Religions*, 5th ed. (Belmont, CA: Wadsworth, 2002), 1.

2. *Systematic Theology*, vol. 1 (Chicago: University of Chicago Press, 1951), 11ff.

do is look in a mirror to see that object of worship reflected back at them. The radical devotion to power is, at its core, an exercise of self-idolatry.

"Power" has its symbols. In contemporary America, they include designer clothing, Rolex watches, luxury automobiles, lavishly furnished dwellings, and "high roller" lifestyles, as well as personalities who epitomize the symbols of power. To seek to have one's face on the cover of *Time*, to be seen in the company of a head of state, or to be followed by an entourage of servants, sycophants, and supplicants is to indulge in wallowing in the symbols of power.

Certainly, the religion of power has its myths and stories, its saints and priests, its heroes of the faith and its fallen angels. In the twenty-first century, it is sufficient to mention only the names of Sam Walton, Lee Iacocca, Bill Clinton, Saddam Hussein, Michael Jackson, Oprah Winfrey, Donald Trump, and Martha Stewart.

To read the doctrinal literature of the religion of power, there are many places to turn. Those who have made contributions in the past include Plato, Machiavelli, Nietzsche, Lenin, and Dale Carnegie. In a bookstore or on Amazon, you can find an abundance of titles: *In Search of Excellence, Seven Habits of Highly Effective People, The Dynamics of Power, The Way of the Superior Man, Execution: The Discipline of Getting Things Done*, etc. Such literature sets forth the basic doctrines of the contemporary religion of power.

All religions contain systems of ethics. The religion of power is no exception. A number of years ago, I stood in the office of a mid-level academic administrator and expressed my concern regarding an action he had recently taken. It was my position that his decision had compromised the integrity of the final exam process for graduating seniors that semester. When I asked why he had taken that particular action, his response was straightforward and direct. Without batting an eye, he said, "I did it that way because I can!" His response was the classic expression of what I described to my philosophy students as the "Ethics of Power." It is propounded in Nicolo Machiavelli's treatise on human government, *The Prince*. In *The Prince*, Machiavelli advised Lorenzo De'Medici that a leader was justified in the exercise of any action or conduct that achieved the leader's aims, including violence, falsehood, and deliberate deceit. Machiavelli wrote, "It is necessary to know well how to . . . be a great pretender and dissembler; and men are so simple . . . that he who seeks to deceive will always find someone who will allow himself to be deceived."[3] Such an attitude is, I fear, all too pervasive in much of corporate, political, and religious America. It is an attitude that says, "If I have the power to do, I have the right to do; and it is right for me to do what I have the power to do." I contend that anyone who allows such an ethical posture to guide their conduct has been worshiping at the altar of "power."

And finally, the religion of power has its ritual behaviors. Some of them we call "dressing for success," "power lunches," "playing hardball," and "spinning the facts." Others include "seeing and being seen," "working the room," and "brokering a deal." These ritual behaviors, from who pays for lunch to who gets invited to play golf, are no less complex, stylized, and powerful than those of High Mass in a cathedral, of a World Series game, or of how one arrives at an Academy Awards ceremony.

By now, many of you are quite distressed and are saying to yourselves, "He's talking about the conduct of people out there in the 'lost' world, but you don't find that kind of behavior among God's people." Sadly, I've attended too many denominational conventions, too many ministers' conferences, too many faculty meetings on church-related seminary, college, and university campuses, and too many decision-making meetings in local congregations to be blind to the misuse and abuse of power by those who claim the name of Jesus Christ. Those within the Christian community are as susceptible to worshiping at the altar of "power" as those outside the church. And often we are remarkably adept at camouflaging such behavior behind a screen of pious God-talk that amounts to no more than the "pretending and dissembling" recommended by Machiavelli.

If the above is true, and I'm not just a jaded, cynical old Baptist preacher, it's time to address the question, "What are the distinguishing characteristics of the 'power of God'?" The Bible points

---

3. Machiavelli, *The Prince*, in vol. 25 of Great Books of the Western World (Chicago: Encyclopaedia Britannica, 1954), 25.

out many characteristics that, if looked for carefully, will help us remain open to the "power of God" while avoiding the idolatry of the "god of power." First, God's power creates (Gen 1:1), liberates (Deut 4:37), and opposes evil (Luke 11:20); the power of God is not destructive or enslaving, and God does not connive with the false "god" of power. Second, God's power is redemptive, not punitive. Even in judgment, God's power is exercised in redemption and restoration, not in punishment. Third, within the biblical revelation, God's power is presented to us in the forms of persuasion, not coercion. God reasons (Isa 1:18), God pleads (Isa 3:13), God draws "with bands of love" (Hos 11:4), and God stands at the door and knocks, waiting for us to open the door and invite God to come into our lives (Rev 3:20).

Finally, and most importantly, God's power expresses itself in humble servanthood, not prideful selfishness. Jesus starkly contrasted the difference between those who know the "power of God" and those who serve the "god of power." The writer of Matthew tells the story of how the mother of James and John, the sons of Zebedee, went to Jesus requesting that when he came into his kingdom, her sons would be granted the chief seats of power on his right and left hand. In indignation, the other ten disciples protested this blatant attempt to grab for power, perhaps because they had not thought of it first. Jesus responded with these words:

> Ye know that the princes of the Gentiles exercise dominion over them, and they that are great exercise authority upon them. But it shall not be so among you: but whosoever will be great among you, let him be your minister; and whosoever will be chief among you, let him be your servant. Even as the Son of man came not to be ministered unto, but to minister, and to give his life a ransom for many. (Matt 20:25-28)

Only a short time later, Jesus would act out his words by girding himself with a towel and washing the feet of the disciples (John 13:4-5). In this humble act of servanthood, Jesus closed the door on all our prideful posturing and selfish desire for attention and personal glory. It is in the experience and exercise of the "power of God" through humble servanthood that we are most in tune with the mind of Christ (Phil 2:5), whom Paul described as the One who "made himself of no reputation, and took upon him the form of a servant . . ." (Phil 2:7).

One of the greatest men in medieval Christianity was Pope Gregory I, known to history as Gregory the Great. Gregory's *Regula Pastoralis* or *Pastoral Rule* was written fifteen hundred years ago, but it still offers insightful counsel to those of us who, while charged with proclaiming the "power of God," are often seduced by the wiles of the "god of power." In it Gregory cautioned,

> There are some who, through the outward show of rule within the holy Church, affect the glory of distinction. They . . . covet superiority to others, and . . . they seek the first salutations in the market-place, the first rooms at feasts, the first seats in assemblies.[4]

Gregory contended that such a posture disqualifies one for roles of leadership within the Christian community. Instead, the authentic Christian leader is called to be the *servus servorum Dei*, "the servant of the servants of God." This is all the real power a Christian has; and it is all the power a Christian really needs.

---

4. *The Book of Pastoral Rule of Saint Gregory the Great, the Nicene and Post-Nicene Fathers*, 2nd ser., vol. 12, pt. 1 (Grand Rapids: Eerdmans, 1976), 1–2.

Only an *I* Separates *Run* from *Ruin*

The world is filled with people who want to "run" our lives. Among them are politicians, parents, preachers, persecutors, etc. What these people have in common, even those among them who are good people, is a deep-seated conviction that they are more qualified at, and capable of, running your life than you are. Their favorite phrases are, "If I were you . . . ," "Let me give you some advice . . . ," "God told me to tell you . . . ," "I'm just trying to help . . . ," and "I know better than you." Under these assumptions, such people license themselves to instruct, manage, manipulate, coerce, and bully their way into a domineering position where they wrest meaningful decision-making from others. Unfortunately, one of the consequences of this abuse of power in the lives of others is that such people often "ruin" the lives they wish to "run."

Now, before you become overly upset, let me acknowledge that sometimes there is the need for an assertive, managing role in the lives of others. Children, the mentally and/or physically challenged, the addicted, the elderly, etc. sometimes need another person who will assume a positive role in aiding them with matters they are unable, at the time, to manage for themselves. However, there remains the need for restraint even in these situations. Children do not remain children forever. The mentally and/or physically challenged still need the opportunity to exercise their limited faculties. The addicted don't need to exchange a substance addiction for an emotional/psychological addiction. And the elderly, while sometimes needing assistance, do not need to be deprived of the dignity of aging gracefully. So please do not hear me disparaging the loving, supportive help that we all need, or will need, from others who care. My concern addresses the problem created by those who demand that others submit to being dominated and having their lives run by the self-appointed "I know best" egotists, and sometimes sociopaths, of the world. The obsessive need of such people to "run" inevitably leads to "ruin" as they deprive their victims of indispensable qualities needed for a meaningful life.

Those with an obsessive need to "run" our lives often "ruin" them by robbing us of our independence. Some wish to keep others economically dependent. Some want to control how others think, believe, worship, vote, and engage in relationships. Their victims are subtly, and sometimes not so subtly, told that to have an opinion or engage in an activity that is not approved by the domineering personality is wrong, or sinful, and deserves to be punished. The result is to be enslaved by the biases, prejudices, and ambitions of the self-appointed "runners" of people's lives. And to rob another of appropriate independence is to ruin their lives by depriving them of the freedom to learn, grow, question, reject, embrace, and decide for themselves the values, opinions, and loyalties that they internalize and live by. Julius Caesar, Adolf Hitler, Joseph Stalin, and Mao Zedong were all sure they knew better than anyone else and, thus, were justified in denying others the independence of their personhood. Many preceded those named above, and still others have followed them. What they all have in common is the trail of ruin they leave in their wake.

Those with an obsessive need to "run" our lives may also "ruin" them by robbing us of our integrity. Integrity is robbed when it is compromised in order to keep a job threatened by a domineering employer. Integrity is robbed when it is tempted to betray those who are trusting us by another's manipulative promise of reward. Integrity is robbed when we surrender the responsibility of determining "right" and "wrong" into the hands of another instead of cultivating and maintaining our own values. Integrity is robbed when we embrace, out of one form of fear or another, a belief system that runs contrary to plain reason and experience. Integrity is robbed not only when we do what we know we should not have done; integrity is lost when we don't do what we should have done. The biblical writer was correct when he concluded, "Therefore to him that knoweth to do good, and doeth it not, to him it is sin" (Jas 4:17).

Those wishing to "run" our lives may "ruin" them by depriving us of a healthily integrated self. In geometry, two triangles are said to be "congruent" when their sides and angles are both the same. Psychologists use the term "congruence" to refer to the circumstances when one's perception of "self" and one's actual "self" correspond as closely as possible to one another. The Apostle Paul was referring to this lack of congruence in his reference to people who tended to "think of [themselves] more highly than [they] ought to think" (Rom 12:3). While perfect congruence of "perceived self" and "actual self" are probably impossible for us to achieve, the closer the correspondence between "perceived" and "actual," the healthier our personhood. However, Paul was sure that it would help if we learned "to think soberly, according as God hath dealt to every man the measure of faith" (Rom 12:3).

The problem created by others wishing to run our lives is that such people are attempting to force our personhood to be congruent with theirs. Instead of permitting us to be who we are, they insist on forcing us to be, as close as possible, who they are. And because, by its nature, this controlling attitude is psychically and spiritually unhealthy, the result is that their unhealthiness infects our personhood as well. The more the coercive other "runs" one's life, the more they "ruin" the possibility of one becoming a whole, integrated personality in one's own right. The result is the tragedy of neither being able to be the other nor being able to be fully one's own self.

Finally, those wishing to "run" someone's life may "ruin" it by robbing the person of their individuality. To Socrates is attributed the phrase, "Know thyself." He is further quoted as saying, "To know thyself is the beginning of wisdom."

Jewish philosopher/theologian Martin Buber suggested that human identity is determined by two primary relationships, that of *I-Thou* and *I-It*. The implication of this insight is that one may rightly relate to "*Thou*—the other" or to "*It*—an object" only if one understands oneself as an *I*. The failure to understand who one is in distinction from others and the world about us is to lose one's self in the "many" and the "much." Mark 5 tells the story of a man completely divorced from his personhood, possessed by insanity, a danger to himself and others. Jesus encountered him and asked, "What is thy name?" The fragmented, distraught man answered, "My name is Legion; for we are many." The 1957 movie *The Three Faces of Eve* introduced many of us to the psychological phenomenon of multiple-personality disorder (now known as dissociative identity disorder). This poignant, tragic story graphically illustrated what happens when one loses one's sense of *I* and becomes hopelessly lost in the many.

It seems to me that many today have lost, or been robbed of, their *I*-ness by the dominating people and movements that would submerge personal individuality under the dark waters of many and much. I am astounded by how many people seek to define their individuality by tattooing themselves like everyone else. Have you noted how many appear unable to articulate their own thoughts and opinions and thus are reduced to parroting the thoughts and opinions voiced by those who are sure they are entitled to run everyone's lives? I've never quite been able to understand how personal autonomy is asserted by allowing advertisers and cult personalities to dictate how we should dress, smell, speak, and behave. I'm amazed at how many people, while vociferously announcing, "I'll say and do what I want to say and do," repeatedly do and say the things the people who want to "run" their lives tell them to do and say.

Where is the "ruin" in this? The "ruin" is in spending money I can't afford to spend because another says I should. The "ruin" comes when I indulge in self-destructive behaviors because another tells me I'm not cool if I don't. I am "ruined" when I commit literal or existential suicide by embracing the insanity of the many and the much.

Is there a way to avoid those who would "ruin" our lives in their attempts to "run" them? Remember, I began with the statement that "only an *I* separates 'run' from 'ruin.'" The answer is in that *I*. It is the *I* of personal responsibility and accountability. To be truly *I*ndependent involves learning to think maturely for one's self and then to express that independence in responsible behavior. To be a person of *I*ntegrity is to elect to do what is right regardless of the consequences and even when no one else will ever know. To be a whole, *I*ntegrated person is to be able to realistically compare who one is and who one wishes to be and then to work tirelessly to bring those two selves into congruence with one another. To be an *I*ndividual is to acknowledge that each *I* lives in the world of *Thou* and *It*. And the truly individual *I* never treats a *Thou* as an *It* or an *It* as a *Thou*, for to everyone else the individual is a *Thou* who should also never be treated as an *It*.

Is this easy? Of course not! But an irrefutable fact is that if you don't develop the capacity to "run" your own life, someone else will "run," and perhaps "ruin," it for you. Am I suggesting that we should never permit others to exert influence within our lives? Again, of course not! We all need role models, mentors, friends, teachers, parents, ministers, and others who can guide, instruct, warn, and encourage us as we make our way through life. To willfully deprive ourselves of what others have to contribute would be a great personal disservice. All I'm suggesting is that it is difficult enough to live with the consequences, particularly if they are negative consequences, of our own decisions and behaviors. It is even more difficult to live with the negative consequences resulting from the decisions of those who insist on running our lives for us.

One last thought. When we allow another to "run" and perhaps "ruin" our lives, we never have the opportunity to learn from our own mistakes. Nor do we get to revel in the pleasure of knowing we got it right. If we are successful, it is because, robot-like, we followed the programing inculcated into us by the domineering personality. If we fail, the domineering personality will assure us that we failed because we did not follow their instructions correctly. The result is that when we let others "run" our lives, we never get the credit for the good; and if there is "ruin," we always get the blame.

Because the above is true, I suggest that one additional *I* be included in our list. It is the *I* of *I*nitiative. It is a truism to say, "There are two types of people in the world: those who let things happen and those who make things happen." The fact that the phrase is a truism does not mean there is no "truth" in it. Another person can "run" and perhaps "ruin" your life if you permit them to do so. Remember, if you don't "run" your own life, someone else will "run" it for you, and they may "ruin" it.

How Deep Does the Water Have to Be?

His name was Carl, and he had begun to attend the church I served in Rainbow City, Alabama, during my undergraduate days at Gadsden State Junior College and Jacksonville State University. Carl, in his late forties, was a remarkable personality whose life had been tragically disrupted as the consequence of an automobile crash when he was a young man. He was paralyzed from the chest down, had limited arm movement, breathed through a tracheotomy in his throat, and voided his body wastes into a colostomy bag attached to his side. I first met Carl, a veteran of the Korean War, at a Veterans Hospital when one of the deacons took me there shortly after I became pastor of the church. Through the Veterans Administration, Carl had been provided with a chair-lift van, modified so his wheelchair could be rolled under the steering wheel. He could and did drive himself almost anywhere he wished to go.

Carl had been visiting the church for some time and we became good friends. On a variety of occasions, I talked with him about his relationship to God, and on one occasion I drove with him to Memphis, Tennessee, for his appointment at the VA hospital there. Needless to say, a portion of that long drive was devoted to reflecting on the spiritual realities of our lives.

By the time I met Carl, he had pretty much processed his way through all the emotional baggage associated with his paralysis. He and a few friends had consumed entirely too much beer one night, were driving much too fast on a curvy road, and the result was the death of one of his friends. Carl was the most severely injured of the survivors. He had been through it all: grief, remorse, guilt, anger, a frustratingly long rehabilitation, the stares of the morbidly curious, and the pity of those who meant well but did not really understand. Somehow Carl managed to make it through all that physical and emotional trauma a sane, balanced, happy person. He was a joy to be around and to call my friend. What Carl still lacked, however, was the assurance of God's presence in his life. Though raised in a church-going family, he had never embraced Jesus Christ as Savior and Lord.

One Sunday evening during the invitation following my uninspiring sermon, I watched as Carl unlocked the brakes on his wheelchair and began to roll himself down the long center aisle toward where I stood in front of the Communion table. He stopped his chair, awkwardly extended his partially paralyzed right arm, grasped my hand, and said, "Larry, my time has come. I want to ask Jesus to come into my life and save me." I choked back tears as the congregation continued to sing. Composing myself, I knelt beside Carl's wheelchair so we could talk, and then I listened as he prayed, confessing his sins and inviting Jesus to save him. When he finished, I rose from my knees and shared Carl's decision with those present. It was an answer to the prayers of many, and you can imagine the rejoicing that took place as people stood in line to express their joy to Carl at the conclusion of the service. However, standing to one side as the people passed by, I realized I had a problem; I had a big problem. I had several big problems. And how I handled them was important not only for Carl but also for the future of that congregation and for my ongoing ministry in the years to come.

Without doubt, and with sufficient reason, Baptists have traditionally placed great emphasis on the importance of believer's baptism by immersion in water following a conscious decision to accept Jesus Christ as Savior by a person who is cognitively, emotionally, and psychologically competent to make such a decision freely of their own volition. While the preceding sentence is long, every phrase within it is important, for they all serve to protect the practice of Christian baptism, from the Baptist perspective, from misuse and abuse. Allow me to illustrate.

First, Baptists do not subscribe to the concept of baptismal regeneration, i.e., that the water, when appropriately applied by the properly consecrated officiant, has the miraculous capacity to effect salvation in a person's life. Baptists maintain that water baptism bears witness to a spiritual regeneration that has already taken place in the new believer's life as that person trusted Christ as Savior and was thereby indwelt by the presence of the Holy Spirit.

Second, Baptists have traditionally maintained the importance of a conscious, free choice made by cognitively, emotionally, and psychologically competent people. By this I mean Baptists do not practice *pedobaptism* (the baptism of infants), nor do we perform proxy baptisms on behalf of others living or dead. While Baptists do baptize children, it is hoped that care is taken to ensure that such children have arrived at a level of maturity making them competent to choose Christ consciously and freely. Regrettably, the contemporary concern of many with annual baptismal statistics suggests that, in many instances, perhaps not enough deliberation takes place before the very young are escorted to the baptistry. This has led to the practice of infant baptism among some Baptists who, at the same time, deny that they are doing so.

Third, for centuries Baptists have maintained that the word "baptize" is an English transliteration of the ancient Greek word *baptizo*, which literally means to "dip" or to "submerge." Therefore, Baptists have held across the centuries that the most consistently scriptural mode of believer's baptism is that of immersion.

As important as these matters are among Baptist Christians, they did not constitute my existential dilemma in the face of Carl's decision to accept Christ as Savior. My problem was all the holes in Carl's body that would fill up with water if we immersed him completely as Baptists are wont to do. As both his pastor and his friend, I wanted to baptize Carl; I didn't want to kill him.

The next day, I went by Carl's house to have a chat with my cherished friend and now my new brother in Jesus Christ. Carl understood the problem as well as I did, and before I could say anything he observed, "Larry, if you put me under water, all these holes in my body are going to fill up. I can get an infection. I can drown. I can die!" Nodding my head in agreement, I replied, "I understand, Carl. I lay awake most of the night trying to figure out what to do."

We continued to talk at length about how to respect the biblical injunction, the church's practice, and Carl's personhood all at the same time. Finally, he threw the whole problem into my lap by saying, "Larry, I want to do what's right. You tell me what I've got to do, and I'll do it if it kills me." Oddly enough, I was relieved by Carl's statement, for the seed of an idea had already begun to sprout in my mind. "Thanks, Carl," I said. "That's all I needed to know."

Later that week, a special meeting of the church's deacons was convened to discuss the matter. They were collectively in a quandary; the situation had been the talk of the small community for days. As traditional "Baptists," they were not prepared to consider sprinkling or affusion (pouring) as alternatives. They did not want to set a precedent for exempting a person from baptism who joined the church on profession of faith. And, certainly, they did not want to imply that Carl's physical disabilities preempted him from becoming a Christian and a member of the believing community.

Stymied, they asked if I had a suggestion. I had been waiting for someone to give me a chance. I related the conversation I'd had with Carl days before and quoted verbatim his statement, "Tell me what I have to do, and I'll do it if it kills me." Then I suggested we baptize Carl in the same manner we baptized everyone else who made a profession of faith in Jesus Christ, with the single exception that in this instance we put no water in the baptistery. I proposed that if we couldn't use all the water we wanted to use, we would just not use water at all.

The men sat in stunned silence for a moment. Some, I am sure, were wondering if their twentysomething pastor had gone completely off his rocker. Then eyes began to light up and broad smiles split faces. I could see from their expressions that these fine Christian men, all of whom were old enough to be my father, and some my grandfather, were getting it. They understood that baptism was not about water; it was about the humble willingness to be obedient to the commands of Jesus Christ in one's life, even at the risk of one's life.

After brief discussion, one of them made a motion that my recommendation be passed along to the congregation in the upcoming church conference, and the motion was unanimously adopted. Two weeks later, the congregation in conference unanimously adopted the same recommendation. The following Sunday evening, I descended into the baptistery and explained once again what we were doing. Then a group of burly young men lifted Carl, wheelchair and all, down into the baptistery in front of me. After relating some of the details of Carl's conversion experience I said, "Carl, in obedience to the commands of our Lord and Savior, Jesus Christ, and upon the profession of your faith in him, I baptize you my brother in the name of the Father, and of the Son, and of the Holy Spirit." With the assistance of one of the men, we leaned Carl's wheelchair backwards until he went out of sight in the baptistery, then we raised him up once again. A resounding "Amen!" went up from the congregation, and all present were sure Carl was as genuinely baptized as anyone else in that Baptist church, or anyone else's Baptist church for that matter.

During my college and seminary/divinity school teaching years, in Old and New Testament classes I talked to students about hermeneutics, or the process of taking an artifact or written record from one time period and cultural setting and transferring and applying it in another time period and cultural setting. Every time we take the words of Scripture and seek to apply them to our present-day circumstances, we are practicing the art of hermeneutics. Every time we struggle with "what the Bible says" and "what does what the Bible says mean?" we are engaging in hermeneutics.

The author of the Gospel of Matthew relates these words of Jesus: "Go ye therefore, and teach all nations, baptizing them in the name of the Father, and of the Son, and of the Holy Ghost: teaching them to observe all things whatsoever I have commanded you: and, lo, I am with you always, even unto the end of the world" (Matt 28:19-20).

As a Christian, as a Baptist Christian, and as for more than fifty years a Baptist Christian minister and academician, do I take this Great Commission seriously? You bet I do! But, because I take it seriously, I must seek to apply it redemptively as well. I have two choices. I can legalistically adhere to the absolute "letter" of the command to "baptize them" and become so preoccupied with the water that I fail to pay attention to the injunction to "teach them to observe *all* things that I have commanded you." My other alternative is to be sensitive to the "spirit" of the commandment. Here I turn to the larger body of New Testament literature and discover that the authenticating evidence of one's Christian experience is not found in how much water was used at one's baptism but in the Christ-likeness of one's life as one lives after the example of Jesus. Is the water important? Yes. Is the obedience important? Yes. If I must make a choice between the importance of the water and the importance of the obedience, which should I choose? I choose the obedience, for experience demonstrates and the Scripture teaches that those who have water without obedience are just "all wet."

In his powerful exposition of the Sermon on the Mount, Dietrich Bonhoeffer observed, "only he who is obedient believes."[1] It was submissive obedience to the will of God that led Carl to say, "Tell me what I have to do, and I'll do it if it kills me." In doing so, he echoed the words of Paul when he said of Jesus, "he humbled himself, and became obedient unto death . . ." (Phil 2:8). Authentic Christian experience is validated not by the depth of the water at baptism but by the depth of Christ-likeness reflected in one's daily living.

---

1. *The Cost of Discipleship* (New York: Macmillan, 1969), 69.

Making Idols of What We Believe

All people believe some things; we embrace certain foundational assumptions that constitute the lens through which we interpret reality, look at life, make decisions, and relate to others. This is a universal reality grounded in the nature of human personhood. This universal axiom of human existence is summarized in Anselm of Canterbury's (1033–1109) famous dictum *credo ut intelligam*, "I believe so that I may understand."

I recall an encounter many years ago with a gentleman who was stridently accusing me of doing something I had not done. When he paused to catch his breath, I said, "I think you are working with a mistaken assumption." His immediate and angry response was, "I don't make assumptions!" At that point, I elected to walk away from the confrontation because I wasn't prepared to assume I could have a reasonable conversation with a person who had embraced the assumption that he didn't make assumptions. If we don't regularly inhale and exhale, we will die. And if we can't accept the truth that our beliefs are rooted in assumptions about the origin, nature, and functioning of the world we live in, we are condemning our own selves to intellectual, psychological, and spiritual death.

The problem, particularly from the perspective of Christian faith and practice, lies in the danger of elevating one's beliefs/assumptions to a quasi-divine status of ultimate truth that cannot be challenged, revised, or ignored. At this point, God has been dethroned and the divine place has been usurped by infallible beliefs/assumptions that, when pushed to the extreme, become demonically destructive to self and others. My introspective reflection upon myself, and my attempt at objective observation of those around me, has led to the conclusion that there are at least four idolatrous beliefs/assumptions that constitute serious threats to our personal lives and possibly to the future of human civilization.

The first of these idols I call theological *hubris* (pride). It is the belief/assumption of many that the only correct way God can be understood and experienced is the way they understand and experience God. It is a matter of irrelevance whether one is Christian, Muslim, Jew, Hindu, Buddhist, etc. It is a matter of irrelevance whether one is theist, polytheist, atheist, agnostic, or simply indifferent. What is relevant is the insistence of some that they "drink from the spout where the glory comes out" when it comes to understanding God and that they are called to compel others to believe and behave as they do. This idolatry of the exclusive superiority of one's own beliefs/assumptions about the divine has been the occasion of much, some would say most, of humanity's long dark history of religious intolerance, persecution, warfare, and genocide. People holding such a dogmatic posture regarding their understanding of God have only to look into the mirror to see who they really think is god reflected back at them.

The second idol is chauvinism. Taking its name from one of Napoleon's soldiers, chauvinism is the belief/assumption that one's own national, ethnic, racial, cultural heritage is superior to all others. It is the underlying assumption of conquerors, empire builders, extreme nationalists, bigots, racists, and hate-mongers of all varieties. Past worshipers at the altar of chauvinism have clothed themselves in the garments of Crusaders, the Ku Klux Klan, Mussolini's Black Shirts, and Hitler's Brown Shirts. Contemporary expressions are seen in ethnic cleansing, racial profiling, hate speech, and extreme political ideologies. Claims to some form of collective exceptionalism inevitably lead to attempts to drive out or exterminate those deemed to be inferior genetically, physically, socially, ethnically, and economically. Hiding behind the smokescreens of blind patriotism, religious and political fundamentalisms, and just plain fear, those who worship the idol of chauvinism are compelled to draw stark distinctions between "our kind" and "that kind." And once "that kind" has been distinguished from "our kind," it becomes necessary for "that kind" to be marginalized, ostracized, and figuratively, sometimes literally, eliminated.

Yet a third idol, akin to the previous ones, is the belief/assumption of self-righteousness. Those who worship at the altar of self-righteousness are sure their own moral/ethical values are superior to all others. Such people are committed to the belief/assumption that there is only one correct answer to life's complex moral/ethical questions, and any answer other than the one they have embraced is categorically wrong, dishonest, and immoral. Such folks may quote Aristotle, Jesus, Confucius, Kant, Joseph Fletcher, or simply what they were told when they were growing up. They may proof text the Qu'ran, the Bible, the Book of Mormon, Karl Marx's *Das Kapital*, or Mao Zedong's *Little Red Book* to shore up their position. However, the bottom line is "I know better than you do and if you disagree with me you are wrong." And based on this belief/assumption, such people feel entitled to dictate to the rest of us how to worship, whom to love, how to vote, and the correct positions we should take regarding poverty, abortion, immigration, gender identity, national and international policy, health care, etc. If there's anything we need to know, or any difficult decision we must make, we should ask those who worship at the altar of self-righteousness, for they know the answers.

Last, at least for the sake of this exercise, there is the idol of self-projection. Those who worship at this altar believe that all others are motived by the same urges and drives that motivate them. Thus misers assume that everyone else is as stingy as they are. Power brokers assume that everyone else is as manipulative and ambitious as they are. Bigots are sure that everyone else is equally biased in their attitudes toward those considered to be racially, ethnically, or culturally inferior; they just don't have the "guts" to publicly admit it. This list goes on interminably. The person who worships at the altar of self-projection is sure that they are the only genuinely honest person and that everyone else is a hypocrite because they won't openly declare and practice their various biases and predilections in the public square.

There is another aspect of this tendency to worship at the altar of self-projection. As surely as one may project the negative aspects of one's personhood onto others, it is equally possible to uncritically project positive aspects as well. Here people may naively believe/assume that others are motivated by the same loving, altruistic, genuinely honest predispositions that motivate them. Believing that everyone is transparent and trustworthy, they find it difficult to make realistic assessments of the motives and intentions of others.

The failure to have a balanced understanding of one's self from either the negative or the positive direction may result in one becoming predator or prey. In either instance, there is a lack of wholeness in the individual's personal self-understanding that makes it impossible to realistically accept and deal with the multiplicity of drives, compulsions, and motives, both positive and negative, that are expressed in our interactions with one another. While we share a common humanity, we are not all alike, and it is a serious mistake to make our own self-perception the paradigm for understanding what makes others "tick."

By now some are asking, "Is he going to leave us with nothing within which we may anchor our personhood and engage in interpersonal relationships?" It is a fair question. The answer lies in my original assertion: "All people believe some things, embrace certain foundational assumptions that constitute the lens through which we interpret reality, look at life, make decisions, and relate to others." There is nothing wrong with a profound and abiding sense of identity with Ultimate Reality, however that reality is perceived and experienced. There is nothing wrong with a deep commitment to one's nationality, ethnicity, and social consciousness. There is nothing wrong with embracing a comprehensive and coherent sense of values that provide the guardrails for one's moral/ethical decision-making. There is nothing wrong with looking at reality through the lens of one's own sense of personal identity. It could be said that there is not only nothing wrong with these things but also that they are absolutely essential to making our way meaningfully through life and relationships. The problem is not in our having beliefs/assumptions about ourselves, others, and the world in which we live. The problem lies in elevating those beliefs/assumptions to godlike status where they are beyond question by ourselves or others.

One may then ask, "How do we keep our foundational beliefs/assumptions from becoming idols?" First, we must know what they are and how we came by them. Many appear to have done no disciplined reflection on the core commitments of their lives; they have absorbed them from their social/cultural environment. Nor have they tested the reliability, integrity, and judgment of those people from whom they unconsciously acquired their beliefs/assumptions. Not reflecting or testing is to risk simply making the idols of a previous generation one's own idols. To Socrates is attributed the insight that "the unexamined life is not worth living." I would add that the unexamined belief/assumption is not worth holding.

Second, we must be open to the need to correct our beliefs/assumptions when we find them to be less than adequate for our needs. One may attempt to open a can of beans with a plastic spoon, but the effort will only lend itself to frustration and failure. Tools should be suited to the tasks, and if tools are found to be inadequate and even counterproductive, one should search for more suitable tools. Beliefs/assumptions should adequately enable one to live positively and harmoniously with self, others, and the Ground of one's being.[1] When one's basic beliefs/assumptions prove inadequate or counterproductive to this task, one should correct them. And if they are demonstrably wrong, they should be abandoned and replaced by more adequate beliefs/assumptions.

Third, we must make the attempt to understand the foundational beliefs/assumptions of others, even those that may be markedly different from our own. Understanding does not require accepting or embracing the beliefs/assumptions of other people; all it requires is the recognition that genuine diversity exists in these matters. Many factors—environmental, cultural, religious, economic, genetic, educational, etc.—influence how people understand themselves and the world in which they live. We all start from a beginning, but all beginnings are not exactly the same. Thus it should surprise no one

---

1. See Paul Tillich, *Systematic Theology* (Chicago: University of Chicago, 1963), 1:110.

that diverse beginnings result in diverse paths of comprehension and conduct. It is only by seeking to understand the beliefs/assumptions of others that we can rid ourselves of the notion that others don't genuinely believe what they say they believe, and therefore they are not being honest when they interact in the world differently from how we do.

Finally, once we have clearly determined that our foundational beliefs/assumptions are reliable guides for living and relating, we must commit ourselves to being faithful to them despite the temptation to temporarily abandon them for the sake of economic reward, pleasure, acceptance, or mere expediency. It is easy to declare our absolute commitment to the beliefs/assumptions we have embraced when we are safe, warm, well fed, economically secure, affirmed by others, and never challenged by the vicissitudes of life. Frequently, people declare their willingness to die for what they believe. This is not a reliable guide. Authentic commitment to our beliefs/assumptions is seen in our willingness to live them, and if in the process of living them we are called upon to die for them, then we die. This is the difference between suicide and martyrdom.

If That Don't Just Beat a Hog a Peckin'

The West Alabama of my childhood and early adolescence in the 1950s and 1960s was an easygoing Southern environment of ordinary working people who thought a trip to Birmingham was one of the year's highlights. Apart from the veterans of World War II and Korea, most of the people I knew had never been outside of Alabama and many had never left Tuscaloosa County. While at the public level our society writhed in the anguished throes of the assassination of John Kennedy, the civil rights movement, the political antics of George Wallace, and the early years of the Vietnam War, only occasionally did these circumstances intrude upon our day-by-day existence. These things were the substance of the evening news with Chet Huntley and David Brinkley, but life in those days was more about whether Roger Maris was going to hit sixty home runs, if the *Beverly Hillbillies* was based on anyone we knew, and if Alabama's Crimson Tide was going to win yet another NCAA football national championship.

Summer was a particularly laid-back time. Mornings were devoted to working in the garden, helping Mother with canning green beans, corn, and tomatoes, or running the laundry through the old wringer washing machine. There's nothing like getting your fingers caught in the rollers of one those torture devices pretending to be a home appliance. But in the hot, sweltering afternoons, things slowed down. Most everyone gathered in the living room after lunch—we called it dinner—to watch game shows, soap operas, and cartoons on the black and white TV set. Evenings, after dinner—we called it supper—were devoted to sitting in the shade listening while the grown-ups talked or to watching TV while shelling peas and butter beans and snapping green beans. There was hardly ever a time when you did nothing.

It was at that time in my life that I began to absorb the quaint but often profound colloquial expressions of the region and time period. To have everything going your way was "to have the world by the tail in a downhill pull." Men who imbibed too much beer or corn liquor were "three sheets in the wind" or "high as a Georgia pine." Uppity, snobbish people had "their noses so high in the air they'd drown if it come a shower." The overbearingly pompous and aggressively assertive had their oversized egos deflated with the question, "Who died and left you king?" And suggestions about what we could do "if . . ." were usually responded to with, "Yeah! An' if a frog had wings he wouldn't bump his"—well, you can fill in the rest for yourself.

It was a language everyone understood, and it worked with remarkable effectiveness in communicating the basic principles of practical living. Today, all these decades later, something will happen or someone will say something, and I find the first words that pop into my mind are those colloquial expressions from my childhood and youth. I have to be careful with them because many are not suitable for public expression. However, others remain highly useful for clarifying my understanding of the events and people around me.

One of my favorites among such expressions was used frequently by my mother in response to some action or statement she considered suspect or incredible. Observing the behavior of another, or hearing gossip about something someone had said or done, frequently prompted her to say, "Well, if that don't just beat a hog a peckin'!" The juxtaposition of familiar visual images from the chicken coop and the hog pen was so dramatic that anyone hearing her had no difficulty understanding what she meant. It was a wonderfully colorful and ironic way of saying, "That's almost impossible to believe."

I spend a great deal of time with religious people—mostly, but not exclusively, Christian religious people. For the most part they are sane, sensible, reasonable, thoughtful people whom it is a joy to know. But occasionally one of my fellow Christians will do something or say something that seems diametrically opposed to the basic tenets of their Christian faith. In such instances, while I rarely express my thoughts aloud, the statement "Well, if that don't just beat a hog a peckin'" leaps into my consciousness. It is amazing to me how many attitudes and behaviors some people can embrace without recognizing how incredible it is to maintain those attitudes and behaviors while claiming Christian identity at the same time. Permit me to surface a few of them for consideration and reflection.

First, I find it incredible that many think that because they made a public profession of faith and got baptized as children, they are automatically Christian believers regardless of their day-to-day behaviors. They seem to think some sympathetic magic was effected in shaking the preacher's hand, letting the little old ladies come by and cry on them, and getting dunked later in a baptistery or stream. While public profession and baptism are important aspects in the shaping of Christian identity, nowhere does the New Testament teach that simply going through such ritual activities makes one Christian. The Bible clearly teaches that identity with Jesus Christ is reflected in Christ-like behavior. I frequently encounter people whose lifestyles demonstrate not one shred of Christian character and conduct; yet they're sure they will spend eternity in heaven with God because they joined the church and got baptized when they were children. I come away from such conversations thinking, "Well, if that don't just beat a hog a peckin'."

Second, I find it incredible that many professing Christians think racial and ethnic prejudice, crass materialism, deceitful behavior, violent political and social extremism, and moral and ethical misconduct are acceptable Christian behaviors. Many have so compartmentalized their thinking that they espouse one set of values in their religious lives and practice an alternative set of values in their daily conduct. Biblical ethics have been attenuated to the extent that, in a society preoccupied with debates over the propriety of prominent displays of the Ten Commandments and the imposition of "Christian" practices on the public square, we have lost our focus on Jesus's teachings of respect for the personhood of others, prayer in the closet of one's personal being, and humble servanthood in a needy world. When I witness Christians militantly insisting that all legislation and court decisions regarding social issues must conform to their perspective without giving due consideration to the fact that all American citizens are entitled to the civil liberties rooted in the Constitution, whether they are Christians or not, I find myself thinking, "Well, if that don't just beat a hog a peckin'."

For the sake of driving home the point, let me mention one more. I find incredible the assumption of many that, because they are Christians, they are supposed to be immune to the stresses and hardships of life. Amid difficult circumstances, I often hear someone say, "I just don't understand why God let this happen to *me*." Behind the statement is their apparent belief that it's OK for God to let nasty stuff happen to other people; it's just not supposed to happen to them. Such an attitude is at the height of vanity and self-centeredness. It is the tacit expression of a posture that "God loves me more than he does other people" or "God is obligated to me in a special way" or "as a Christian, I'm a superior human being." Such things are implied by people who claim identity with one who took upon himself the common lot of humanity, who experienced the rejection and ridicule of those around him, who knew poverty, homelessness, and oppression, and who suffered and bled and died an excruciating death at the hands of corrupt, contemptuous political and religious leaders.

Such an attitude is diametrically opposite to that expressed by the imprisoned, aged, physically impaired Apostle Paul who identified with both "the power of [Jesus's] resurrection" and "the fellowship of [Jesus's] suffering" (Phil 3:10). In response to the apparent complaint of some among the Philippians regarding their loss of material possessions Paul said, "I have suffered the loss of all things" (Phil 3:8). To Timothy, who appears to have written Paul to protest the difficulties of living faithfully for Christ, the apostle asserted, "I also suffer these things" (2 Tim 1:12). If both our Lord Jesus Christ and such a giant of the Christian faith as the Apostle Paul were not immune to the ordinary and extraordinary sufferings of human existence, why should the contemporary believer presume that they should be? When I hear people bemoaning the fact that God permitted things to happen to *them* that happen to other people as well I find myself thinking, "Well, if that don't just beat a hog a peckin'." And sometimes I am tempted to ask, using another of those colloquial expressions from my youth, "Just who the pea turkey do you think you are?"

Before I close, let me quickly point out another, more positive side to this. With wonderful frequency, people, both Christians and others, do astonishingly generous, totally unselfish, and refreshingly gracious things as well. One needs only to point toward the remarkable outpouring of assistance afforded to those victimized by devastating natural disasters. People around the world, at great risk to themselves, jeopardize their own lives to rescue others marooned by rising floodwater, earthquakes, wildfires, hurricanes, and tornadoes. Countless volunteers force themselves to endure horrendous circumstances to assist in recovering the remains of the dead and decomposing. Churches, mosques, synagogues, temples, civic clubs, and businesses contribute financial resources, previously earmarked for other important uses, to relief and recovery efforts. Communities open their homes, schools, and public buildings to house, feed, clothe, and care for refugees. In an environment that often decries the absence of human kindness and compassion in a modern technological, materialistic culture, even the most cynical must stand back from such incredible outpourings of sympathetic, compassionate assistance and say, "Well, if that don't just beat a hog a peckin'."

As the years continue to pass, and if I continue to live, there is no doubt that I am going to lose many things. I have already lost most of my hair. Middle age has inexorably segued into senior adulthood. I am rapidly approaching the time when I can remember the names of more people who are no longer alive than I can of those who are. Bones creak, knees ache, vision and hearing are fading, and there are lots of things I used to be interested in that don't matter nearly as much as they once did. And there's not much I can do about these inevitable by-products of the passage of time.

On the other hand, I'm determined never to lose my appreciation for the fact that some things, some people, some events, and some opportunities are almost too incredible to believe. Sometimes reflecting on them causes my heart to ache and makes me pray that both I and the people around me would strive harder to become the people God has always intended for us to be. But there are other times when I catch my breath in astonished joy at how noble, how gracious, how thoroughly Christ-like we demonstrate ourselves to be, both believer and nonbeliever, from time to time. And I pray, "God, help me never to become so complacent and self-satisfied with either the positive or the negative that I lose the capacity to think, 'Well, if that don't just beat a hog a peckin'.'"

Never Push on the Hinges

We were walking into a local discount store. Both Peggy and I were in something of a hurry. I had a class scheduled to begin in about half an hour, and I prided myself on my reputation among students for never being late. It happened to be a class in which Peggy was enrolled, and she knows how impatient I become with students who are tardy as well. With this in mind, Peggy stepped briskly up to the glass door, pushed assertively on the aluminum door facing, and proceeded to walk directly into the glass. Being a step or two behind, I was blessed with her bewildered expression as she bounced, unharmed, off the door. Turning toward me, while rubbing the spot where her forehead had struck the plate glass, she chuckled ruefully and said, "I guess that's what happens when you push on the hinges."

It was one of those remarkable moments when I had the good sense to keep my mouth shut and nod in agreement, for there was nothing I could have said that would have been the right thing. But the suggestion of the moment was too good to allow myself to forget. So, as this time she pushed on the correct side of the door, I followed her into the store grabbing for a scrap of paper and my pen in order to write down her laconic observation, "That's what happens when you push on the hinges."

Occasionally someone will ask, "Gregg, where in the world do you get the topics you speak about in your Facebook devotions, Believing Thinker essays, and books?" Now you know the answer. They just pop up. Something happens, sometimes the most innocuous and insignificant thing happens, and it triggers a response in my cerebral cortex. I'm about half a bubble off of level to begin with. Because this is true, I often find myself looking at life sideways. The truth is, it's great fun, and often there is something to be learned from observing life from a perspective that is somewhat askew. So the next day I sat down to reflect on the apparent truth that when opening a door, one should never push on the hinges.

Buildings have doors and rooms have doors, but the concept of door is also a time-honored metaphor for human life with its diverse decisions and opportunities. We speak of "open doors" and "closed doors" of opportunity. We lament over "doors slammed shut in our faces" and rise enthusiastically to answer when "opportunity comes knocking at the door." Both the literal and metaphorical use of the term "door" is quite common in the Bible; I counted more than two hundred and fifty times the words "door" or "doors" are used in Scripture. I know, you're thinking, "If he has time to calculate the frequency of word usage in the Bible, we need to find something useful for him to do." Well, let's don't tarry too long on that thought. I'd prefer to move on to some observations regarding why, when attempting to pass through a door, one should never push on the hinges.

First, doors are designed to open in a particular way. Some open from the right, and others from the left. Some open into a building or room, and others open out. Some doors open by sliding horizontally or vertically, and others open by folding. Some open only for entering, and others are only for exiting. This could go on forever. But there is a point. As one approaches a door, it is important to take note of how the door is designed so it may be used properly.

Much of what goes wrong in life is the result of not paying attention to how our most significant relationships are designed to be used. Marriages often fail because people seek to use the marital relationship inappropriately. Friendships are broken because they are misused and abused. People who do things with their bodies that are detrimental to their physical well-being often suffer a breakdown in their physical health. Even our relationships with God in prayer, Bible study, worship, giving, and ministry founder in meaninglessness because we pray to manipulate God, study Scripture to win our arguments, attend worship to be seen and entertained, give to get in return, and minister so that others will talk about what good people we are. Then we find ourselves saying, "I don't seem to be able to get through to God," without realizing the problem is that we have been pushing on the hinges, and the doors of access to intimate fellowship with our Maker simply don't open that way.

While some may be inclined to snap, "Why don't you tell us something we don't already know?" I intend to continue laboring this point for a moment longer, for there are some who, even though they know how the doors of life and relationships are supposed to work, still refuse to try to open them in the appropriate ways. Such behavior always results in negative consequences. Doors get damaged. Those attempting to open them get frustrated and/or hurt. We end up looking foolish to ourselves and to others because we insist on refusing to turn the knob or handle, push on the correct side of the door, or take the time to be sure it is unlocked before we go ramming and slamming into it. We must recognize that if we get injured or end up looking foolish because we always insist on pushing on the hinges, it's not the door's fault.

Now, let's try to carry this a bit further. A second reason that there is no sense in pushing on door hinges is that it is completely unnecessary. By their nature, hinged doors are for opening and passing through. All that is necessary is that we use them as they are designed to be used. This leads to a number of other generalizations about literal doors. Some doors are open all the time; we can pass through them whenever we please. Some are such that we cannot open them alone; we need the assistance of others. Some doors are time sensitive; they may be opened only at designated times. Other doors we encounter have hinges that are rusty from neglect and disuse. They can be opened only after an investment of time and energy to make them work properly once again. Yet other doors open only from the inside; we pass through them only by permission and/or invitation. Finally, there are some doors that are just as well left closed anyway, for they aren't our doors and we don't need to go through them to begin with.

While there are many ways the preceding analogies may be applied to our professional careers, our social relationships, our educational opportunities, etc., these analogies are particularly useful when applied to one's ongoing relationship to God. Knowing the nature of the doors of divine-human relationships and how they work enables us to avoid pushing futilely upon hinges and to open the way to a vital and transformative life in the presence of God.

The Scripture speaks of one door through which we must pass before we can even begin to access any of the other doors of spiritual growth and development. This is the door of salvation. Passing through this doorway requires a couple of absolutely essential understandings. First, the doorway to salvation is not some "thing"; it is "Someone." Jesus said, "I am the door: by me if any man enter in, he shall be saved . . ." (John 10:9). Too often people assume salvation is acquired through the mastery of a set of theological facts or doctrinal concepts related to God. This assumption is mistaken. The way to salvation is not through mastery of data about God but through meaningful relationship with God in and through Jesus Christ. It is a relationship of knowing and being known. Second, we pass through this door not by banging and beating it down but by accepting the reality that it has been standing wide open all the time. If today you find yourself on the outside looking in, all that is lacking is for you to accept the invitation God has been offering for as long as you have been alive.

Once we have passed through the door of salvation, God has many other doors awaiting us. There are doors of spiritual growth and development that open wide as we study the Scripture, commune with God in prayer, and clarify our thinking by engaging the assistance and insight of others within the believing community. God will set before us what the Apostle Paul called "great" and "effectual" doors of ministry (1 Cor 16:9). Without doubt, there will be adversaries and obstacles along the way, but we also live in God's promise that though we are not strong in and of ourselves, God will set before us open doors of ministry that no one can close, regardless of how hard they try (Rev 3:8).

One of the most difficult things for many to comprehend and accept is that sometimes God closes doors as well. In Acts 16 we are told the story of Paul's journey, along with Silas and several other companions, westward across Asia Minor. Coming to Troas on the Aegean coast, they wanted to turn north and east toward Bithynia, but the Spirit of God simply would not permit them to do so.

Later, as he reflected on this frustrating experience, the Apostle to the Gentiles celebrated the fact that though the door to Bithynia was closed, another "door was opened unto me of the Lord" (2 Cor 2:12). Bithynia was just not one of Paul's doors, and by God's grace he had the good sense to walk through the door to Macedonia that God had opened instead of continuing to bang against and push on the hinges of the door that God had closed.

A number of years ago, a door was slammed shut in my life. On the other side of the door was something I had desired passionately and prepared for assiduously over many years. For a long time after the door was slammed shut, I stood outside and pounded, pouted, and pled to be permitted inside, all to no avail. All I accomplished was depression, excessive weight gain, and frustrated lack of direction. But a time finally came when I heard the voice of God saying, "My son, I love you dearly. And I have much in store for you as you live before me in faith. But you will never experience what I have in store until you accept the fact that that door is closed and it is not going to open again. You must turn around, for the doors I am opening are in another direction." And sure enough, when I gave up pushing on the hinges of a closed past and turned toward the future, I discovered that God had set before me more than one open door.

Do not misunderstand me. This is not an exercise in sour grapes, nor is it the callow assertion that I didn't really want what was lost anyway. I miss what was taken from me. I regret its loss. I wish that things that were done and words that were said that eventuated in the loss had never been done and said. But one cannot live one's life simply regretting the past and lamenting over what might have been. There is no future in that.

The future lies in another direction. The author of the book of Revelation put it this way: "I looked, and behold, a door was opened in heaven: and the voice which I heard . . . said, 'Come up hither . . .'" (Rev 4:1). Having walked by faith through the door of salvation in Jesus Christ, I wait patiently for the time when I shall see "a door opened in heaven" and hear a voice say, "Come up hither." Between now and then, I can trust the God who has saved me and who will ultimately call me to experience the glory of the fullness of God's presence in heaven, to set before me the doors through which I need to walk. Meanwhile, I keep myself reminded that the door to salvation did not open because I pushed on the hinges; it was always open, waiting for me to pass through in faith. The door to heaven will open one day, not because I bang on the hinges of its gates but because they will be thrown open to me by God's grace. And I have no need to push on the hinges of God's doors of growth and ministry here and now; God will open them in his time and in his way. When God closes a door to me, no amount of pushing on the hinges will open it; and when God sets an open door before me, no adversary can close it.

Because I Am a Rich Man: An Exercise in Reflective Thanksgiving

We sat on the deck above the boathouse of friends who have a place on the lake, eating pizza and chatting at the end of a busy day. Most of that unusually warm late fall Saturday had already been devoted to taking our grandson to the Renaissance Festival in Charlotte. We spent hours watching magicians, jugglers, troubadours, and jousters recreate a microcosm of the world of late medieval Europe. If the day had simply ended with pleasantly munching pizza and visiting with friends, it would still have been a fine day.

But Jamison had come for the weekend with something else on his mind. While he had enjoyed immensely the strangely costumed jousters, jesters, and jugglers at the festival, he wanted to go fishing. So, after driving back from the Renaissance Festival, we ordered a pizza to pick up on the way and headed for the lake. Jamison had a brand new rod and reel won at a boat show he had attended with his father a few weeks before. All I had for bait were several slices of stale sandwich bread that had dried out in the refrigerator. And I made him agree we wouldn't keep anything he was lucky enough to catch unless it was a really impressive fish. We consumed the pizza as quickly as possible, thanked our friends for the use of their pier, and headed for the water, because Jamison had serious fishing he wanted to do and not much time to do it in.

The next two hours were a delight. As darkness descended, I baited this eight-year-old's hook with stale bread so many times I lost count. He would cast out onto the water, and we both watched intently, waiting for the round, red and white float to be snatched below the surface by a hungry fish. More times than not the bait was stolen by fingerlings who got the bread without getting caught on the hook. But I continued to bait, and he continued to cast, and the fish began to cooperate. Gleefully he caught first one, then another, and another, until he had caught five, matching his record from an earlier outing on the same lake. The score was Jamison ten, "Gee Daddy" one.

Later that evening I mellowed out on the den sofa, feet propped on the coffee table, sipping Irish Cream coffee. Clancy, our Yorkshire terrier, sat proprietarily in my lap while Jazz, the cat, napped on the sofa back behind my head. In the background, I could hear Peggy reading from one of the Harry Potter novels while Jamison drifted off into contented sleep. I couldn't help but think, "It would be pretty hard for a little boy to have a better day than this one has been." Then I thought, "It would be pretty hard for a grandfather to have a better one either."

One of my favorites of the grand musicals of the twentieth century is Joseph Stein's *Fiddler on the Roof*. I am particularly fond of the Jewish actor, Topol, who portrayed Tevye, a beleaguered Russian Jew in pre-Bolshevik Revolution Tsarist Russia, who is always talking to God about his troubles. In one scene Tevye, bemoaning the lameness of his horse, contemplating the sale of his milk cow, agonizing over how to marry off his daughters, and attempting unsuccessfully to avoid the nagging of his wife, sings to God about what he would do "If I Were a Rich Man." One of the themes underlying this powerful movie musical is that Tevye does not truly realize how "rich" he is. In remembering days like the long past Saturday described earlier, I recognize what a truly rich man I am.

Most of us fail to recognize the difference between being "rich" and being "wealthy." I am far from being a wealthy man, as most everyone who knows me understands. I drive an old Ford pickup truck that is well into its second 100,000 miles. We live in a more than fifty-year-old house that is comfortable because of the immense amount of sweat equity we have poured into it since 1993. While our retirement income is adequate to meet our needs, like most everyone else today, we wonder about whether future economic upheavals will result in our undergoing drastic changes in lifestyle. Like most everyone else we know, we are far from impoverished, but we are also far from being wealthy. But while we are not wealthy, we are infinitely rich. And if there is a choice to be made between being wealthy and being rich, I'll take being rich, the way Peggy and I are rich, every time.

I thank God daily for those who have enriched my life by sharing who they are and investing their personhood in who I am. Space does not permit the listing and commenting upon family members, teachers, mentors, neighbors, friends, church families, students, fellow ministers, and educational colleagues who have imparted incalculable value to my life by simply being who they were at places and times when I needed people just like them. Some I see and share life with daily; others I have not seen in years; and some I am likely never to see again. Many are no longer among the living. But I am rich for having the blessing of who they are, or were, become a part of who I am. Because this is true, I am a rich man.

More than five decades of my living have been shared with the woman who is the love of my life. Many men have women who love them, but rich is the man blessed with a spouse who not only loves him but believes in him as well. God has blessed me with a mate who, through some of the darkest nights of my soul, has never ceased to believe in me. Because this is true, I am a rich man.

Together Peggy and I raised two sons, each of whom has blessed us in the person he is. Though unique in their own personhood, both sons are blessed with gifts I pray they will continue to develop, through God's grace, with all the potential that lies within them. Because this is true, I am a rich man.

Through the resources of generously endowed academic scholarships, and the gifts to theological education of Baptist churches across the country, I have been blessed with educational opportunities my parents could never have imagined. I was the first person in my extended family to graduate from high school. For many years, I remained the only one to earn a four-year college degree. And to my knowledge, I continue to remain the only member of that large extended family to acquire educational credentials beyond a bachelor's degree. Some might conclude, "Well, that's just because you're smart." I happen to know better. While I may be somewhat brighter than average, over a teaching career I looked into the eyes of students every semester who were "smarter" than I am. While the degrees that hang on the wall of my home study have my name on them, they are the product of the work, sacrifice, generosity, and dedication of a vast number of people, a few of whom I have known personally but most of whom I shall never meet, who made it possible for me to attain anything significant I have done. Because this is true, I am a rich man.

Since the late 1960s, the people of various congregations have trusted me to provide them with pastoral leadership and nurture. From the tiny congregation outside Greensboro, Alabama, that called me to be its pastor when I was eighteen and didn't have a clue what I was doing, to the present when I still sometimes don't have a clue what I am doing, I am deeply indebted. I have known people who were in the truest sense of the phrase "saints of God." They have followed faithfully when I deserved to be followed, rebuked and instructed when I needed to be called to accountability, comforted and consoled when I hurt and grieved, and rejoiced and celebrated the victories we shared. Because this has been true across a long career in vocational Christian ministry, I am a rich man.

God has abundantly blessed me with the richness of grace. Through God's grace, I know Jesus Christ as Savior and Lord of my life. Through God's grace I have a calling to participate in what God is doing as "pastor-teacher" and as "equipper of the saints for the work of the ministry" for "the edifying of the body of Christ" (Eph 4:12). Through God's grace, I was afforded the opportunity to challenge the minds and hearts of young people who walked into the college, seminary, and divinity school classroom and allowed me to help them hone their critical thinking skills. Through God's grace, I am able to convert the thoughts of my mind, and the feelings of my heart, into words in which many report they have found comfort, challenge, hope, and encouragement. If this is true, I am humbled, for I am truly a rich man.

The writer of Ephesians spoke of God's intention to "shew the exceeding riches of his grace in his kindness toward us through Jesus Christ" (Eph 2:7). While, contrary to the materialist preoccupations of those who proclaim the "prosperity gospel," God has never promised to make those who follow God wealthy, God has promised the faithful "riches of his grace" beyond the broadest reaches of their imaginations. It is my prayer that, as you have read my grateful enumeration of personal riches, you have begun to reflect on the "riches of God's grace" in your own life. Perhaps you have begun to realize, as I have, that you are infinitely richer that you ever supposed.

The difference between wealth and riches is that wealth is, one way or another, acquired and must be hoarded and protected or it will be lost, while riches, on the other hand, are pure gift. Because they are pure gift, they can be clutched to the heart and given away indiscriminately at the same time and never be lost or diminished. This is one of the great ironies of life. Many possess vast material wealth, but they are not rich for they live with impoverished souls. Others, with little or no material wealth, live lives shaken down and overflowing with richness because they have learned to inventory the things that are truly, infinitely valuable. Such things cannot be stored in vaults, accounts, certificates, and deeds. The infinitely valuable is laid up, in the short-term, in the minds and hearts of those who are truly grateful and, in the long-term, in the "treasures of heaven, where neither moth nor rust doth corrupt, and where thieves do not break through nor steal" (Matt 6:20).

My friend, this is why a Saturday in the company of a loving spouse, an adventuresome child, and dear friends is such a wonderful thing. Such days are foretastes, signs along the way, arrows pointing in the direction of the fullness of riches in the kingdom of heaven. They are reminders that heaven is not "pie-in-the-sky-by-and-by-when-we-die." Heaven is a present reality in the lives of those who choose to experience it by recognizing how rich they truly are.

Please do not hear in these words the pious platitudes of a Pastor Pollyanna. I am not unaware of the sufferings that result from being bereft of one's material possessions, the loss of family members, and deprivation of one's means of earning a living, as well as the shattering trauma occasioned by natural disasters, meaningless violence, endless wars, and grinding poverty. If all the "stuff" Peggy and I have accumulated over a lifetime were suddenly washed away or razed to the ground, I would be as shocked and frightened and dismayed as anyone else. While what I have accumulated in terms of wealth is not great, I do not wish to lose it any more than anyone else does. But I hope and pray that, faced with a similar set of circumstances, I would not confuse loss of wealth with loss of riches. Bereft of all the material wealth he has, that man who sat on the sofa in his den, sipping coffee and listening to his wife read to his grandson, would still be a rich man. Why? Because those who are truly rich recognize that the real treasures of life are the intangibles, and such intangibles are gifts, not possessions.

Just 'Cause Somebody Says "Boo!" Don't Mean We Have to Jump

We have all played the game; sometimes we have been the trickster, sometimes the victim. Oblivious to the fact that someone is sneaking up on us, we pursue whatever we are doing until we hear the sudden "Boo!" announcing we have been surprised again. Involuntarily our "fight or flight" instincts kick in, the adrenal gland floods our system with a massive dose of adrenaline, and our muscles ready themselves for instant action.

We learned the game from our parents and siblings, we practiced it as children on our friends and unsuspecting bystanders, and from time to time we still play, or are played with, by those around us. Like many things, if not done with malicious intent or at inappropriate times or too often, the game of "Boo!" is fun. Everyone gets a laugh, even the unsuspecting victim, and life goes on. Unfortunately, there are those who take too much pleasure in seeing the distress of another, who don't choose their times well, and who don't seem to know when enough is enough. We dread seeing them come in sight, and we dread even more when they are not in sight, for we suspect they are lurking somewhere waiting for the next opportunity to make us jump when they say "Boo!" One of life's most important lessons is that just 'cause somebody says, "Boo!" don't mean we have to jump.

Over the years I have worked with many congregations that had recently gone through tumultuous times and were attempting to recover from the trauma and move on with productive ministry. The list of causes for the trauma is almost endless: the forced termination of a pastor or staff member; conflict between two influential members who had elected to make the church the battleground on which they discovered who was the stronger; stress over too much money or not enough and over who gets the credit or the blame; a doctrinal dispute about speaking in tongues, or about women deacons, or about which biblical translation should be used in the pulpit, or about how deep the water should be in the baptistery and whether it should be hot, cold, or lukewarm.

Whatever the causes, when congregations go through such traumatic experiences, almost everyone gets their sensors tuned so high that someone can whisper "Boo!" and everybody in the place goes into a panic. Angry voices get raised, hands get wrung, almost forgotten slights are dragged to the surface of consciousnesses and rubbed raw again, and everybody writhes in agony over the prospect of having to wallow once more in the briar patch of ill will, forced politeness, and only thinly veiled hostility.

Congregations and their leaders have become accustomed to my making two deliberate assertions when I agree to work with them in improving their conflict management skills. First, I say, "I'm not interested in hearing your lists of good guys and bad guys. I'll probably have my own list soon enough." Second, I say, "We must learn that just 'cause somebody says 'Boo!' don't mean we have to jump. If we jump every time somebody says 'Boo!' all we're ever going to do around here is 'Boo!' and jump."

The pertinent question is, "Why do some people sneak up on unsuspecting ministers, congregations, volunteer organizations, educational institutions, governmental structures, and businesses in order to shout 'Boo!' at the top of their lungs?" While I can't speak for every situation or circumstance, I have been watching religious people and institutions for a long time, and I do have some opinions regarding why various people within them elect to shout "Boo!"

Sometimes the shouting of "Boo!" is a test of leadership. Some people are the self-appointed testers of whether a new pastor, elected official, CEO, etc. is going to go into a panic at the first sign of trouble or conflict. When not done maliciously, or capriciously, this kind of "Boo!" shouting can be a good thing. While people may vote to give someone the title of pastor, county commissioner, president, etc., they most often wait until the person has weathered some crisis before deciding to follow their leadership.

The Presbyterian academic and former seminary president James D. Glasse published a book in the 1970s titled *Putting It Together in the Parish*. In it, Glasse introduced would-be ministers to the concept of "paying the rent" in their ministry positions. His thesis was that until people have concluded their minister is "trustworthy," they are not likely to follow their leadership into new and untried arenas of ministry. Further, people decide the minister is trustworthy by observing how the rent is paid, i.e., how the minister manages the day-to-day tasks of ministry. Put more directly, people don't ordinarily follow a leader until they have determined the leader is stable and self-assured enough not to jump and run every time somebody shouts "Boo!" at them.

On the other hand, sometimes when someone shouts "Boo!" it is a threat. These "Boo!" shouters are not trying to be helpful; they are trying to intimidate and manipulate. I remember the first such "Boo!" shouter I encountered as a young minister of eighteen, in my first pastorate. She was the church pianist, the Women's Missionary Union Director, the wife of the church's only deacon, and the daughter of a deceased charter member of the church. One day she said to me, "Young man, as long as my daddy was alive, he pretty much ran this church the way he wanted to; and as long as I'm alive, I'm going to run it the way I think he would want it to be run." Now that's a pretty long sentence, but essentially what she said, menacingly, was "Boo!" just to see if I'd jump. The sad truth is that I did jump, and because I jumped that time, I spent the remainder of my ministry there jumping every time she said "Boo!" I found no comfort in the knowledge that her husband, and everyone else within the scope of her influence, jumped when she said "Boo!" as well. This overbearing woman needed somebody to "Boo!" back at her.

Such threatening "Boo!" shouters are often only a distracting nuisance. At other times they are as dangerous as the sting of an adder. In a power position (supervisor, trustee, major financial giver, family member of an influential person, etc.), the threatening "Boo!" shouter seeks to intimidate and coerce others into bowing to their will by warning of the dire consequences that will result from crossing them. "Boo!" shouters threaten to have faculty members fired because they didn't get the grade they wanted in a class. "Boo!" shouters redirect their financial gifts from the church's undesignated budget into special funds in order to "starve out" an unwanted minister or "kill off" an unwanted ministry. "Boo!" shouters sometimes even threaten physical violence toward those who stand between them and what they expect to receive. Among the favorite phrases of "Boo!" shouters are, "I'll call my lawyer." "You haven't heard the last of me." "Wait till I tell 'so-and-so' what you did." "God told me to tell you . . . ." A person, church, or other institution that repeatedly caves in to the "Boo!" shouter's threats soon finds they can no longer breathe in and out without the "Boo!" shouter's permission. And that is no way to live.

So we have concluded that some "Boo!" shouters, while what they do is irksome, may be helpful as they test the quality of the leadership others are exercising. We have concluded that other "Boo!" shouters are consistently unhelpful because they are motivated solely by their own ego needs and lust for power and control. What these two classes of "Boo!" shouters have in common is that each, to a large degree, consciously chooses if they are going to shout "Boo!" Their conduct, positive or negative, is the result of a deliberate choice. There are at least two other classes of "Boo!" shouters who may act more from compulsion than from choice. For instance, sometimes the shouting of "Boo!" is a plea for attention and reassurance from a desperately lonely and insecure personality; it is a cry for help. Like the serial abuser who leaves telltale clues at the scene of each crime, or the teenaged binge drinker, or the pornography addict who puts various salacious websites in the favorites list of a computer shared with coworkers, the compulsive "Boo!" shouter is doing the abuser's or the binge drinker's or the addict's equivalent of crying, "Catch me! Help me! Stop me before I hurt myself or others again!"

Such a person needs for those around them to recognize that shouting "Boo!" or crying "Wolf!" or "stomping on the brakes" is only a presenting symptom of a deeper problem. Psychologically unable to acknowledge loneliness, fear of rejection, a deep-seated sense of personal inadequacy, etc., the compulsive "Boo!" shouter cries out for someone to grasp their hand and pull them to safety before they are completely swept away by the psychological, spiritual, or circumstantial *tsunamis* they fear are about to swamp them.

And then there are "Boo!" shouters who are simply crazy-makers. There is no other explanation for their behavior. Like the "berserkers" of Norse mythology, some people seem to thrive on creating as much confusion, consternation, and chaos as they can. I've watched them in committee meetings, church business meetings, pastor's conferences, and faculty meetings. It can happen in a group as small as two and as large as the annual meeting of the Southern Baptist Convention, the US House of Representatives, or the US Senate. For no apparent rational reason, the "Boo!" shouter explodes, doing indiscriminate damage to everyone and everything within the range of their vocal concussion. Stunned survivors of such happenings stagger away wondering, "Who set them off?" or "What was the cause of such behavior?" Too often there are no answers, and we are left with the sad conclusion that so-and-so is a habitual crazy-maker who may not even understand why they behave the way they do.

The question remains: "How do we avoid jumping just 'cause somebody shouts 'Boo!' at us?" First, we school ourselves to pay attention to what is going on around us. The "Boo!" shouter's most effective weapon is the element of surprise. Take this away and they are, for the most part, disarmed. Don't hear me encouraging paranoia. All I'm suggesting is that leaders should pay attention to the people around them. "Boo!" shouters are usually as recognizable as "yes-men," "naysayers," and "wet blankets" to leaders who are not so self-absorbed they aren't paying attention.

Second, don't overreact to the "Boo!" shouter. These people get their kicks out of seeing their victims melt into quivering bowls of emotional jelly. Take away the source of their gratification and the behavior usually goes away. If the person persists in shouting "Boo!" even when they get no reaction, they become the victims of their own disruptive pathological behavior.

Third, all organizations (churches, civic clubs, government agencies, etc.) need a clearly defined, commonly shared sense of purpose that guides what they do. When this is true, the disruptive "Boo!" shouter is unable to derail progress by creating confusion. If everyone understands why the organization exists and the nature of its mission, the temporary disorientation of one, or a few, cannot wreck the whole institution.

Finally, regardless of how satisfying it may appear to do so, don't become a "Boo!" shouter yourself. What I said earlier about how someone should have responded to the overbearing woman in my first pastorate was probably wrong. To descend into "Boo!" shouting ourselves simply sucks more and more people into this childish behavior. We do so frequently with little or no positive result. Strategies like "If you shout, I shout," "If you quit, I quit," and "If you become a 'berserker,' I become a 'berserker'" have dealt the death blow to more friendships, family relationships, church fellowships, and cooperative civic endeavors than anything I know. Just 'cause somebody says "Boo!" don't mean we have to jump; and just 'cause somebody makes us jump don't mean we should become "Boo!" shouters ourselves.

Between *Rosh Hashanah* and *Yom Kippur*

For as long as human beings have existed, we have experienced the need to acknowledge the progression of time and to mark the significant events that take place in time. All peoples observed the cyclic pattern of lengthening and shortening days and learned to connect this pattern with those of seasonal change. Because ancient peoples recognized the relationship between seasonal changes, their agricultural harvests, and the birth cycles of their domestic animals, such events came to be closely associated with their understanding of God and the nature of their relationship to God.

In late summer/early fall each year, the Jewish people, and those of us who while not Jewish have a deep appreciation for that religious tradition and its people, pass through a series of days that are deeply enshrined in the biblical religious tradition. One is *Rosh Hashanah*, literally the "head of the year" or the Jewish New Year. The other is *Yom Kippur*, or the Day of Atonement. *Rosh Hashanah* marks the beginning of a new lunar year in the religious calendar of Judaism. *Yom Kippur* observes the deliberate confrontation of the religious community with its sin and addresses the need to remove any and all obstacles that stand in the way of a right relationship with God and with others. These two days are about starting over and about the things that need to be done in order for "starting over" to be effective and meaningful. They contain many lessons worth reflecting on, even if the shape of one's religious understanding is in a tradition other than Judaism.

At the heart of *Rosh Hashanah* is the call to look back and remember the original creative activity of God. The community is drawn back to the Genesis creation narrative in which a good God creates a good universe and places good people in it, with good instructions regarding how to be responsible for that created environment. Tragically, the people choose to go their own way into disobedience and take the good environment with them into their fallenness and estrangement. But God comes walking in the garden in the cool of the evening and calls the man and woman to accountability for their actions. While the consequences of their disobedience cannot be undone, it is possible, through God's grace, for their nakedness to be covered and for their lives to continue. There is a new beginning.

For thirty days prior to the Jewish New Year, the *shofar* is blown in the morning synagogue service as a call to attention, accountability, and contrition. The eerie, otherworldly blast of the ram's horn pierces the consciousness with its reminder that all humanity is called to stand before the God who created them and who sustains their being.

Rosh Hashanah is followed by the *Ten Days of Awe*. It is a time of personal and collective assessment in which people are challenged to examine their lives and conduct over the past year. They are called to identify mistakes and deliberate wrong choices that have been detrimental both to self and to others. The *Days of Awe* constitute a deliberate, honest, introspective look into the depths of one's own soul. They are a time for gazing directly into the mirror of conduct to see the genuine truth reflected back with unimpeded clarity.

At the close of this time of introspection comes *Yom Kippur*. Its roots reach back deeply into the original covenant between the ancient Hebrews and God. In ancient times on this one day, the high priest would enter the holy of holies in the temple at Jerusalem. Alone in that most sacred of places, he would vocalize the holy, unutterable name of God and pray for the remission of the people's sins. His hands would be placed on the head of a specially chosen animal, the scapegoat, and symbolically the people's sins would be transferred to the animal, which was then driven out into the wilderness to ritually die, bearing away past sins and guilt so the people could begin anew. Today the observance often involves the asking of pardon from those whom one has injured; and restitution for damages, if necessary, is made. The time of accounting is ended, the books are balanced, the ledger is wiped clean, and individuals and community, after having cleared away all obstacles to doing so, can begin all over again.

Obviously, those of us from a Christian background have taken these ritual observances from ancient Israel's past, and from contemporary Judaism's present, and reinterpreted them through the lens of what we believe God has accomplished in the sinless life, atoning death, and transforming resurrection of Jesus of Nazareth. It is not my intent to pit one of these religious expressions against the other. Instead, it is my intent to remind those of us who are Christian that our faith is deeply rooted in its Jewish heritage and in the thorough-going Jewishness of Jesus himself. Therefore, it is important that we not rip away what we owe to the past from its original context and meaning; doing so risks losing the fullness of the message it contains for us. Sometimes, we who are Christian forget that the God of our Lord and Savior Jesus Christ was also the God of Abraham and Sarah, Isaac and Rebekah, Jacob and Rachel; of David the king; and of Esther, the heroine of the Babylonian exile.

I have been known to observe that if you cut me, I bleed "Baptist." By this I mean that I am deeply immersed in the traditional Baptist affirmation of "the eternal security of the Christian believer," often expressed crudely, and not accurately, as "once saved, always saved." I stand in solidarity with Martin Luther's stirring Reformation call to "faith alone" and "grace alone" as the fountainhead of salvation. However, what I reject is the kind of lazy logic that has led many to conclude that some "profession of faith" in the distant past secures one in an enduring relationship to God while relieving one of any accountability for present-day living and conduct. I affirm that, at the moment we invite God to come into our lives and save us in and through Jesus Christ, our pre-"born again" past is atoned for in the shed blood of the Savior. But nowhere does the New Testament teach that we are not called to accountability before God for how we live our lives after this initial profession of faith. The writer of 1 John is talking to Christians, not to nonbelievers, when he says, "If we confess our sins, [God] is faithful and just to forgive us our sins, and to cleanse us from all unrighteousness. If we say that we have not sinned, we make [God] a liar, and [God's] word is not in us" (1 John

1:9-10). What I am prepared to question is if people who do not acknowledge their ongoing accountability to God for how they live have ever experienced God's saving grace in the first place. You and I are not saved because we say so; we are saved if we have authentically embraced the salvation made available through Jesus Christ.

Now, having said this, how can the Jewish observance of *Rosh Hashanah* and *Yom Kippur* be helpful to Christians seeking to express their faith in the contemporary world? First, we can be reminded of the importance of the public affirmation, and reaffirmation, of the central commitments of our lives. In May 1970, Peggy and I stood before our families and guests at the Green Acres Baptist Church in Birmingham, Alabama, and publicly committed ourselves, before God and those witnesses, in a relationship of husband and wife. Over more than five decades, on many Sundays closest to our wedding day, we have taken a moment to reaffirm those marriage vows in the presence of worshiping Christian communities. We do so not to show off or be piously sentimental; we do so because we understand there is something vital and renewing in publicly reaffirming the pledges we made to one another so long ago. Experience has demonstrated that it's good for us, and it's good for those who witness the renewal of our vows. We are both blessed, and our renewal blesses others as well.

Sadly, many Christians have never publicly reaffirmed their Christian experience since first making a profession of faith many decades ago. Don't misunderstand me here. I am not attempting to foster a worship environment where every time an invitation is given, everyone in the sanctuary comes trooping down the aisle in a sloppy display of sentimental emotionalism. What I am saying is that we ourselves, our friends and neighbors, and especially our children and grandchildren need the example of our unashamed reaffirmation of our covenant relationship with God and with God's people.

Second, we can be reminded of the importance of keeping our relationship to God up to date by careful introspective self-examination, where we hold ourselves accountable for our behavior. Too often our prayers for forgiveness fall into the category of generalized, unfocused petitions that "God will forgive us from all our sins of omission and commission, all our failures and shortcomings." While not bogging down in interminable lists of "big" sins and "little" sins, there is something to be said for deliberately acknowledging, "God, I lied. God, I deliberately did injury to another. God, my heart is filled with hate and envy. God, I have done and said things of which I am ashamed. God, *I am guilty.*" We do so not because God needs to be informed but because we need to look into the mirror of our conduct and see the unimpeded truth about ourselves. While we are strongly warned in the Bible about succumbing to the temptation to judge others (Rom 14:10-13), Paul pointed out to the Corinthian believers that if they would accept responsibility for appropriately judging themselves, they would not need to be judged by others (1 Cor 11:31).

Finally, the Days of Awe between Rosh Hashanah and Yom Kippur remind us that this is not just a matter between us and God; it is a matter between us and others as well. Jesus told his disciples, "if thou bring thy gift to the altar, and there rememberest that thy brother hath ought against thee; leave there thy gift before the altar, and go thy way; first be reconciled to thy brother, and then come and offer thy gift" (Matt 5:23-24).

Tragically, too many Christians, particularly American male Christians, believed John Wayne when he said, "Never apologize. It's a sign of weakness." Rarely have stupider words been uttered by an American movie screen idol. The only dumber ones I recall are the words, "Love means never having to say you're sorry." When you've got to make a choice between the gospel according to Hollywood screenwriters and the gospel according to Jesus Christ, choose Jesus Christ every time. The fact that we cannot fix everything we have messed up in the past does not mean we cannot fix some of the things we have messed up in the past. And the truth is that the sooner we acknowledge the injuries we have done to others, sincerely ask for forgiveness, and seek to make restitution when appropriate, the more likely the injury is to be overcome and reconciliation effected. It is in the denial of accountability for our injuries to others that we "sow the wind" and ultimately "reap the whirlwind."

Keeping our relationship to God and our relationships with others up to date are directly related. It is not possible to start fresh, either with God or with others, until we have appropriately dealt with and disposed of the accumulated garbage of a sinful past. People who don't bathe frequently stink, and those who don't haul off their trash regularly begin to wallow in the mire of their own filthiness. Surely I don't have to explain how this applies to regularly dealing with the sin in our lives so we can start fresh with God and others. Authentic Christians don't need to get saved all over again; but periodically we do need to clear out the trash of un-confessed sin and make things right with God and others so we can have a fresh beginning and move on into the blessings of the future. What better time to do so than in the *Days of Awe* between *Rosh Hashanah* and *Yom Kippur*?

Just 'Cause You're Thinkin' about You All the Time Don't Mean Everybody Else Is

The high school English and literature teacher had a point he wanted to make about human self-centeredness to his class of tenth graders, so he suggested an experiment. We were to pay attention to the next person, no matter who it happened to be, who walked through the classroom door that morning. We were not to say anything; we were instructed to simply cease whatever we were doing and look directly at the person.

About ten minutes later, a student office assistant entered the room with a message for the teacher from the principal. She was an attractive redhead, and I had been working up the nerve to ask her for a date for some time. When she walked through the door, everyone stopped and stared at her. The young woman's response was incredible. First, there was shock at the realization that everyone was looking at her. Second, she quickly looked up and down her garments to be sure everything was properly buttoned and zipped. Third, she reached for her always immaculately arranged hair to reassure herself that every strand was in place. Fourth, she looked pleadingly at the teacher for some guidance regarding what was happening. Finally, almost in tears she cried, "What's wrong? Why is *everybody* looking at me?"

At that point, laughter broke out in the room, and the teacher apologized for embarrassing her and explained the experiment. Only slightly mollified, the young woman delivered her message and quickly departed, shaken to the core of her being by the mixed emotions conjured in her mind over the space of less than thirty seconds. But the point had been made: because she spent a great deal of time thinking about herself, she assumed everyone else spent a great deal of time thinking about her as well. She was mistaken, and so are we when we become excessively preoccupied with ourselves. Just 'cause you're thinkin' about you all the time don't mean everybody else is.

As human beings, we are caught on the horns of a dilemma. It is important that we be sufficiently conscious of self so we can be cognizant of what is taking place around us. On the other hand, we don't need to be so self-absorbed that we are seduced by excessive egoism, paralyzed by neurotic fear, or brazenly insensitive to the needs and personhood of others. While it is impossible not to think about ourselves and about what others think about us, we need to guard against addictive preoccupation with ourselves and our personal concerns. Like all addictions, the pendulum of self-absorption continually swings between the extremes of artificially induced euphoria and equally artificially induced depression. Furthermore, like all addictions, self-absorption is ultimately destructive to health, meaningful relationships, the ability to achieve worthwhile objectives, and the respect and goodwill of those with whom we share life.

Excessive preoccupation with self is dangerous for a number of reasons. First, it tends to make us overly sensitive to what we perceive to be the slights or malfeasances of others. Many years ago, I approached the door of the church building where I was pastor and engaged in a few minutes of casual conversation with two of the church's laymen, prior to a midweek prayer service. Not wanting to be late, I glanced down at my wristwatch, noted it was about five minutes before time to begin, and observed, "Well, it's about time for me to go to work." With these words I made my way to the sanctuary for prayer meeting, leaving the two men to join the boys' group they worked with on Wednesday evenings.

At the end of the prayer meeting, I left the sanctuary to take my Bible back to the pastor's study. Waiting outside the door was one of the men I had been chatting with earlier, and he was visibly upset. Before I could ask what was wrong, he shoved his wristwatch in front of my face and shouted, "I own a watch, and I can tell time. I don't need you to tell me when it's time for me to do my job here at church." Needless to say, I was dumbfounded. My casual remark forty-five minutes earlier had nothing to do with any sense that I thought he needed reminding to do his job as a volunteer youth leader. I was simply observing that it was time for me to get on to prayer meeting. I apologized profusely for offending him, but he was having none of it. He was mad, and he intended to stay mad. To this day, I have no idea what set him off that night, but I seriously doubt it had anything to do with my casual glance at my watch, followed by the observation, "It's about time for me to go to work." It was a classic case of his misassumption that because he was thinking about himself, I must have been thinking about him as well. I wasn't. He was simply mistaken, and he elected to take offense at something that was not offensive. And then egoistic pride kept him from being able to acknowledge his overreaction. How sad.

Sometimes preoccupation with self leads us to magnify the proportion of our difficult experiences. Undoubtedly terrible, difficult things happen to us; and for some, those things that happen are profoundly tragic. But the difficulty is only compounded when we allow self-absorption to so cloud our vision that we fail to see that others are struggling with the difficulties of life as surely as we are. Do not hear me minimizing or casually dismissing your suffering. All I am saying is that illness, family stress, the untimely death of a loved one, financial difficulty, and spiritual emptiness from time to time are the common lot of humanity. It does no one any good when we relate in ways that suggest we think our pain is sharper, our struggle is more arduous, our suffering is more profound than that of others in similar circumstances. While it is important that I not make too little of your woundedness, it is equally important that you not make too much of it. The excessively self-absorbed fail to take note of the fact that all of us are wounded.

Akin to the above is the truth that if we spend all our time thinking about ourselves, we never have time or opportunity to think about the needs of others. The English materialist philosopher, Thomas Hobbes, argued that all human beings are, by nature, exclusively self-centered; that we are totally self-absorbed in the gratification of our desires and the avoidance of our aversions. This led him to surmise that it was humankind's realization that if everyone single-mindedly pursued the gratification of their own desires, to the exclusion of all others, we would eventually annihilate ourselves. For Hobbes, this is the foundation of all human covenants, or social contracts. We cooperate in such arrangements, i.e., marriages, business partnerships, societies, governments, etc., because we perceive it is in our self-interest to do so.

May God's grace deliver us from such a negative understanding of human existence! We are better guided by Dietrich Bonhoeffer, who was martyred for his Christian faith near the close of World War II. In an outline for a book Bonhoeffer was planning before his execution, we can read what he intended to explore: "The real meaning of Christian faith." In his annotated outline, Bonhoeffer observed, "The experience that a transformation of all human life is given in the fact that 'Jesus is there only for others.'"[1] Bonhoeffer understood that the only true example of authentic human nature that has ever strode the earth was/is Jesus of Nazareth, the quintessential "man for others." The problem with the thought of Thomas Hobbes, and of ourselves, is that we tend to look at human nature through the lens of human fallenness and sin and conclude that this is our natural, normal state. This is not true. Our fallen sinfulness is not normal; it is subnormal. Human nature as exemplified in Jesus of Nazareth is normal. Our problem is that we have considered subnormal to be normal for so long that, when we encounter the authentically normal, we consider it to be extraordinary.

Once we grasp the reality that our identity with Jesus, the "Man for Others," is a call for each of us to live as "Persons for Others" as well, we find the grace to move away from our personal self-absorption and focus our attention on those with whom we share life, both near and far away. In *Leviathan*, Thomas Hobbes may have been describing human existence as it "is," but he missed altogether

---

1. Bonhoeffer, Letters and Papers from Prison, 380–81.

the biblical message of how it "should" and "can" be. Self-absorption to the exclusion of consideration for others is not a "state of being"; it is the consequence of a deliberate choice. And one indication that we have made the wrong choice is seen in our assumption that "just 'cause we're thinkin' about ourselves all the time, we think everybody else is thinkin' about us too."

Finally, the greatest danger in preoccupation with self is that, because self-absorption is a kind of self-idolatry, it stands between the individual and a right relationship with God. The problem is one of confusion of language. Often we assume that "denial of self" and "self-denial" are the same thing; they are not. "Denial of self" is not the withholding of things from one's self; "denial of self" is the abandonment of the idolatrous assumption that one is the center of reality. Jesus said, "If any man will come after me, let him deny himself, and take up his cross, and follow me" (Matt 16:24). This is "denial of self," the deliberate submission of one's personhood and existence to the will and purpose of God in order to participate in God's redemptive activity in the world. "Denial of self," after the model of Jesus who "made himself of no reputation, and took upon him the form of a servant . . . and became obedient unto death, even the death of the cross" (Phil 2:7-8), leads directly into participation with him in being people whose foremost thought is of others, not self.

"Self-denial" is something else altogether, amounting to no more than the sublimation of the human appetite for food, sexual gratification, the accumulation of wealth, or the exercise of power in ways that benefit us. Often the greatest expressions of human egoism and self-absorption are found in the practices of self-denial. An ascetic can be an egotist. A great humanitarian can be an egotist. A generous philanthropist can be an egotist. The Pharisees of Jesus's day were world renowned for fasting, strict religious observance, and almsgiving. Jesus said that their acts of "self-denial" were done simply for the ego gratification of being seen and admired by others (Matt 6:1ff).

Such acts, performed not for the glory of God but for the glorification of self, are the most blatant expressions of self-idolatry. They are the actions of people who are thinking about themselves all the time and who deliberately engage in behavior designed to cause others to think about them as well. Simon Peter encountered such a self-absorbed individual in the person of Simon the Sorcerer, who sought to purchase the power of the Holy Spirit for his own ego gratification (Acts 8). Simon Peter strongly rejected the other Simon's proposal with the assertion, "thy heart is not right in the sight of God" (Acts 8:21).

There are few challenges in human existence more formidable than this one. But, if we are to live happy, healthy, productive lives that eschew self-absorption on the one hand and, on the other hand, are to be truly deserving of the respect and goodwill of others, we must learn one of life's most important lessons: just 'cause you're thinkin' about you all the time don't mean everybody else is. And if you find yourself "thinkin' about you all the time," you should carefully consider how perilously you are endangering your own self-understanding, your most meaningful relationships with others, and your relationship to God.

To Be Announced

The first time I saw the abbreviation "TBA" was in 1967 as an entering freshman at the University of Alabama. On the registration schedule were a number of places where "TBA" was substituted for a class time, room number, or instructor's name. When I asked an older and much wiser sophomore, she looked at me with haughty disdain and said, "It means 'To Be Announced.'" As she strode away, muttering something under her breath about dumb freshmen, I wondered how one could make a decision about enrolling in a class if one did not know the time it would meet, where it would meet, or who was teaching it. Finally, it occurred to me that, while those matters were not unimportant, what was most significant was the question, "Is it essential that I be in this class?" If it was essential that I enroll, I would have to adjust the other aspects of my life to fit in with the "TBA" when the announcement was made.

Most of us don't like not knowing all the details about stuff we're involved in or think concern us. Without doubt, I am a charter member of the curiosity club, and I keep my dues paid up. Occasionally someone will quote to me the old saw, "Curiosity killed the cat." And I will shoot back the equally old retort, "Satisfaction brought him back." But there is another abbreviation I've become acquainted with as well: "LTA." It means "Learn to Adjust." I began to become a happier person as I accepted the reality that much of the stuff that really matters is TBA, so, whether I like it or not, I might as well LTA.

For many within the Christian community, Acts 1:6-7 is not a favorite passage. After a period of forty days with the disciples following his resurrection, Jesus led them apart and was about to ascend from their presence. Burning with curiosity and feeling that after all they had been through, surely they had the right to know, the disciples asked, "Lord, will you at this time restore again the kingdom of Israel?" (Acts 1:6). It isn't hard to imagine their disappointment and chagrin when Jesus replied, "It is not for you to know the times or the seasons, which the Father hath put in his own power" (Acts 1:7). Then he moved on to tell them their primary responsibility was to wait on the movement of the Spirit of God and then faithfully witness to Jesus and his saving power (Acts 1:8). Essentially, what Jesus said was, "Fellas, that's TBA, and you need to LTA. Meanwhile, I have a task for you to do."

Such an event raises the question of why Jesus would deny information to his followers that concerned them so greatly, both then and now. Why should we have to learn to adjust to the reality that there is much about God's unfolding purposes in the world that remain to be announced? After all, we have inquiring minds, and inquiring minds want to know! Perhaps the answer is to be found in the question. Our own appetite to know leads us to fill in the blanks in our knowledge with speculation on what might or might not be true. Unfortunately, because we find some of our speculation highly attractive, it is easy to conclude that since it is so attractive, it must be true. At that point we substitute our personal and collective wishful thinking for theological truth. Then, with frequent repetition, we subsequently conclude that the Bible must definitively teach what, at an earlier time, we were only speculating about. At that point our speculations become dogmatic assertions, and anyone who doesn't see things the way we do must be wrong, because we couldn't possibly be.

When we examine the Scripture carefully, we discover there are a number of reasons why God, in God's providential purpose, withholds from us information or understanding that we would like to have. Sometimes the answer is that the time is not right. When Simon Peter questioned the Lord about some of his actions, Jesus replied, "What I do thou knowest not now; but thou shalt know hereafter" (John 13:7). Sometimes, in our preoccupation with the passage of time, we lose sight of the rightness or appropriateness of time. Paul made use of the phrase "the fullness of time" (Gal 4:4; Eph 1:10) to emphasize God's disclosure of God's purposes in God's own good time.

Second, often we are not ready to receive the information we would like to have. With great tenderness Jesus told his disciples, "I have yet many things to say unto you, but ye cannot hear them now" (John 16:12). I remember my eagerness to study the biblical languages as a young seminarian. And I remember my frustration and disappointment when I discovered it would take years of disciplined study before I came to a point where I could read the Hebrew or Greek text with the same ease that I read the morning newspaper. First, I had to learn to parse nouns, conjugate verbs, decipher tenses, and memorize vocabulary. Then, I began the practice of translating simple, straightforward verses. Only after much more disciplined study was I ready to take on more complex passages. Regardless of the sincerity of our eagerness, sometimes much work and much time must pass before we are ready to receive with understanding that which we desire. And even now, while I may be more adept in the biblical languages than many, I'm not nearly as good as the ones who are really good at them.

This leads to a third observation. All of us ultimately come up against the limitations of our humanity. While it is possible for us to "get" some of it, none of us "get it all." Paul attempted to help the Corinthian believers keep this in perspective by saying, "now we see through a glass, darkly; but then face to face: now I know in part; but then shall I know even as also I am known" (1 Cor 13:12). A word of caution is needed. Accepting that our humanity limits our capacity to understand is not an excuse for sloppy, slovenly ignorance. The fact that we can't understand everything does not mean we cannot understand some things. By the use of our capacity to reason, the humility of prayer, and the patience to grow, we can polish the mirror of our understanding so that we see more clearly today than we did yesterday.

Next, sometimes we forget that the Divine plan for the universe is an unfolding reality. The writer of Ephesians pointed out to his readers this truth in the observation, "that by revelation he made known unto me the mystery . . . which in other ages was not made known unto the sons of men, as it is now revealed unto his holy apostles and prophets by the Spirit" (Eph 3:3, 5). Do you recall the wonderful story in Exodus where Moses said to God, "I beseech thee, shew me thy glory" (Exod 33:18)? God gently, lovingly told this servant that he was not able to bear the fullness of God's revelation. God would hide Moses in the cleft of the rock, be veiled from Moses's eyes, and reveal only as much of God's self as Moses was able to bear at that time (Exod 33:22-23). The Bible, both Old Testament and New Testament, makes use of phrases such as "it shall come to pass" and "in the fullness of time" to indicate the unfolding nature of the Divine plan and purpose for all of creation. One of the things I love about living in the North Carolina mountains is the beautiful views they present as I travel through them. But I never see all the mountain vistas at the same time. I must cross and experience the wonder of the nearest ridge before I behold the grandeur of the next one.

Finally, the Bible teaches that God has more in store for us than we can possibly imagine. Listen to the wonder and anticipation in the words of the writer of 1 John as he says, "Beloved, now are we the sons of God, and it doth not yet appear what we shall be: but we know that when he shall appear, we shall be like him; for we shall see him as he is" (1 John 3:2). Can't you just hear this wonderful old sage saying, "I don't know all that God ultimately has in store for you and me, but I know that whatever it is, it's going to be wonderful." He would have loved the songwriter's words:

> Trials dark on every hand, and we cannot understand,
> All the ways that God would lead us to that blessed promised land;
> But He'll guide us with His eye, and we'll follow till we die;
> We will understand it better by and by.[1]

The writer of 1 John seemed to have no difficulty with the reality that some things in God's economy were "to be announced." Not only had he "learned to adjust," but he seems to have found joy and peace in patiently waiting for whatever God has in store.

---

1. "When the Morning Comes," *Baptist Hymnal*, 1956, #473.

At this point in my life, I have "learned to adjust" to the reality that there are a number of things "to be announced," and I am content to patiently wait until the announcements are made. I can wait for the sounding of the trumpet of God that announces the end of human history as we know it. It's not that I don't believe it's going to happen. I take Paul's assertion that "the Lord himself shall descend from heaven with a shout, with the voice of the archangel, and with the trump of God" (1 Thess 4:16) at face value. But I also listen when he says, "But of the times and the seasons, brethren, ye have no need that I write unto you, for yourselves know perfectly that the day of the Lord so cometh as a thief in the night" (1 Thess 5:2). There are a great many who need to LTA to the reality that the exact details of the second coming remain TBA. Meanwhile, Christians have a Great Commission that should occupy our time, energy, and resources.

I can also wait to find out who ends up being cast into the "lake of fire" so frequently mentioned in Revelation 19 and 20. I find no place in Scripture indicating that God needs my help in determining who is going to heaven and who is going to hell. While there are many things God has invited you and me to share with God, many need to learn to adjust to the reality that God has reserved the determination of the ultimate destiny of all human beings to God's self alone. For those of you who are frantically looking for the passage where Jesus said, "ye shall know them by their fruits," it is found in Matthew 7:16, 20. There, Jesus is speaking regarding the identification of false prophets, not the determination of who is going to be saved and who is going to be condemned. Do not hear me suggesting that Christian evangelistic efforts are unnecessary. All I am saying is that my calling and yours is to faithfully bear witness to the good news of Jesus Christ in the power of the Holy Spirit and leave the results up to God. The self-righteous "fruit checkers" of the world remind me of people with whom I have played golf, who spent more time keeping up with my score than they did their own. I don't play with them anymore.

I can also wait until the announcement is made regarding the rewards God has in store for me when I get to heaven. The only thing that matters to me is hearing the words, "well done, thou good and faithful servant . . . enter thou into the joy of thy lord" (Matt 25:21).

A fourth thing I can wait for is the discovery of whether the premillennial dispensationalists, and various others who talk as though God has put them on the program and arrangements committee for the second coming, are right in their pronouncements regarding when concepts like the rapture and the great tribulation will take place, who the antichrist is going to be, and what constitutes the great whore of Babylon. I haven't always been this way. In my early twenties, I preached a series of sermons through the book of Revelation that would have led many to wonder if God whispered into my ear things God wasn't telling anyone else. I have kept those sermon notes, though I wouldn't dream of preaching them again. I look at them once in a while to keep myself reminded that even the sincerest people are capable of drivel when they "think more highly of themselves than they ought to think" (Rom 12:3). It's not that I don't care; it's that I see little to be accomplished in spending vast amounts of time pontificating on matters over which I have no influence. It seems to me that all that "stuff" is TBA, and I have LTA.

Lastly, I can wait to discover if I was right all the time. When the time comes, I'm willing to stand before the judgment seat of God and humbly say, "Sorry, Lord. I thought I was doing the best I could with what I had to work with. And from time to time, I blew it. Please forgive me."

The Beach Is a Wonderful Place if You Don't Mind Getting Sand in Your Diaper

Let's face it: there are no toddlers who aren't cute; some are cuter than others, and some are downright adorable. I saw one of the latter while strolling the beach at Panama City. My guess is that he was about eighteen months to two years old, and he and his grandmother were having a grand time digging in the sand on a sunny December morning. The little guy, dressed only in a T-shirt and a toddler-sized disposable diaper, made use of a plastic shovel and pail to excavate a sizeable hole in the damp sand. He romped and played between the surf and the dry sand, chasing sandpipers and giving his grandmother a thorough workout as she panted along the beach trying to keep up with him. Over the space of the half-hour I devoted to watching him, he wallowed in and out of the hole he had dug until damp sand clung to his hair, his arms and torso, his feet and legs. And while I made no attempt at close inspection, without doubt, a fair amount of the sand made its way inside the disposable diaper he wore as well. While watching his gleeful celebration of beach and sunshine and innocence, I found myself thinking, "The beach is a wonderful place if you don't mind getting a little sand in your diaper."

The little boy reminded me of two other little boys I knew many years ago. One was my youngest son who, at the time, was not quite kindergarten age. The other was the son of a couple in the church about the same age as Peggy and me. The adults had become close friends; we socialized together a great deal, and our sons frequently visited with one another. Tim was our second child, about six years younger than his older brother, and Peggy and I had had ample time to discover how durable most little boys are. However, his playmate was an only child, and his parents tended to be somewhat more protective of him than we were of Don and Tim. His mother was an immaculate housekeeper, and when we took Tim over to play, it was evident that toys had been sanitized prior to his arrival and would probably be sanitized again after his departure. The lady never suspected the existence of a germ, a bacterium, or a virus she did not wish to kill.

One Saturday we were asked if their son could spend the day with Tim while his mom and dad did some shopping. They dropped him off shortly after breakfast, and it was almost sundown before they returned. In the intervening hours, both boys spent most of that summer day outside. By the end of the day, both were in great need of a bath. Unfortunately, the boy's parents arrived before Peggy had time to get the boys in the tub to wash off some of the accumulated grim of a hard day of play. They pulled into the driveway and found us all sipping Kool-Aid under the shade of one of the silverleaf maples in our front yard. It was all I could do to restrain my amusement as our friend looked her thoroughly grimy little boy up and down for several seconds. She noted the necklaces of dust and perspiration around his neck and the smudge of leftover peanut butter that remained from his hurriedly eaten mid-afternoon snack. Her nose wrinkled at the scent of mint that clung to his body. Most recently, the boys had been wallowing in a bed of mint that grew on the terrace below our deck. Some of the leaves still clung to their hair and T-shirts. Finally, she ruefully observed, "I don't think he's ever been that dirty before."

A short time later, the mom and dad gathered up their son, thanked us for looking after him that day, and departed in the darkness. I would have paid good money to have overheard the conversation that surely transpired as they drove homeward. Without doubt, the boy was sleeping the sleep of exhausted contentment by the time they reached home. And while his mom was sure she had never seen him as dirty as she found him that evening, I was sure I had never seen him happier than he was that day. And no, you're wrong: it wasn't a long time before the boy was permitted to spend another day in the unsupervised care of the Greggs. You see, he didn't come down with some dread disease as the consequence of being allowed to have a great time getting thoroughly dirty one pleasant summer day. And it was so evident to his mom and dad that he had had the time of his life that day that soon the boys were taking turns spending the entire weekend at one another's homes.

Now, let's go back to the little guy playing in the sand at Panama City Beach. As I made my way down the shoreline, I began to think about how many people I've met across the years who have denied themselves much of life's joy because they, figuratively, refused to risk getting a little sand in their diapers along the way. I'm not suggesting the little guy I watched that day enjoyed having sand in his diaper; all I'm suggesting is that the joy of playing in the sand in the company of a person he loved, and who loved him, more than made up for the discomfort occasioned by a little sand. Lots of people have much to learn from that little boy, and more than a few of them are devoutly religious people who need to learn that "church is a wonderful place, too, if you don't mind getting a little sand in your diaper."

I'm astounded at the number of people, both inside and outside the church, who have completely unrealistic expectations of a Christian community of faith. They have convinced themselves that it must be idyllically perfect all the time, and the slightest manifestation of human imperfection sends them spiraling into disappointment, disillusionment, and rejection. The first hint that a little of the sand of human imperfection has crept into their diapers sends them scurrying off the beach of Christian fellowship, many vowing never to return.

There are no perfect churches as surely as there are no perfect days at the beach; some are just better than others at certain times and places. The December day when I watched the little boy and his grandmother was far from a perfect day. Though the sun was shining, the air was chilly enough for a light sweater or heavy shirt. The wind was strong enough that signal flags snapped in the breeze, warning swimmers of the danger of wading too far into the roiling surf. Before noon a storm blew ashore with pelting rain that drove everyone to take cover. The genius of the little boy was that he understood it wasn't necessary to have a perfect day at the beach in order to have a good time while there. All that was necessary was that he use well the opportunity the less-than-perfect day afforded him. So, under the watchful eye of his grandmother, he refused to permit the chill of the air, the approaching storm, and the grit in his diaper to rob him of a chance to thoroughly enjoy himself.

Perhaps you are reading while remembering some disappointment, some disillusionment that happened in your life that now keeps you from sharing together in the worship and ministry of a Christian community. Someone said or did something that injured or disappointed you. You found that it's not always exciting and beautiful at church; sometimes it's thoroughly dull and mundane. Changes took place that made you uncomfortable, or with which you did not agree, and you chose to absent yourself instead of adjusting to new circumstances. Other people, sometimes deliberately and sometimes inadvertently, messed up something you had invested much time and energy in, and you have elected to harbor a grudge instead of forgiving and moving on. One way or another you got a little personal, theological, relational, or institutional sand in your diaper, and you decided if you couldn't have a beach without sand, you just wouldn't go to the beach anymore. I wish to make the gritty sand even more uncomfortable by saying, "That's a pathetically sad way to deliberately choose to live your life when you don't have to."

Perhaps some of you are thinking, "For a man who lives in the mountains, he sure is fascinated with the beach." The truth is that I'm fascinated by both the mountains and the seashore, and for the same reasons. To enjoy them fully one must take both mountain and shore as one finds them. In the mountains there are splendid vistas, babbling brooks, cascading waterfalls, and mysterious shadows. There are also dramatically changing seasons, flash floods, rockslides, and rattlesnakes. On the coast there is the rhythmic music of the tide, the sunrise on a misty, distant horizon, scudding clouds and circling gulls, and glistening white sand. There are also hurricanes, enervating heat, beaches often stained by the effluvia of oil spills, and sharks.

One must also take the Christian community of faith as one finds it. There one will find profound spirituality, nobility of spirit, generous selflessness, and godly acceptance and grace. One will also find crass sinfulness, meanspirited spitefulness, grasping greed, and bigoted prejudice and rejection. In the church one always finds people who are considerably less than they are capable of being, and one always finds people who are infinitely more than they used to be. The Christian community, in all its manifestations, is always between the "already" of the experience of God's redemptive grace in Jesus Christ and the "not yet" of fully orbed Christ-likeness. Therefore, one must always be prepared to experience the best, the worst, and everything in between. Those who insist that a church must always be the best all the time are as naïve as those who assume they will find perfect conditions every time they go to the beach or visit the mountains. It just ain't gonna happen. And that's not automatically a bad thing.

During the years the boys mentioned above were best friends, our friend's son was sick more often than Tim; he was more susceptible to whatever "bugs" other children he came in contact with were carrying. The reason, I suspect, was that his system lacked the opportunity to build up the antibodies necessary to ward off various childhood infections. Conversely, Tim's mother understood that to have a healthy, clean home did not require spotless cleanliness all the time. Therefore, his body developed more natural resistance to the "bugs" of others.

While analogies are never perfect, they are quite useful in helping us understand how to relate to the world in which we live. Genuinely healthy Christians this side of heaven live somewhere between the ideal of Christ-like perfection and the dissoluteness of unrestrained depravity. All of us are somewhere along the continuum between "as good as we are meant to be" and "as bad as we are capable of being." This business of "being in the world, but not of the world" requires that we have enough contact with the world to develop the resistance necessary to ward off corrupting infections that would destroy us. It also requires that we continually remain focused on a loving God's ultimate intention for us and that we strive daily to be more and more the people God has always intended us to be.

Under the benevolently watchful eye of the God who created us and is redeeming us in and through Jesus Christ, we are called to find joy in living, even when our circumstances are not always perfect. The truth is that we can't make it through life without getting some sand in our diapers; but we should never permit the sand in our diapers to prevent us from having a wonderful day at the beach—or a wonderful life in the company of our fellow Christians. So why don't you stop insisting on perfection and join the rest of God's children in enjoying the goodness of each day we are given in the blessed, though less than perfect, company of one another? Both the beach and the church are wonderful places if you don't mind getting a little sand in your diaper.

Larry, You're Gonna Miss the Mandevilla This Year, and It's Nobody's Fault but Your Own

One of my favorite things about the acre and a quarter Peggy and I live on in Shingle Hollow is the diverse abundance of flowering plants and trees that grow on the property. With the first rays of springtime sunshine, brash yellow jonquils leap from the ground to joyfully proclaim the end of winter. A few weeks later, the dogwood and forsythia blossom with their characteristic white crosses and yellow bells. Soon they are joined by the riotously profuse blossoms of the azaleas planted in clusters behind the house. Following closely on their heels, our single rhododendron, a wedding anniversary gift from a church I served in the area many years ago, reminds us that May has come once again. Soon the time comes for the tall, stately poplar trees to blossom in peach-pink and yellow, while spring breezes waft the wispy "helicopter" seeds of the maple trees through the air and into the gutters and downspouts on the house.

By this time, the massive redbud that grows out beside the old swimming pool is tinged with burgundy-colored new foliage. Meanwhile, tightly compacted rosebuds have opened their petals of red and pink and white. In mid-summer, the ivory puffs of the snowball plant bounce up and down in the rain showers. Later the tall crepe myrtles blossom at the tips of long boa-constrictor-looking trunks and then dust the ground with mauve snowflakes. Meanwhile, mandevilla, after spending all summer winding their vines around fences and climbing strings that lead upward to the eaves of the house, open up in glorious pink flowers. Then there comes the multihued pallet of fall leaves as first the poplars and sweetgums and finally the maples show off for us once again. Last, the stubborn camellias insist on exposing their delicate, easily wounded blossoms to the cold and snow of wintertime.

I love it all, but I am particularly partial to the mandevilla with its slithering vines, broad forest-green leaves, and saucy, impertinent pink flowers. But this year, for the most part, Larry and Peggy are going to miss the mandevilla, and it's nobody's fault but my own.

Much of what is planted around our house requires almost no direct attention from me. Obviously, the poplar, dogwood, maple, redbud, and crepe myrtles pretty much tend to themselves. The azaleas, camellias, rhododendron, and forsythia are not particularly demanding. Only the roses require deliberate care and feeding. But the mandevilla is altogether different.

Because it is a tropical plant, the mandevilla cannot handle the cold and occasional snow of western North Carolina. Therefore, every fall I take them in and prune away all the vines down to gnarled stubs barely sticking out of their pots. Then I place them in a dark, dry corner of my workshop and leave them there for the winter. As spring draws near, I begin to water them a bit and move them near a window to wake them up and stimulate the development of new foliage. When the weather is warm enough, I take the pots outdoors, place them in our favorite locations, run the strings I want the vines to climb, and water and feed them regularly while waiting for them to begin to bloom in August and September.

This year, because of a number of things taking place in our lives, we were well into June before I took the time to get the mandevilla outside in the sunshine. Now we are in September; their usually lush and abundant vines are stunted, and they have only barely begun to blossom. While we will see some blooms, the chill of October will prevent us from enjoying the mandevilla nearly as much this season as we have in years past. And again, I say it's nobody's fault but my own. I knew what needed to be done, I knew how to do it, I knew when to do it, and I knew if I didn't do it no one else would. Still, I tarried over long, and even though I knew better, I didn't do better.

By now some of you are wondering, "Does he have a point in all this whining about his mandevilla?" Indeed I do! My point is that there is a direct connection between how we do the things we do and the quality of the results we get from doing them. Your response may be, "Boy, he really has a gift for saying the obvious!" I know I'm not saying anything original. What I am doing is wrestling with the evident fact that many people apparently do not comprehend the logical connection between their actions and the consequences of those actions. Therefore, when something inconvenient, troubling, or disastrous takes place in their lives, they look around for something or someone to blame instead of acknowledging the truth that frequently it's "nobody's fault but their own."

This failure to perceive the causal connection between actions, or the failure to act, and their consequences manifests itself in a number of ways. One way is that we know what we should do; we just don't do it. Another is that we do what we should, but we don't do it in a timely fashion. A third is that we know how to do things the right way, but we insist on doing them the wrong way anyhow. A fourth is that we depend on others to do for us what we can only do for ourselves. A fifth is that we attribute the problems and difficulties in our lives to the failure of others to act properly, while we take the credit ourselves when everything is going well.

I presume by now you have gotten my drift. With amazing speed and variety, human beings can spin out a list of reasons that they should not be held accountable for the consequences of their actions. Shifting responsibility away from ourselves is not just something we're good at; it's something we are really, really good at! Undoubtedly there are physical, social, cultural, economic, educational, geographical, and psychological factors that place constraints upon us all. Because we like the sound of the statement "Anybody can do anything he/she really wants to do," we often ignore the reality that this statement is not true. I maintain that "anybody *cannot* do anything he/she really wants to do," but most of us can do a good deal more than we do. The fact that we are limited does not absolve us of responsibility for the consequences of our decisions and actions. Even Jimmy Buffett's old boy "wasting away in Margaritaville" understands, according to the lyrics of the song, "it's [his] own damn fault."

One of the saddest consequences of the way the message of God's saving grace in Jesus Christ has been proclaimed in modern times is that many have concluded that "knowing Jesus" absolves one of all responsibility for one's life and conduct. A shallow interpretation of Martin Luther's recovery of the Pauline principle "for by grace are ye saved through faith; and that not of yourselves; it is the gift of God; not of works . . ." (Eph 2:8-9) has led to the conclusion by many that everything in the Christian's life is "all of God and none of me." Thus, they have ignored the equally Pauline assertion that we are to "work out [our] own salvation with fear and trembling" (Phil 2:12). Both Paul and Luther understood that the authentic relationship between grace and works is one in which we trust God to do for us what only God can do while accepting responsibility, under God, for doing for ourselves what God expects us to do.

There is a great need for many contemporary Christians to cease using their so-called "faith in God" as an excuse for not living responsible, productive lives. The biblical writers understood the direct connection between authentic "belief" and appropriate "behavior." The writer of 1 John asserted, in relation to our authentic knowledge of God, "hereby do we know that we know him, if we keep his commandments" (1 John 2:3). It was this author's conviction that "he that saith, I know him [God], and keepeth not his [God's] commandments, is a liar, and the truth is not in him" (2:4). When he examined our relationships to others, his conclusion was similar. He said, "he that hateth his brother is in darkness" (2:11). Again, these are the biblical writer's words, not mine: "If a man say, I love God, and hateth his brother, he is a liar . . ." (4:20). His conclusions regarding our moral/ethical conduct in the world follow the same logical progression: "Love not the world, neither the things that are in the world. If any man love the world, the love of the Father is not in him. For all that is in the world, the lust of the flesh, and the lust of the eyes, and the pride of life, is not of the Father, but is of the world" (2:15-16). Clearly, the writer of 1 John knew absolutely nothing about a Christian faith that absolved one of responsibility for the consequences of one's conduct and decision-making.

In my introduction to ethics classes, the students and I discuss the term "culpability," a word used to indicate the degree of a person's moral responsibility for their actions. Many use the Latin term *mea culpa*, commonly understood to mean "my fault," when they make a mistake or error in judgment. The problem with this popular usage of the term *mea culpa* is that it is only half right. While it means "I am the one who is at fault or to blame," it also means "I am the one who is responsible." Too many in today's world are willing to readily acknowledge their "fault" or "blameworthiness" for the circumstances of their lives while, at the same time, seeking to shift responsibility onto others. To say "it's my fault" and "it's not my responsibility" at the same time is an oxymoron, a contradiction in terms. That's why both I and the "old boy" in Margaritaville need to clean up our act and acknowledge that the reason it's our fault is that we failed in our respective responsibilities.

Perhaps you're wondering why I'm making such a big deal of this. The purpose is not that we wallow in our fault and blameworthiness; it is the truth that until we accept appropriate responsibility for ourselves, we are not likely to take the steps necessary to fix the problems we have created. As long as we project responsibility for our circumstances outside ourselves, i.e., onto those around us, our environment, our hereditary characteristics, our upbringing, our economic circumstances, or how we were treated as children, we are not likely to acknowledge that such factors, both positive and negative, are part and parcel of everyone's life. Indeed, it is true that "I am a part of all that I have met," but it is not true that "all I have met is all that I am." I was taught as a child, and I have learned from subsequent reflection and experience, that the first step toward solving the problems of my life is owning the truth that they are "my" problems. They do not belong to someone else, and if I do not actively assume responsibility for them and take proactive steps toward dealing with them, the negative consequences that follow are nobody's fault but my own.

What is the implication of such thinking for Christian behavior and conduct? Essentially, it is that based on the clear content of the New Testament document we call 1 John, I maintain that while it may be possible for one who is not a Christian to live as though they are, it is not possible, under ordinary circumstances, for an authentic Christian to live as though they are not. By this I mean that Christians do not have a corner on morality, integrity, behavioral discipline, and various other qualities associated with Christian living. There is great similarity between the ethical values espoused by the Apostle Paul in the New Testament and those found in the philosophical Stoicism of his day. It is possible to be a "good" person without being a "Christian" person.

However, the Bible is clear in its assertion that the reverse is not true. It is not possible to be a "Christian" person without actively striving to be a "good" person. The New Testament writers know nothing of authentic Christian people who do not accept responsibility for their lives, their decisions, their actions, and their relationships. This means, as tough as it is to hear, that if you claim Christian identity and you have made a royal shambles of your life, it's nobody's fault but your own. Your brokenness is self-inflicted. And the solution, by God's grace, is found in owning responsibility for living your life. Others can help, others will help, others want to help, but no one else can do it for you.

If There Weren't Writers Who Aren't as Good as Shelby Foote, There Wouldn't Be Any Shelby Footes

Many of my friends are amused, and some are annoyed, by my obsessive interest in various topics and pursuits. For many decades, one of my passions has been the study of the American Civil War, its politics, its personalities, its battles, and its consequences. This endeavor has led to extended visits to places such as Ft. Sumter, South Carolina; Manassas Junction, Virginia; Antietam Creek, Maryland; Perryville, Kentucky; Gettysburg, Pennsylvania; Petersburg, Virginia; Vicksburg, Mississippi; and Appomattox Court House, Virginia. A number of years ago my wife told me that if I took her to one more battlefield, she and I were going to have a war.

Innumerable hours have been devoted to reading the literature of the war from both primary and secondary sources. And my personal library contains dozens of volumes—some I have collected myself, some I received as gifts—and among the most treasured are those from the private collection of a dear friend who died a number of years ago.

Among civil war authors, I have found some of the finest writers I have ever read. Many are familiar names to those who are interested in the war, and their books are classic examples of outstanding research combined with fine narrative style. Numbered among them are James M. McPherson, who wrote *Battle Cry of Freedom*;

Stephen W. Sears, author of *Landscape Turned Red: The Battle of Antietam*; Michael Shaara, who wrote *The Killer Angels*; and Bruce Catton, whose works are numbered by the Book of the Month Club as "essential classics of the Civil War."

But beyond doubt, Mississippi-born and North Carolina-educated Shelby Foote was the finest writer of civil war history in the twentieth century. When he died, all students of the war mourned the loss of an outstanding intellect and one of America's preeminent historians. When Foote's *The Civil War, A Narrative* was first published, *Newsweek* asserted, "to read this chronicle is an awesome and moving experience. History and literature are rarely so thoroughly combined as here . . . ."[1] Truly, Shelby Foote was a great historian and a great writer. But, though this is true, why am I taking the time to devote so much attention to his talent and skill? The answer is that I wish to observe, "If there weren't any writers who aren't as good as Shelby Foote, there wouldn't be any Shelby Footes."

Now let's get to what's on my mind. Contemporary American culture, including American religious culture, is obsessed with the idolization of the most outstanding examples of achievement in sports, politics, business, entertainment, and even religious leadership. The result is a pervasive attitude that suggests that if you don't win the Super Bowl you're a loser; if you are not as economically successful as Elon Musk, Steve Jobs, Bill Gates, or Martha Stewart, you're a financial failure, etc. You know the litany of glib phrases used to justify our preoccupation with the super-achievers of our culture. As we elevate them to the status of cultural nobility, we fail to recall that they weren't born at the top of their fields or professions. They worked hard to get where they are, and others helped by coaching, mentoring, running interference, and instructing them along the way. Those who seem limitless in their power to achieve have all arrived at the pinnacle of success through the assistance of others who are often only slightly less talented, intelligent, beautiful, motivated, etc. than they.

This is not a call for the super-achievers of the world to be sure to thank the "little people" who helped to make their success

---

1. See *Book Review Digest* (New York: H. W. Wilson Co., 1976) 71:423.

possible. Instead, it is a call to realize that nobody would recognize the accomplishments of the super-achievers were their achievements not contrasted with the significant achievements of others. Therefore, the only way to recognize that Shelby Foote was a great writer is to compare and contrast his work with that of many other good writers, many of whom are almost as good as Foote himself.

I am convinced that this comparative principle needs to be given more attention in many aspects of our culture, particularly in the realm of religious leadership and devotion among both clergy and laypeople. Contemporary American Christianity needs to get over its idolatrous obsession with idealizing "great" Christians and recognize the profound influence of men, women, and young people who, without notoriety and fanfare, live faithfully as merely "good" Christians.

Let me tell you about those whose contributions to the "kingdom of God" I contend exceed those of popes, mega-church pastors, erudite theologians and teachers, senior executives in religious bureaucracies, world-renowned evangelists, and flashy contemporary Christian musicians and entertainers. First, let's begin with ordinary Christian parents who conscientiously seek to live their faith and model Christian commitment and conduct day by day in their homes and before their children. These are the people who teach their children to pray, read the Scripture, relate respectfully to others, and cherish the values of biblical faith and practice. They bring children into the world, provide them with a secure environment in which to grow and mature, teach them to walk and talk, help them potty train, show them how to play catch, provide transportation, and persevere through insufferable amounts of preadolescent and adolescent petulance, defiance, and disrespect. And all the while they work at their jobs, scrimp and save to pay mortgages and provide college educations, serve as volunteers in churches, civic clubs, and charitable organizations. They give of themselves, they give their resources, they give time, energy, talent, and faithfulness. And they do these things, for the most part, because they love God and wish to express their gratitude through worship and service in their homes, their churches, and their communities.

Closely akin to this first group is another body of people who deserve enduring respect and gratitude. While our religious culture tends to focus on the "professionally religious," i.e., the "hired holy people" who serve on church staffs, church-related university faculties, denominational boards and agencies, and missionary organizations, most of these people have a story deeply rooted in the gracious Christian love and nurture they found in a Sunday school teacher, deacon, missions organization leader, choir member, etc. who modeled for them Christian living and provided for them an environment in which they could respond to the call of God to vocational Christian ministry.

It is these faithful laypeople who "get it done" in the work of the kingdom of God. While they are sometimes treated condescendingly by religious professionals, it is this vast army of volunteers who teach the classes, serve on the committees, respond to the call for disaster relief personnel, give the money, bear the witness, and minister to the hurting. They are the "body of Christ," the physical extension of the Incarnation in the midst of a suffering, lonely, bewildered, searching world. These are the "sheep" for whom Christ died and rose victorious over death. They are the ones through whom Jesus continues to live and for whom one day he will return to receive unto himself, that where he is there they may be also (John 14:3).

Yet another group consists of those "hired holy people" I sounded somewhat critical of a bit earlier. While from time to time one of them embarrasses us all, for the most part, vocational Christian ministers are godly, compassionate, selfless people who invest themselves lovingly in their congregations and communities. Most will never serve as pastor or staff member in a mega-church, deliver the commencement address at a college or high school, speak at a denominational convention, be asked to serve as trustee or board member of an important organization, or even lead their state in evangelism and church growth statistics.

Yet these people, often inadequately compensated, accused of working only one day per week, and liable to the unfocused criticism of those who don't have a clue what ministers do, are always there. They stand by the bedside of the sick and dying. They offer comfort to the grieving, hope to the desperate, acceptance to the lonely, encouragement to the faltering, and grace to the fallen. These people, in response to the call of God in their lives, seek to be "all things to all men, that [they] might by all means save some" (1 Cor 9:22). And substantial numbers of them, when they retire, live out their days on meager pensions, live in inadequate housing, and never hear words of appreciation from those who owe them debts of gratitude beyond calculation.

In whatever realm of endeavor we consider, it takes nothing away from the accomplishments of the most talented, the most skilled, the most gifted, to acknowledge the talents, skills, and gifts of those who don't quite measure up to the mega-achievers of the world. The word "great" is an adjective of comparison; it means nothing apart from comparative association with that which is "almost as good." Were it not that there are writers who are almost as good as Shelby Foote, that great writer's literary accomplishments would go unacknowledged. Without the ordinary, and the better than ordinary, it is not possible to recognize the extraordinary.

Why is the recognition of this comparative principle so important? Allow me to begin the answer by asking some questions. How drab and colorless would the world be if the only art in it were what is contained in museums? How dull and soundless would our world be if its only music was that of the great musicians? From a Christian perspective, how bereft would our world be of love, mercy, grace, and goodness if it were dependent only on those qualities as reflected in the lives of the so-called "great" Christian personalities of today?

Adorning the walls of the Greggs' house are several nautical paintings and charcoals done by a gifted artist. While they are not great, they are very good; and I am grateful that the artist has blessed my life and the lives of others simply by being somewhat better than average. It would be a tragedy if she ceased to paint simply because she is not Michelangelo, Picasso, or Grandma Moses. And I would be an insensitive boor to dismiss her work as insignificant because she is not one of them. After all, an original Michelangelo, Picasso, or Grandma Moses will never adorn the walls of my house, but several of hers do. My life is richer and more meaningful because she has blessed me through her artistic gift.

Before this day is over, you are likely to be in the presence of someone, perhaps several someones, who, while not great, are pretty fine people. Why don't you take the time to express a measure of gratitude for the difference they make in your life; offer a word of encouragement to help them persevere when their burdens are heavy and their hearts are weary. And who knows, perhaps you are one of these people yourself. Don't despair because you're not a "great" spouse or parent or child. Don't give up because you're only average in your profession. Don't allow frustration to overwhelm you because you give the best you can and it never seems to be enough. The best you can give is all anyone should expect of you, all you should expect of yourself, and, more importantly, all God expects of you as well. My guess is that as a writer, I'll never be as good as Shelby Foote, but I have no intention of allowing that to keep me from writing something every day of my life. After all, if there weren't writers who aren't as good as Shelby Foote, there wouldn't be any Shelby Footes.

God's Family Is Larger than Just the Part of It I Know

No one was more startled than I when I met the great Christian gentleman. It happened this way: In 1996, I was doing a summer sabbatical at the University of Notre Dame. I had gone there expressly to participate in a graduate seminar on "Christology" or the "Study of Christ" taught by an eminent Roman Catholic theologian, Gerald O'Collins, from the Gregorian University in Rome. Over the years, I had read a number of O'Collins's books and had been particularly interested in studying with him. However, as much as I enjoyed O'Collins, I am not writing about him.

Upon arriving at Notre Dame, I discovered that George Carey, who at the time was Archbishop of Canterbury, was scheduled to deliver a series of lectures on Anglican Theology during my weeks at the university. I quickly sought out the dean of the graduate school of religion to acquire permission to attend Archbishop Carey's lectures as a visiting scholar. He graciously granted the permission, and I began attending the evening lectures.

On the third night, I arrived at the auditorium classroom about forty-five minutes early and took a seat high at the back. I had brought my Greek New Testament along with me to do some work related to my Christology seminar while waiting for the lecture to begin. As I pored over the text, I was surprised to hear a voice say, "Hello." Looking up, I was astonished to find the Archbishop of Canterbury standing beside me, his right hand extended as he said, "My name is George Carey." I quickly rose from my seat, took his outstretched hand, and shared my name with him. He observed that there was some time to spare before his lecture began, and he wondered if I minded if we "sat and chatted a bit." I assured him I would be honored by his company. For the next twenty minutes, we talked amiably about what was going on in our lives. He seemed just as interested in hearing about me and my work as a Baptist Associate Professor of Religion and Philosophy as I was in hearing about his work as Archbishop of Canterbury, England's leading prelate. Finally, looking down at the Notre Dame dignitaries who had gathered on the speaker's platform, and who were staring curiously up at the two of us, he remarked that it was about time for things to begin.

We rose to shake hands and I said, "Archbishop Carey, I have colleagues and friends who will not believe me when I tell them about our chat. Do you mind signing my Greek New Testament?" He replied, "Not at all." Lifting the volume and opening it to one of the blank pages in the front, in green ink he scribbled, "Larry, with my prayers for your ministry." Then he signed it, "George Carey."

Up until that evening, I had never asked anyone for an autograph; nor have I asked anyone since. But I shall never forget the evening I met personally a man who had served God from the same place as the great missionary Augustine of Canterbury, who died in 604 CE and was known as "the apostle to the English"; Anselm of Canterbury, one of the great Christian theologians of the late Middle Ages; Thomas Becket, the archbishop who refused to reduce English Christianity to a tool of King Henry II and who was martyred at the altar of Canterbury Cathedral while he knelt in prayer; William Temple, who from 1942–1944 led the Church of England through the devastating Nazi Luftwaffe bombing of Britain; and Ian Ramsey, whose book *Sacred and Secular* was the first serious piece of contemporary Christian theology I ever read.

Down across the decades, God has gifted me with the opportunity to engage in worship and fellowship with a diverse collection of people from various religious traditions, racial and national ethnicities, social and economic classes, and contrasting political persuasions. Among Christians, I have worshiped with various Protestants, Catholics, Anglicans, Greek and Russian Orthodox, Coptics, Quakers, and Charismatics of various stripes. Ethnically they have been Caucasian, Hispanic, African American, Polish, Egyptian, etc. In addition, I have been a guest in both synagogues and mosques.

In each instance, I have found gracious welcome, deep faith, and profound hope rooted in the belief that there is One who caused us to be, who sustains our being, and who is moving the created order toward an ultimate goal of unity and peace. In the circles of professional scholarship, the academic classroom, parish ministry, and day-to-day living, I have encountered so many graciously godly people that I have become convinced that *God's family is infinitely larger than just the part of it I know.*

The author of Hebrews said, "Wherefore seeing we also are compassed about with so great a cloud of witnesses, let us lay aside every weight, and the sin which doth so easily beset us, and let us run with patience the race that is set before us, looking unto Jesus the author and finisher of our faith . . ." (Heb 12:1-2). Often we take note of this passage only as we recall the faithful who have already gone home to be with the Lord. While that is appropriate, I suggest that the "great cloud of witnesses" includes many who are alive and well and who are faithfully serving God today. Many of them are our neighbors, friends, family members, and those with whom we worship regularly. They are people like us.

There are multitudes of others who are from different Christian confessional groups, whose worship patterns we find unfamiliar and strange, and whose languages we do not speak but who are members of the family of God as well. They are as much a part of the "body of Christ" as are we, and their commitment to God, passion for the truth, devotion to Christ-like living, and desire to bear faithful witness is no less sincere than yours or mine. They are fellow believers in Jesus Christ, for we all confess "one Lord, one faith, one baptism, one God and Father of all, who is above all, and through all, and in all" (Eph 4:5-6). It is not necessary—I contend that it is not even desirable—that we all be "cookie-cutter" clones of one another; but it is required that we recognize that we are "the children of God . . . , and joint-heirs with Christ . . ." (Rom 8:16-17). In truth, because of what God has done and continues to do in and through Jesus Christ, even with all our differences, believing Christians are still more alike than they are different. And I, for one, am committed to fostering the elevation of our similarities while at the same time recognizing and valuing our differences.

In 2006, Peggy and I traveled to Oxford, England, so that I could participate in a gathering at Saint Anne's College, Oxford University. Along with approximately forty others, I had been invited to participate in a gathering of ministers, academics, political and business leaders, and educators to present position papers and engage in dialogue around the theme *Religion, Education, and the State*. Subtopics for discussion included (1) boundaries of state involvement in religion; (2) government control and accountability of religious institutions; (3) evolution and intelligent design, science or religion?; (4) vouchers, charter schools, and public funding for religious schools; and (5) secular schools, religion, culture, and ethnicity. I had been invited to present a paper and make a formal presentation on one of those topics when the symposium convened at St. Anne's College. I was both honored and humbled to have been invited to participate in such a gathering. I was particularly excited about this gathering because it was an outstanding illustration of the principle of collective interaction to search for solutions to many of the troubling issues of contemporary culture, both religious and secular.

Often in my college classes, and in various occasions within the church and community, I raise the issue of the importance of recovering the fine art of civil discourse as an effective tool for meaningful human interaction. Western civilization owes a great debt to the fifth-century BCE Greek Sophists, who taught their peers to engage in carefully thought-out discussion and debate regarding the issues concerning their society. In doing so, they laid the foundations for the development of the first expressions of democratic forms of government. In American culture, these principles were embraced and used with great effectiveness by political figures who became founding personalities of the American republic and by influential religious figures among Baptists, Methodists, and other religious groups. Some of these people were both political and religious leaders at the same time. History records the tremendous significance of the dialogue between James Madison, one of the framers of the US Constitution, and John Leland, a Virginia Baptist leader, that led to the adoption of the First Ten Amendments, or the "Bill of Rights."

Unfortunately, in recent decades, Americans seem to have lost the capacity for civil discourse as we have embraced various unyielding instances of what I call "true believerism" in the realms of religion, politics, education, economics, and social values. The proponents of "true believerism" are not automatically conservative or liberal, religious or nonreligious, Democrat or Republican, Protestant or Catholic. The "true believer" is one who assumes the posture that their position, understanding, political persuasion, or religious conviction is the only right way a matter can be understood and that everyone else can either agree with them or be wrong. Many such "true believers" then move on to the conclusion that any tactic or behavior that exalts their position is justified on the basis of their rightness. Thus, character assassination, manipulation of information, lying, and, for some, even various forms of terrorism are justifiable because they are being used to further the agenda of the "true believer." The result has been the loss of civil discourse as various flavors of "true believers" simply shout at one another in an environment where everyone is speaking but no one is listening. The tension is only heightened and made worse by various claims made by such "true believers" that their position coincides with the position of God.

Several times I have made use of the phrase "civil discourse." I suppose it is time to explain what I mean by the phrase. First, let's examine this word "civil." It is the root of so many important words in our language: civilization, civilized, civilian, civic, civility, etc. In this context, two meanings of the word seem particularly important. The first is the idea of public, i.e., out in the open in an environment where everyone has the opportunity to participate. The second is the idea of civil, i.e., done with respect, decorum, and a measure of dignity. The other important word in the phrase "civil discourse" is the word "discourse." It implies dialogue rather than monologue, debate rather than diatribe, open discussion rather than closed assertion, and as much willingness to listen and hear as to speak and be heard.

Now let me return to the title of this little piece of reflective thinking: "God's Family Is Larger than Just the Part of It I Know." You and I, and everyone else, have no control over the fact that we were born in a particular place at a particular time and into a particular set of cultural, religious, and social assumptions. Nor does this particularity constitute anything for which we should be ashamed or embarrassed. Often I refer to and express appreciation for my West Alabama 1950s and 1960s heritage. There was much about the environment that Forrest Gump and I grew up in that was not perfect; but there was also much I will treasure until the day I die.

On the other hand, it was also important that I discover and learn to appreciate that while the world included West Alabama, it was not confined to West Alabama; while the world included "my South," it was not confined to "my South"; and while the world includes the United States of America, it is not confined to the United States of America. While human beings certainly reflect distinctive racial, ethnic, cultural, political, and religious differences, the basic challenges with which we struggle are essentially the same. Therefore, it is important that we not allow our preoccupation with our differences to prevent us from addressing our commonly shared needs and aspirations.

We did not solve all the problems of society at the Oxford symposium, but, as we gathered from around the world to participate in civil discourse, we at least addressed and sought possible solutions to some of them. Surely similar discussions ought to take place in town halls, local churches, classrooms, religious denominational gatherings, political conventions, and legislative assemblies. All that is required is the commitment to being true to our cherished beliefs while refusing to descend into the various "true believerisms" that make us unwilling to hear anything other than ourselves being repeated back to us.

I believe that all human beings are the creation of God; therefore, I maintain that all people are a part of God's family, both those who acknowledge God's Fatherhood and those who don't. Remember the question of the prophet Malachi: "Have we not all one father? Hath not one God created us?" (Mal 2:10). It is not necessary that we equate being part of God's family only with being "saved," being "Baptist," being "American," being "Republican" or "Democrat," or being "for" or "against" any particular hot-button social issue. Remember, it was Jesus who said, "Other sheep have I, which are not of this fold . . ." (John 10:16). Truly, God's family is larger than just the part of it I know.

Not Every Foot Leaves the Same Print in the Sand

I hope you're not tired of my occasional reflections on my experiences of visiting the beach, because I'm not quite through thinking about them yet. Recently I've been reflecting on my leisurely daily walks up and down the beach, luxuriating in the sight and sound of crashing waves while watching people enjoy their mid-winter getaway. I've spoken of infants and grandmothers playing in the sand, treasure hunters with their metal detectors, the clientele of a local oyster bar, and a mother and daughter taking pictures of one another with a digital camera.

One day, as I walked the firm, damp sand near the water's edge, I noted the hundreds upon hundreds of footprints others had left behind. I saw large prints and small ones; some were bare feet, while others evidenced the distinctive marks of jogging shoes, sandals, and flip-flops. Tracks crisscrossed one another from every direction. Some had gone down the beach only to return sometime later, leaving parallel patterns of identical tracks going in opposite directions. From the way sets of tracks were spaced, I could tell who had been jogging, who had been simply strolling along at leisure, and who had been venturing down into the water and back on that blustery, chilly December day. I could even distinguish the prints left by those who had been alone from those who had been walking together in step.

As I strolled along, taking note of the hundreds of footprints, an unexpected wave surprised me by flooding my own feet with rushing water, reminding me that the tide had shifted and, as the day progressed, would march inexorably up the beach, erasing every trace of the myriad footprints I found so fascinating. Then the words leapt into my consciousness, "Not every foot leaves the same print in the sand, but ultimately they all wash away."

I know Shakespeare has already said, "life's but a walking shadow, a poor player that struts and frets his hour upon the stage, and then is heard no more" (*Macbeth*, act 5, scene 5, line 17). I know the biblical sage observed that human existence passes "swifter than a weaver's shuttle" and that "life is wind" (Job 7:6-7). Writers far wiser and more eloquent than I have reflected, time and again, on the frailty of human life and the brevity of our tenure on the earth. The fact that earlier generations have paused to take the time to reflect on these matters, however, does not mean those who live in the present should not take the time to do so as well. It is only as we do that the wisdom of the Bard of Avon or the long-suffering Job becomes our own. So I decided to take the time to do some thinking about all those sandy footprints that would be washed into oblivion within just a few short hours. Here are some of my thoughts.

First, there are limits to how much one can tell about another by examining the fleeting tracks, literal or metaphorical, they leave behind. In today's world of forensic investigator television shows, we are often left with the impression that another's entire life history can be reconstructed from the most innocuous physical remains. What such "Crime Scene Investigator" entertainment fails to acknowledge is that deducing "stuff" about another from the physical remains of their existence does not automatically equate to knowing them.

I could deduce much from the tracks left in the wet sand by those who arrived at the beach before I did that day. Imprinted brand name logos from the soles of shoes made it possible for me to distinguish those willing to spend $125 to $200 for beach shoes from those who elected to do other things with their money. Telling the prints of children, especially the barefoot ones, from those of adults was simple enough. Viewing the size of footprints and their depth in the wet sand, I could even surmise things about the relative weight and body mass of some. An eye with better training than mine could probably have discerned even more.

But, examine as I might, footprints in the sand told me nothing of hair color, complexion, and dress other than footwear or the lack thereof. Nothing I found imprinted in the sand revealed whether these people were happy or sad, enjoying themselves or bored, locals or out-of-towners. I could not tell if they were laughing or crying, drunk or sober, moral or immoral, Christians, Jews, or Hottentots. The best I could do was conclude the tracks were left by human beings, more or less like me.

Perhaps I'm just getting older, but I'm not nearly as sure about my judgments of others as I was at earlier stages in my life. Looking back, I am prepared to admit that often I judged too harshly the contributions of the former pastors of congregations I have served. I dismissed the insights of professional colleagues, community leaders, church members, and total strangers for superficial and irrelevant reasons. Often I jumped to conclusions that turned out to be erroneous because I misinterpreted, undervalued, or just plain ignored the tracks they left behind in the sand of human interpersonal relationships. I failed to understand that, while their tracks could tell me some things about those people, they could not tell me everything. And furthermore, that what the tracks could tell me was not necessarily important.

At this point, I am willing to be content with the knowledge that the traces left behind by the passage of others, at best, merely tell me they were human beings, more or less like me. And to be more or less like me is to be like the girl with the curl in the middle of her forehead of whom it was said, "When she was good, she was really good; and when she was bad she was a real stinker."

It's time to listen again to the words of Jesus: "Do not judge others, so that God will not judge you, for God will judge you in the same way you judge others, and he will apply to you the same rules you apply to others" (Matt 7:1-2, Today's English Version). When we take the time to truly know another, as opposed to jumping to hasty judgments on the basis of our knowledge of some things about them, we are likely to be less harsh and unforgiving in our conclusions. Like the humble publican who went down to the temple to pray, I am inclined, with increasing frequency, to beat my breast in contrition and cry out, "God, have pity on me, a sinner!" (Luke 18:13, TEV). Once I thought justice was the most important thing; now I'm sure it's mercy that we all need most. Again, listen to the words of Jesus, "Blessed are the merciful: for they shall obtain mercy" (Matt 5:7, KJV).

My second thought was the fact that there are tracks at all may mean infinitely more than how long they endure. The tracks we leave along the beach of life say a number of things about us. One thing they say is that we were there. Most everyone knows the story of the World War II GIs who left the words "Kilroy was here" painted on walls, scratched on stone, carved into tabletops, and chalked on roadways across Europe and the island fortresses of the South Pacific. There is an instinctive need, on the part of human beings, to leave some evidence of their passage through the fleeting years of life. Sometimes what we leave behind is the refuse and wreckage of our passage. But at other times we leave monuments like Stonehenge and Notre Dame; documents like the Magna Charta and the Constitution of the United States of America; memories enshrined in the consciousness of our children and grandchildren that challenge them to aspire to stand on our shoulders and reach beyond anything we could possibly have attained ourselves. Such markings along the beach of life bear witness to the nobility, the courage, and the greatness of the human spirit.

But as surely as the many tracks left in the beach sand during my day of reflection were as varied as the footwear, or lack thereof, of those who had traversed the sand before me, the tracks we leave behind are stark reminders that human beings are not all alike and that our diversity is one of our greatest strengths. How sad life would be if every sunrise were exactly like all those preceding it, how dull if every voice was the same pitch and tone. Some human tracks are worthy of following to discover where they are leading. Others should be ignored, for they lead to brokenness, despair, and tragedy. Were all tracks the same, we would be unable to distinguish which paths are leading in positive, hopeful directions, which are just wandering aimlessly and are going nowhere, and which would lead us into the mire of confusion or over the ledge of disaster.

Having said this, all positive and hopeful paths are not identical to one another. There may be more than one good and useful path one may follow while traversing the beach of life. Sometimes I hear a well-meaning voice say, "God has one perfect plan for the life of every person." I question whether this is true. While not denying the reality of Divine purpose and intentionality in the universe, I still maintain that, as human beings, we have been created with a measure of freedom to choose the pathway of our lives. While we are not absolutely free, we are also not absolutely determined either. Often we pray, "God, I can choose between this or this or this. Which path do you want me to follow?" I think on many such occasions God's response is, "My child, either of the paths that lie before you is fine with me. Choose whichever is most pleasing to you. All I desire is that you live faithfully before me, whatever path you follow." Some of you are thinking, "Is he saying that God doesn't have a plan for our lives?" I'm not saying that. What I am saying is that God's plan is for us to be "conformed to the image of his Son" (Rom 8:29), Jesus Christ. But the choice of the path we follow while becoming more and more the person God has always intended us to be is left pretty much up to us.

Finally, the tracks we leave in the present may be more valuable than any we anticipate leaving for the future. Human beings spend entirely too much time preoccupied with regrets over the past or fretting about the unknowns of the future. Centuries ago the great Christian theologian Augustine of Hippo pointed out, "neither future nor past exists . . . . The present considering the past is the memory, the present considering the present is immediate awareness, the present considering the future is expectation" (Augustine, *Confessions*, xx.26). While not repudiating the past or discounting the future, it was Augustine's contention that only in the realm of *immediate awareness* are we able to exert any influence on our own lives or on those around us. We have no assurances that our choices or actions will endure much beyond our own existence. While some have left enduring marks on human history, many of those marks are more the scars of past trauma than signposts pointing the way to the future. The truth is that most people have lived and died without leaving tracks that endured more than a generation after their passing. The tide of human experience washed up on the shore, and when it receded it left a smooth, unmarked beach on which others, oblivious to the existence of those who had been there before, would make new marks of their own.

Do not hear in these words resignation or surrender, for they are not meant that way. I am asserting that it is enough to leave marks that make a positive difference in the present. We have lived lives of value and worth if the traces of our passage bring hope, joy, peace, and grace into the lives of those we meet each day. It was not in despair that James said, "you know not what shall be on the morrow. For what is your life? It is even a vapour, that appeareth for a little time, and then is vanished away" (Jas 4:14). On the contrary, he simply echoed the sentiment of the author of Hebrews, who challenged his readers to "exhort one another daily, while it is called 'Today'" (Heb 3:13). It matters almost nothing at all that my tracks or yours be preserved indelible for generations far in the future. All that is necessary is that we leave a clear path in the present for those who are following close behind. If we do, we can trust them to leave equally clear paths for those yet to come, long after our own tracks have all washed away. I gave up a long time ago any concern I had about making a difference for the future. All I want to do, by God's grace, is make a positive difference in the present. And by faith, I believe that if I do, those following behind will perpetuate that difference into the future. That's good enough for me.

Things I Gave Up when I Gave My Heart to Jesus

The nature of my work in the local church and the college classroom has often placed me in situations where I listened as people told the story of their Christian conversion experience. Often it is a great joy to listen as people share from their hearts regarding how they became aware of the need to place their trust in God's grace, made known in and through Jesus Christ. The sheer diversity of the stories is one of their greatest blessings. Each man, each woman, each young person bears witness to their unique experience with the transforming power of God. While there are similarities between the stories, each is, to some degree, person specific. They all met Jesus, but no two met him in exactly the same way.

On the other hand, there are occasions when I must confess that I experience a degree of distress in listening to the conversion testimonies of some of my church family. While many have been redeemed from the deepest, darkest enslavement to sin and its various manifestations in drug and alcohol addiction, abusive behavior, and crass sensuality, some, it seems to me, spend an inordinate amount of time describing all the salacious details of their past lives. When they begin to speak of what they "gave up" when they gave their hearts to Jesus, they speak of lifestyles steeped in self-destructive behaviors, greed, and the pursuit of luxury and pleasure.

Sometimes such people linger wistfully over the details of their former lives. They remind me of the story told of the young woman who repeatedly went to confession and recounted the details of the same sexual misconduct. One day, in exasperation, the priest spoke from behind the screen, saying, "Daughter, you have confessed and received absolution for this sinful act before. Why do you keep confessing the details of the same sin?" The young woman replied, "Well, Father, it's just such a pleasant memory." When people lay bare the details of their past in public settings such as revival services, crusades, Christian TV broadcasts, etc., I often find myself wondering if they're "testifying" or "bragging."

Do not hear me belittling the courage, faith, and determination required on the part of those who, by God's grace, overcome the ungodly behaviors of past lives. My concern is with what seems to be an excessive preoccupation with having to "give up" the sins of destructive self-indulgence because one has chosen to become a follower of Jesus Christ. Often people sound as though they think they have made a great sacrifice in order to be a Christian. There is no sacrifice in "giving up" murder, adultery, theft, gossip and slander, lying, and covetousness. There is no sacrifice in ceasing to live and conduct ourselves in ways we should never have been living and conducting ourselves to begin with. To wallow in self-pity because God will not connive with us in the continuation of such behavior reveals that we have little or no interest in genuinely living a Christ-like life.

Furthermore, preoccupation with these behaviors keeps us focused on only the surface details of the problem of human sinfulness. There are much deeper issues that, until faced and dealt with appropriately, will always keep us from being able, as Christians, to distance ourselves from what the writer of 1 John called "the lust of the flesh, the lust of the eyes, and the pride of life" (1 John 2:16). Therefore, I wish to draw attention to the deeper things I was challenged to "give up" when I gave my heart to Jesus. I draw attention to them because you were called to give them up as well.

First and foremost, when I gave my heart to Jesus, I gave up the right to choose who I was going to love. The "good news" of the gospel is that God expressed God's love for me completely and unreservedly in Jesus Christ. The writer of 1 John said, "Herein is love, not that we loved God, but that he loved us . . ." (1 John 4:10). Paul wrote to the Romans, "God commendeth his love toward us, in that, while we were yet sinners, Christ died for us" (Rom 5:8). God has declared love for all of creation, including all of humankind, in the oft-repeated words "for God so loved the world, that he gave his only begotten Son, that whosoever believeth in him should not perish, but have everlasting life" (John 3:16).

In his last extended conversation with the disciples prior to his crucifixion, Jesus chose to speak to them about the quality of their love. Listen as he said to them, and continues to say to us, "A new commandment I give unto you, that ye love one another; as I have loved you, that ye also love one another. By this shall all men know that ye are my disciples, if ye have love one to another" (John 13:34-35). To the best of my understanding, there are no "optional" commandments. The truth is that my relationship to God can be measured by the quality of the love I express to those around me. Undoubtedly it is easier to love the "lovely and those who love me" than it is to love the "unlovely and those who do not love me." But I have not been left with the option of picking and choosing; I have been commanded to love consistently, to love sacrificially, and to love selflessly after the example of my Savior.

The British New Testament scholar William Barclay put it this way: "The only way to prove that we love God is to love the man whom God loves. The only way to prove that God is within our hearts is constantly to show the love of men within our lives."[1] When I gave my heart to Jesus, I gave up the right to choose who I was going to love, and you did too.

Second, when I gave my heart to Jesus, I gave up the right to choose who I was going to forgive. The New Testament teaches clearly that "forgiveness" is not optional on our part either. Paul said to the Colossian believers, "Forgive one another. If any man have a quarrel against any: even as Christ forgave you, so also do ye" (Col 3:13).

Paul understood well the interconnectedness of our willingness to be forgiving toward others and our ability to experience the forgiveness of God in our own lives. Jesus taught his disciples to pray, "forgive us our sins, for we also forgive every one that is indebted to us" (Luke 11:4). In a parallel passage from Matthew 6, Jesus said, "if

---

1. Barclay, *The Letters of John and Jude* (Philadelphia: Westminster Press, 1960), 116–17.

ye forgive men their trespasses, your heavenly Father will also forgive you: but if you forgive not men their trespasses, neither will your Father forgive your trespasses" (Matt 6:14-15). To refuse to forgive others is to shut ourselves off from the forgiveness of God. One of the major reasons we should be open to a spirit of forgiveness toward others is the truth that the price of not forgiving is much too high a price to have to pay.

The biblical message is clear; when we harbor hate or envy or resentment toward others in our hearts, we cannot possibly be in right relationship with God. "If a man say, I love God, and hateth his brother, he is a liar: for he that loveth not his brother whom he hath seen, how can he love God whom he hath not seen?" (1 John 4:20).

Often I hear well-meaning people say, "What we need to do is to learn to forgive and forget." While I appreciate the sentiment, I think this is precisely the problem. We set ourselves up for failure in forgiving because it is truly impossible to forget the injury, the pain, the injustice done to us by another. And the Bible does not teach that we are called to do so. Godly forgiveness is not forgetfulness; it is an infinitely costly and precious way of remembering.

Forgiveness is what Fisher Humphreys, in his wonderful little book *Thinking about God*, called "costly remembering."[2] Humphreys asserted that when someone does me an injury, I have three options: (1) I can try to forget the whole thing and act as though it never happened. But, if I do this, I become implicated in the injury and fail to help the one who has injured me because I absolve that person of any accountability for their deeds. (2) I can seek to punish the one who has injured me. However, in seeking to punish I must descend to the same level of insensitivity and violence as the one who has injured me. This is why retaliation is ultimately self-destructive. (3) I can absorb the injury into myself, forgive the one who has injured me, and relate to him as though he has not injured me, even though I know he has. This is biblical forgiveness.

To say that God has forgiven me is to say that God has taken the injury I have done God in my sin, absorbed it into God's self in

---

2. *Thinking about God: An Introduction to Christian Theology* (New Orleans: Insight Press, 1974), 115.

Jesus Christ, and cut short its power to do the ultimate evil to me, to destroy me. To forgive another is to take the injury the other has done to us, absorb it into our ourselves after the example of Jesus Christ, and cut short its power to perpetuate the evil in both ourselves and in the other. Nobody ever said this was going to be easy, just that it is what must be done. When I gave my heart to Jesus, I gave up the right to choose who I was going to forgive, and so did you.

Finally, when I gave my heart to Jesus, I gave up the right to choose who I was going to serve. I cannot genuinely be Christian without being willing to serve. Jesus told the disciples, "Not every one that saith unto me, Lord, Lord, shall enter into the kingdom of Heaven; but he that doeth the will of my Father which is in heaven" (Matt 7:21). In obedience to the will and purpose of God, Jesus lived a life of redemptive servanthood in our midst. To embrace Jesus Christ as Savior and Lord in our lives is to embrace the servant ministry of the "body of Christ" in the world. For it is in ministering to the needs of others, in a spirit of Christ-like servanthood, that we demonstrate the authenticity of our Christian experience.

Such servant ministry requires acknowledging that we do not have the right to choose who we will or will not minister to in the name of Jesus Christ. Jesus sternly rebuked the scribes and Pharisees who, though deeply religious, neglected the needs of those around them, dismissed Gentiles and women as socially inferior and unworthy of respect, and deliberately interpreted the Law in ways that impeded the ability of others to minister to them as well. In contrast, Jesus asserted that when one ministers to the least, the lowest, the loneliest, one is ministering to him as well (Matt 25:40). We are most like the Father who created us, the Son who died and rose again to save us, and the Holy Spirit who indwells us when we humbly and willingly accept our calling to be servant of all. When I gave my heart to Jesus, I gave up the right to choose who I was going to serve, and you did too.

Herein is the critical issue. The chief measures of the authenticity of our Christian experience are not found in what immoral and self-destructive behaviors we "gave up" when we gave our hearts to Jesus. The authenticity of our Christian experience is measured by what we embraced when we gave our hearts to Jesus. We can practice keeping the Ten Commandments until the Lord returns, and it will avail us nothing at all if we have refused to embrace "love," refused to embrace "forgiveness," and refused to embrace "servanthood." And inevitably we will fail in our legalistic commandment keeping because a heart that refuses to be motivated by Christ-like love, a heart that refuses to receive and accept forgiveness, a heart that will not serve with humility lacks the resources necessary to abstain from murder, adultery, theft, gossip and slander, lying, and covetousness.

This is our calling as Christians: to love as we have been and are being loved. To forgive as we have been and are being forgiven. And to serve after the example of the one who "took upon him the form of a servant" (Phil 2:7). There are no options here. I cannot be Christian and not love. I cannot be Christian and not forgive. I cannot be Christian and not serve. I gave up the right to refuse to do these things when I gave my heart to Jesus, and you did too.

Son, They Sell Produce Down at the Grocery Store

I was on a quest for my first job. It was summertime in central Florida in the late 1950s, and I wanted to earn money. The reason was pretty straightforward. Not far from the house where I lived was an Army/Navy Surplus store. Now, I'm not talking about what passes for an Army/Navy Surplus store today. I'm talking about the kind that cropped up across the country in the aftermath of World War II and the Korean War. They contained the vast quantities of old uniforms, official insignia, tent halves, helmets, web belts, combat boots, defused grenades, and various other paraphernalia of the world's, at the time, most recent military conflicts. It was all genuine, GI-issue military surplus—not the manufactured-for-sale stuff one finds in today's pseudo-surplus stores.

The merchandise fascinated me. I would spend hours just standing and staring at the shiny brass buckles and corps emblems, the cloth rank and unit patches, and the silver-and-gold-colored cap insignia. By age ten I could recite, in ascending or descending order, every enlisted and commissioned rank in the US Navy and its corresponding rank in the Army, Marines, or Air Force. My most prized personal possession was my father's campaign ribbons from his service as a Gunner's Mate on a destroyer in the Pacific during World War II. They contained five bronze stars, one for each major battle in which his ship was engaged. The only thing I considered greater than looking at the unused equipment of that global conflict was the personal possession of some of it. Therefore, I wanted a job so that, the next time I went to the store and the indulgent owner asked, "Son, are you ever going to buy anything?" I could respond with a confident "Yes sir!"

Not far from the Army/Navy Surplus store was an old building an elderly man was in the process of refurbishing and turning into a secondhand store. That spring, on my walks back and forth to school, I had passed the store daily and had kept an eye on its progress toward opening day. I even stopped and chatted with the old man once or twice. On this summer day, emboldened by my desire to purchase a cap insignia like the one I had seen in a recent photo of my older brother, an Air Force enlisted man, I strode up to the door of the secondhand shop and pushed assertively against it. As the door opened, its top struck a small set of bells intended to alert the owner that a customer was entering. The old man quickly appeared from the back, and walking behind the counter he asked, "What can I do for you today, son?"

Stumbling for words I replied, "I was wondering if you needed somebody to help you sell your produce?"

A broad smile split the old man's face and he chuckled, but at least he didn't laugh out loud. "Son," he drawled kindly, "we don't sell produce in a place like this. Produce is vegetables. They sell produce down at the grocery store."

Stuttering, and with embarrassed tears welling in my eyes, I replied, "I'm sorry. I didn't know."

"Would you like a Coke?" he asked.

"I don't have any money," I answered.

"Don't worry about it. This one's on me." With these words he turned to an old refrigerator behind the counter, extracted two icy cold Coca-Colas, and popped the tops off using a brass opener nailed to the wall beside the refrigerator. Coming out from behind the counter, he pointed toward a couple of empty wooden orange crates that passed for stools. I climbed up on one and he sat down on the other, a frosty Coke in each hand. He passed one to me, and we both took a long sip and I luxuriated in the astringent sting of the sweet liquid upon palate and throat.

"Ah, that's good," he said, taking the bottle from his lips. "Thanks for coming by. I needed a break." For the next twenty minutes we sat and chatted about his store and his plans for the future. Finally he said, "Son, I'm sorry I can't give you a job. I don't have enough business yet to pay somebody to help me."

I said I understood and, thanking him for the Coke, I rose to leave. "There's one more thing before you go, son," he said. "Yes sir?" I queried. "Before you ask anyone else for a job, learn some things about what kind of business they're in. You need to be careful about using words you don't understand."

"Yes sir," I replied. "Thanks again for the Coke." The bells jingled as I pulled open the door and left the secondhand shop, not much older but at least a little bit wiser.

Perhaps you are wondering, as I have, why this childhood story has been retained in my consciousness for well over half a century. I have no simple explanation, but I do have some thoughts on the matter. It may be that this boyhood recollection has remained fresh because I happened upon the old man and his secondhand store at a particularly teachable moment in my childhood. It came at a time when I failed to get either of the things I thought I wanted, i.e., the job, the money, or the silver-colored enlisted man's cap insignia. But what I got was something infinitely more precious than what I desired. Even so, it took decades for me to fully appreciate what was given to me freely that day. What I received were the seeds of what may be the three most important insights I have ever understood. I profoundly hope you are thinking, "Tell us about them."

First of all, I began to learn that day that while it is not necessary that one know everything, it is desirable to know some things. It matters not what the endeavor—gardening, architecture, sailing a ship, or becoming a neurosurgeon—one has to begin somewhere. There are certain rudimentary concepts and ideas that must be a part of one's consciousness, even if it is as simple as knowing the difference between what is sold in the fresh market of a grocery store and what lines the shelves in a secondhand junk store.

Over a career as minister and teacher in the academic disciplines of Biblical Studies, World Religions, Philosophy, and Ethics, I began each semester telling incoming students that these disciplines have basic vocabularies, ideas, and concepts that must be mastered if one is to move forward successfully in learning anything about the larger subject matter. This is not exclusive to the areas in which I taught; it is true of Mathematics, Language Arts, the Physical Sciences, and the Social Sciences. Those who will not make the effort to grasp these rudimentary ideas and concepts, and the meanings of words, usually don't last long or do well in the learning endeavor. Frequently I heard the plaintive wail, "It's just too hard." Too often, what the person was ashamed to say was, "I just don't have the interest level and/or the discipline to try."

Sadly, I find that many Christian believers are profoundly ignorant of the content of Scripture and have almost no grasp of the essential concepts and ideas of their faith. Somewhere back in the 1960s and 1970s, we abandoned the teaching of basic Christian doctrines in the educational programs of our churches; the consequence is that we have raised several generations of Christians who, increasingly, don't have a clue about what they profess to believe and why they should believe it. Thus, to use the words of the writer of Ephesians, many are "tossed to and fro, and carried about with every wind of doctrine" and end up being manipulated "by the sleight of men, and cunning craftiness" of those who "lie in wait to deceive" (Eph 4:14). Because they do not recognize sound doctrine when they see or hear it, they become easy prey for those who would victimize them spiritually, emotionally, and even physically. When challenged to deepen their knowledge of basic Christian truths, many say, "It's just too hard to understand." What they really mean is, "I just don't have the interest level and/or discipline to try."

Now I know some of you are making faces and thinking, "Well, Dr. Gregg, doctrine is not everything." I completely agree. All I am asserting is that while sound doctrinal understanding is not everything, it is also not nothing when it comes to expressing the depth of one's Christian experience and witness.

I said previously that the seeds of three important life truths were sown in my consciousness in the secondhand shop that day. The second was that it is a noble thing to treat another person respectfully, even when you don't have to. In the world of the late 1950s, it was required that children be respectful toward adults but not necessarily that adults be respectful toward children. Without doubt there were many who, had they been witness to the display of my gross lack of understanding of retail sales, would have hooted in derision without giving a thought to the damage they might have done to an impressionable boy's self-esteem and sense of value. On the other hand, they would have been much more restrained in their reaction to a similar *faux pas* from the lips of an adult who might have punched them in the face for making fun of them. Even though he didn't have to, what the old man did was to treat me respectfully, heedless of the disparity of our ages or the depth of my ignorance.

Some years ago I ran out of patience with two young women who constantly whispered and giggled during my lectures, distracting me and the rest of the class. One day I stopped, mid-lecture, and asked them if they had information they would like to contribute to the rest of the class. When they both vigorously shook their heads, I moved on to explain, in explicit detail and in the hearing of the class, that there would never be a time, inside or outside the class, when I did not treat them with respect; and under no circumstances would there ever be a time when it was permissible for them to be disrespectful toward me or their fellow students by blatantly displaying such lack of maturity while class was going on. I further explained that if they found that expectation unacceptable, they needed to be somewhere else because I didn't want them in my classroom if they insisted on being grossly disrespectful to the learning process. With these words, I told them the class was over for them that day and that they could both leave immediately. Sheepishly they gathered their belongings and exited the room. Needless to say, there were no further interruptions for the remainder of the class.

Later that afternoon, I looked up from my desk to see one of the young women standing in the office doorway. Nervously she asked if she could speak with me. I assured her she could and motioned her toward a chair. With tears flowing down her cheeks she said, "I'm sorry for the way I've been acting, Dr. Gregg. My parents didn't raise me to act that way. And if you'll let me come back to class I'll never be disrespectful again." Assuring her the incident was over, I said I looked forward to seeing her in the next class meeting. I returned to my work hoping the other young woman would come by as well.

She didn't, and I never saw her again in class. But the first young woman not only returned; she did well in the class and continued to take courses with me during the balance of her academic career in that institution. I suspect she shall never forget the lesson that respect given evokes respect in return and that to be blatantly disrespectful toward others is never acceptable regardless of one's position, wealth, or status in life.

Finally, reflection on my encounter with the kind old man in the secondhand shop suggests that the injuries others inflict on us aren't the only things that can be remembered for a lifetime; the kindnesses of others can be retained in our consciousness as well. I contend that if you're going to remember things for a lifetime, it's better to recall the kindnesses than the injuries. Why? Because old injuries, actual or perceived, lying hidden in consciousness behave like the dormant chickenpox virus that occasionally manifests itself in the intensely painful medical phenomenon called shingles. Anyone who has ever had an episode of shingles never looks forward to the next one. But remembered kindnesses have the capacity to evoke, once again, the pleasure of having been related to with dignity and grace. Remembering such acts makes us wish to emulate them in our own daily conduct. In the realm of kindness, it is appropriate that we act kindly toward others because we recall the kindnesses that others, often many years earlier, have bestowed upon us. No one should contaminate those around them with the shingles of ill will and chronic resentment. But when it comes to kindness, we should spread it around hoping that everyone will become infected with it.

Thank God for a gracious, generous old man who shared a Coke with a lonely boy and planted seeds that have meaningfully influenced his life for decades. They may not sell produce at the secondhand store, but the world would certainly be a better place if more of us emulated the behavior of the old man who graciously shared a Coke and a teachable moment with me that day.

You Take My Picture, and I'll Take Yours

It was in the days before cell phone cameras became ubiquitous but after small, handheld digital cameras became available. Mother and daughter strolled down the beach together; no two women could so closely resemble one another and not be genetically related. The older woman appeared to be in her early fifties, the younger in her late twenties. Dressed casually in cool-weather beach attire, it was evident from broad smiles, easy laughter, and uninhibited antics that both were having a wonderful morning. Between them they carried a small digital camera that passed from hand to hand as they made their way westward along the beach. Every few yards they would pause in their journey; one would pose or gawk for the camera while the other shot a photo. Together they would inspect and laugh at the image on the display screen, the camera would change hands, and they would move on down the beach till the mood hit to take another picture. In sublime good spirits, and oblivious to whether anyone was observing them, they had great fun playing, "You take my picture, and I'll take yours."

I found myself charmed by these two because of their obvious sheer enjoyment of one another in the bright sunlight and cool breeze of that late December morning on the Gulf Coast. Their spontaneous laughter and unselfconscious playfulness marked them as people comfortable with themselves and comfortable with one another. Suddenly I was aware that, while they were the ones with the camera, I was taking pictures as well. The only difference was that they were using a sophisticated piece of modern technology to capture digital images while I was recording memories in my mind.

At that moment it occurred to me that almost every human interaction is, at its simplest level, a game of "You take my picture, and I'll take yours."

To tell the truth, I'm not much of a photographer. Back in 1981, while preparing for my first visit to the Middle East, I was chatting with a dentist friend in Birmingham, Alabama, about my upcoming trip, and he asked if I had a good SLR to take along. He laughed when I admitted I didn't have a clue what an SLR was; then he patiently explained that the letters stood for a "Single Lens Reflex" camera, ideally suited for shooting 35-millimeter film, both slides and prints.

I asked the dentist what kind of camera he thought I ought to buy. Immediately he replied, "You don't need to buy anything yet. You need to learn to use one before you tie up any money in an expensive camera and lenses."

With these words he rose from the chair in his den, where we had been sipping coffee after a pleasant dinner, and promised to return in a moment. I remained in the comfortable room watching the fire and listening to our wives chat in the kitchen. Soon he returned, carrying a black camera bag from which he withdrew a Canon AE-1 with the interlocking circles of the Olympic logo stamped on the lens cover. When I inquired about the marking, he said the camera was one of a select number manufactured by Canon as part of the promotion of the 1980 Olympics.

We sat back down and my friend began to explain how the camera worked. We talked of lenses, F-stops, shutter speeds, and film types. While I nodded in understanding, both of us knew I only barely comprehended what he was saying. Finally he said, "Here's what I want you to do. Take the camera, the manual, and the rolls of film in the case home with you. Shoot up the film and have it developed. In a few days we'll talk about how you're doing. Then, if you want to, you can take the camera with you to Israel. If you're satisfied with the quality of your photos when you get back, the camera's yours."

Flabbergasted at his generosity, I agreed to do as he proposed. That was in 1981. Now, decades later, even though photographic technology has advanced by light years, when I get serious about taking pictures I pull out my old Canon AE-1 and remember the dentist's final smiling words: "Don't worry, Pastor. We can set this thing up so an idiot can take good pictures with it."

Over the years I have learned there are four essential factors involved in the process of taking photographs of other people. They are (1) the quality of the camera, (2) the skill of the photographer, (3) the characteristics of the environment, and (4) the goodwill, or lack thereof, between the photographic subject and the photographer.

Earlier I suggested that almost every human interaction is, at its simplest level, a game of "You take my picture, and I'll take yours." By this I mean that at first meeting, and in every subsequent encounter, our minds record impressions, make judgments, and fix in our consciousness mental images of people. Through these mental snapshots we make judgments about others—about the quality of their personhood, whether we like them or not, and our willingness to work with them or become involved with them at deep interpersonal levels.

Stored in the picture albums of our minds are innumerable mental photos we have taken over a lifetime. In them we have recorded value judgments about our world and the people with whom we share life; and those value judgments profoundly affect the decisions we make and how we conduct ourselves in our relations to others. Consequently, it is imperative that we develop the skills necessary to take good mental photos. Otherwise our blurred, out of focus, poorly lighted, and carelessly framed impressions will lead us to make decisions and take actions predicated upon bad, inaccurate, or distorted information. Such decisions and actions frequently do great injury both to ourselves and to others. More often than not, we stand back from such experiences and say, "I didn't see as clearly as I thought I did" or "I just didn't get the picture" or some other admission that we have made a mistake. And, in our mistake, we have harmed ourselves, harmed others, and possibly created an environment where the consequences of our actions will extend far into the future. This business of the mental photos we take of one another is far too important for us to just point and shoot.

If this is the case, how can we improve our skills at mental picture taking so our interpretations are more truthful reflections of reality? I suggest we employ the same four essential factors involved in taking good camera photographs: camera quality, skill of the photographer, environment, and good will between subject and photographer. Having said this, let me elaborate on each one for a moment.

The first factor is the quality of the camera. Immediately, I must point out that "most expensive" does not automatically indicate "best quality" when one is shopping for cameras. Lots of expensive things are not necessarily well made. A similar thing is true of human minds. Many people have high IQs, hold degrees from prestigious educational institutions, and give the outward appearance of being mentally astute and well focused. Unfortunately, closer inspection reveals that some such people still think sloppily, allow sentiment, prejudice, and fear to impair their judgment, and permit poorly formed earlier impressions to harden into inflexible refusal to continue to learn and grow. The result is that they are unable to form good mental images of others because the instruments they are using, in this case their own minds, are not up to the task.

This failure to cultivate and develop a healthy mind is especially unfortunate on the part of religious people. I am always astounded at those who seek to substitute religious fervor, sentimentalism, and dogmatic Bible-thumping for what can only be accomplished through the careful cultivation of Christian critical thinking skills. The writer of 2 Timothy counseled his readers to develop a "sound mind" (2 Tim 1:7). In 1 Peter, believers were told to "have your mind ready for action" (1 Pet 1:13, TEV). It is not possible to take consistently good photographs without a good-quality camera. And it is not possible for Christians to form good mental images of others without a mind that is attuned to the mind of Christ (1 Cor 2:16).

The second factor is the skill of the photographer. In most things we learn by doing. The photographer develops their skills by taking many, many pictures; but this does not equate to randomly shooting up roll after roll of film or megabyte after megabyte of digital memory. The novice who really wants to become a good photographer spends time studying the shots taken by others, asking questions about composition, lighting, exposure time, and dozens of other things. She spends a lot of time testing lenses to find the best one for a particular shot and then carefully focuses the lens before clicking the shutter. Once the film is developed, time must be devoted to careful analysis of the results to be sure that the best-quality photo was taken, given the tools and the circumstances. This photography business is challenging work, requiring disciplined practice and the development of a critical analytic eye. The really good photographer can work with a speed that makes it look easy, but the reason it looks so easy is that they have devoted countless hours to the development of the skills of their craft.

The same is true in the formation of the mental photos we take of others. Much too often we rush to judgment, jump to hasty conclusions, and make all the needless errors of the undisciplined and unpracticed. Instead of consulting with those who have demonstrated sound judgment over time, instead of considering the multiple options that may be available, instead of patiently waiting until the facts are in, we just snap the shutter on our mental images, irrevocably fixing our conclusions about others in our consciousness. Then the pride that keeps us from being willing to admit that we may have acted hastily leads us to defend bad images instead of taking the time to formulate new ones.

The third factor is that of environment. Serious photographers are always paying attention to light and shadow, backlighting, color contrasts, unexpected movement, and extraneous clutter as they set up their shots. They know these environmental matters, some that can be managed and others that often cannot, have a significant effect on the quality of the pictures they take. The same is true of the mental impressions we make of others. Quick conclusions that pay no attention to another's life experience, vocational and family background, level of maturity, and economic circumstances often turn out to be erroneous. It takes time and effort to cut through the environmental clutter surrounding the people who enter our lives. But, if we take the time to do so, we are much more likely to make accurate assessments of their personhood. While environmental factors shape us, we are all more than just the product of our environments.

Finally, there is this matter of goodwill between photographic subject and photographer. Ultimately it comes down to trust. The subject must be able to trust that the photographer will not intentionally distort shots or deliberately take unflattering or compromising shots. This is a part of the offense of hidden mini-cams that are used today by sick-minded voyeurs to capture unsuspecting people at their most vulnerable and private moments. Such actions constitute a blatant refusal to respect the personhood of the one whose actions are being recorded.

Similarly, we must be able to trust the mental images we form of one another. If you set out deliberately to find me at my weakest, my most vulnerable, my most unflattering moments, you will get only a negative, one-sided image of the person I am. If you set out deliberately to take note only of my strongest, most secure, most admirable qualities, you will get only a positive, one-sided image of the person I am. Each image will be inaccurate because the truth is that I am both, and so are you.

The joy the two women found in walking down the beach shooting photos of one another was made possible by the evident loving trust they shared together. Each of us should cultivate a posture of thoughtful goodwill and trust toward others. Only then can we safely play "You take my picture, and I'll take yours."

It'll Be Just as Beautiful as It Ever Was; It'll Just Be Beautiful Differently

It took a while for the intensity of our collective grief to pass. The entire church family mourned both the decision and the subsequent fact of taking down the old maple trees that for decades had shaded the main entrance to the church sanctuary. Some members were present when the trees were first planted during World War II. They watched them grow from saplings to full-grown shade trees under which picnics, Vacation Bible Schools, homecoming dinners, and casual conversations had taken place for decades. These were the trees under which old men had smoked, young folks had courted, mourners had gathered for funerals, and brides had waited for the wedding march to begin. But the torrential rains of mid-summer, for the second time, caused significant damage to the roof of the place of worship. The culprits, once again, were the maple trees whose beautiful fall leaves persisted in blocking hard-to-reach gutters and downspouts, causing rainwater to back up on the flat-roofed sanctuary annexes.

For years an ongoing discussion had taken place regarding the damage the trees' root systems were doing to the building's foundation and the problems leaves and squirrels were creating on the roof; but out of sentimental affection for the old trees, no decision had been made regarding them. Finally, the time had come. While the church's insurance company agreed to pay for the repair of cosmetic damages to the interior of the sanctuary, all expenses related to a long-term solution to the problem would have to be borne by the church. Once everyone understood the seriousness of the problem, economic practicality overruled sentiment, and the congregation voted unanimously to have the beloved trees taken down. Over the following weeks the trees were sawn down, cut up into firewood, hauled away, the brush reduced to mulch, and the remaining mess cleaned up. Once the stumps were ground up and new grass planted, the last vestiges of the old, much missed maple trees were gone forever.

The Sunday following the cutting down of the trees, one of the senior adult women voiced the ache in her heart by saying to me, as she looked at the spectacle of the downed trees lying on the ground, "Will it ever be beautiful again?" I responded, "It'll be just as beautiful as it ever was; it'll just be beautiful differently." I understood her question. What lay behind the words, "Will it ever be beautiful again," was the realization that the front of the church building would never be the same. And she understood my response as well. Lying behind my words, "It'll be just as beautiful as it ever was; it'll just be beautiful differently," was the understanding that while things couldn't be the same again, this did not automatically mean they could not be good, or even better, at some time in the future.

Over a teaching career, I frequently pointed out to students the truth that the only thing that never changes in life is the fact that things change in life. Nothing remains the same. The ancient sage Democritus was correct when he observed, "No man steps twice into the same river." For the next time a foot is placed in the water, both the river and the man have changed. To attempt to prevent change in our lives is as futile as to attempt to prevent the tide from ebbing and flowing on an ocean shore. Time passes, and circumstances change; this is an inevitability that defies any attempt we make to prevent it. But what we can manage is how we respond to the changes that take place and whether life's changes eventuate in positive or negative consequences for ourselves and for those around us.

One of the most devastating mistakes made by human beings is that of assuming that because things can't be the same as they once were, they must automatically be worse than they were before. Such logic flies in the face of both common sense and practical experience. While most of us like to reminisce about the "good old days," rarely do I ever hear anyone express the desire to go back and live as we lived in earlier generations. The truth is that most of the "good" in the "good old days" is the fact that they are the "old" bygone days. While we acknowledge that the past has shaped and molded us, and that it helps us to define ourselves in the present, spiritually, psychologically healthy people are oriented toward the future and its flexible possibilities, not toward the past and its fixed "un-alterabilities."

There is not a single one of us who has not wished we could "take something back" or "do something over" or "have another chance." We are sure that, if we had it to do all over again, we would get "it" right this time, not let "it" slip through our fingers, or savor and appreciate "it" more. For the most part, this is simply wishful thinking. The decisions we have already taken make it impossible for us to have exactly the same opportunities we were afforded the first time around. They are gone and they are not coming back. We are wasting our time when we pray, "Dear God, just give me another chance!" if by those words we mean, "God give me the same chance all over again!" You can't step into the same river twice; you can't make exactly the same decision a second time; and you can't rewind the tape of your existence and start over as though what preceded it had never taken place. By God's grace, you and I can have "another" chance; but we can't have the same chance all over again.

I am profoundly grateful that this is true for two important reasons. First, in my life I have messed some things up pretty badly, and I have no absolute assurance that given the opportunity to "do it over" I would not mess it up just as badly the second time as I did the first. On the other hand, there are some things back there that I really got right the first time, and I have no desire to chance messing them up now. All that stuff "back there" is too precariously risky for me to want to do anything other than leave the past in the past.

Now, before you conclude I'm just "chicken," let me move on to the second reason I'm glad we can't have the same chance all over again. I think I have learned some things from past experiences, both positive and negative, that enable me to make better choices for my tomorrows than I did in my yesterdays. While I do not have absolute certitude about this, I am convinced the probabilities are greater that

I can get the future right than they are that I could correct the past if I could do it all over again.

Why do I think this is true? Well, let me count the reasons. First, I'm a better judge of human character today than I was earlier in my life, especially of my own human character. In an earlier time, I see-sawed between either thinking too highly of myself and my abilities or thinking too little of myself and my abilities. Today I am more realistic about both my abilities and my limitations, and I am more comfortable with each. Thus, I spend less time congratulating myself for my achievements and less time pitying myself for my failures. Because I am more comfortable with me, I am more comfortable with those about me. The result is that I am also more discerning in my assessments of myself and of others as well. While I still misread character from time to time and am still subject to failures in sound judgment, such errors are usually less frequent and less harmful than they once were.

Second, I don't value things in the same way I did at an earlier point in my life. It's not that my basic moral/ethical "values" have changed significantly; they haven't. It's that those values have become internalized to the extent that I live by them, not because I'm afraid of being caught and judged by others or by God but because, put simply, I would rather look into my own heart and judge its integrity by God's grace than look over my shoulder to see if anyone else is watching.

Third, while not succumbing to the absolute relativism of the assertion that "beauty is in the eyes of the beholder," I have found that beauty expresses itself in many different ways. Let me illustrate. In 1970, I married an utterly beautiful woman. We have shared life together for more than fifty years. She is no less beautiful to me today than she was five decades ago. Such an assertion does not blindly ignore the reality that over time she has changed. It also does not ignore the truth that the criteria by which I measure authentic beauty have changed as well. And the beauty I find in her now is not only different; it is also better.

Now, let's get back to this business of people's lives. Many have marred the beauty of living in horrendous ways. Through bad choices, addictions, abuses, and much unmitigated selfishness, many have created a set of circumstances where they are beset on every side by the harsh ugliness of life. Yet others have been injured, scarred, and maimed in diverse ways by the choices and conduct of parents, children, siblings, co-workers, employers, governments, and total strangers. Life's beauty has been defaced by divorce, crime, violence, and despair. The damage done is often irreparable. Regardless of the amount of energy, commitment, time, and resources devoted to the task, the fact remains that things can never be the same again. We stand and gaze at the shattered, broken fragments of our lives and wonder, "Will it ever be beautiful again?" The answer is "Yes! Yes, your life can be just as beautiful as it ever was if you will open yourself up to the reality that, for it to be beautiful again, it is going to have to be beautiful differently." All efforts to restore the past as it was are doomed to end in futile frustration. Like with Humpty-Dumpty, "all the king's horses and all the king's men" can't put the broken fragments of the past back together again. Recovering the beauty of life is to be found in living in the present for the future, not in attempting to reconstruct the past.

Many are now asking, "Where does one begin?" We begin by acknowledging the truth that the irreparable is dead, and its ability to continue to do us harm needs to be eliminated. If it can't be eliminated, it needs to be minimized. Once the trees were cut down at the church, we discovered that all three were already dead on the inside. It was only a matter of time before internal rot, a driving storm, or both conspired to topple the trees onto the building, doing tens of thousands of dollars' worth of damage, including the destruction of irreplaceable stained-glass windows. The past is dead. You can learn from the past, and you can treasure aspects of the past, but you can't live in it.

Second, we own our portion of the responsibility for the loss of beauty in our life's relationships. While some ugliness just happens, the most destructive ugliness is that which we perpetrate upon ourselves. This is the dastardliness of human sin; its wounds are self-inflicted. It is in the acceptance of responsibility for ourselves that we are enabled to begin moving beyond the brokenness toward the future.

Next, we must nourish the spirit of hope that, by God's grace, lies within us. The spark of hope has not gone out in your spirit. The hope is there; it may be only the dimmest of flickers, but it is there. Nourish it. Encourage it. Feed it. Help it to grow. Paul told the Roman believers, "We are saved by hope . . ." (Rom 8:24).

Finally, we embrace the truth that our ultimate hope, and the beauty of our lives, lies in someone who wants the best for us. From the Christian perspective, we do not have "hope" in "hope" or "faith" in "faith." Our hope lies in "our Savior and Lord Jesus Christ, which is our hope" (1 Tim 1:1). Our hope lies in the One who willingly entered into the midst of our broken circumstances to do for us what we could not possibly do for ourselves. The author of Hebrews put it this way,

> Wherefore seeing we also are compassed about with so great a cloud of witnesses, let us lay aside every weight, and the sin which doth so easily beset us, and let us run with patience the race that is set before us. Looking unto Jesus the author and finisher of our faith . . . (Heb 12:1-2)

When from the depths of our despair we cry out in anguish, "Will it ever be beautiful again?" God replies, "Sure it will. Trust me, and I will make your life as beautiful as it ever was. I'll just make it beautiful differently."

www.ingramcontent.com/pod-product-compliance
Lightning Source LLC
Chambersburg PA
CBHW051041160426
43193CB00010B/1024